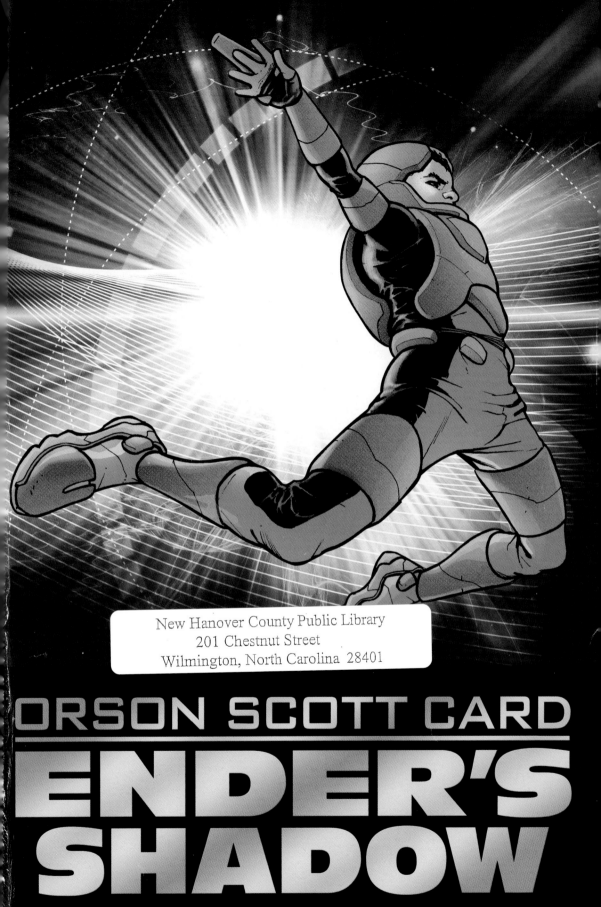

ORSON SCOTT CARD

ENDER'S SHADOW

COMMAND SCHOOL

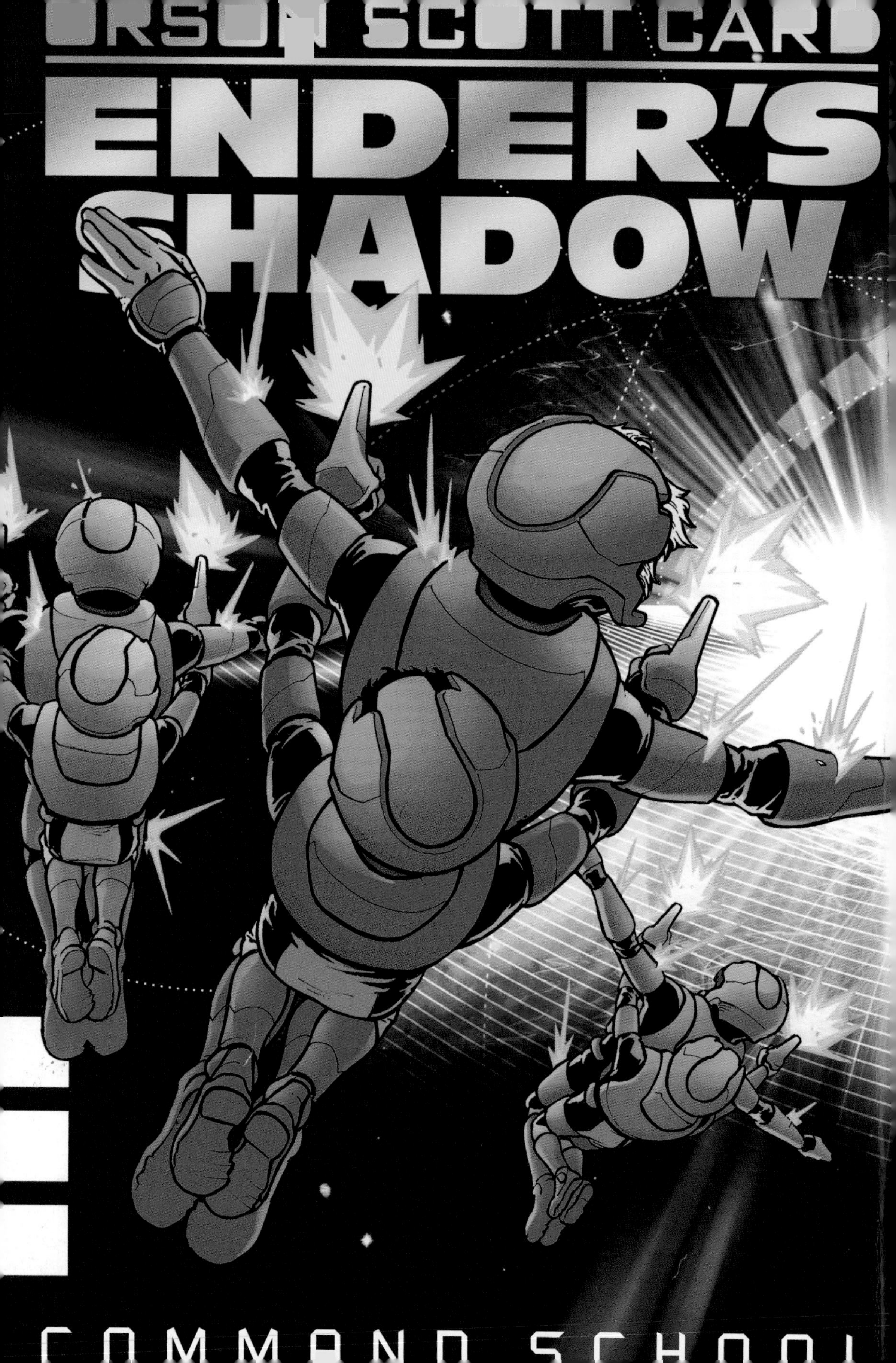
ORSON SCOTT CARD
ENDER'S SHADOW
COMMAND SCHOOL

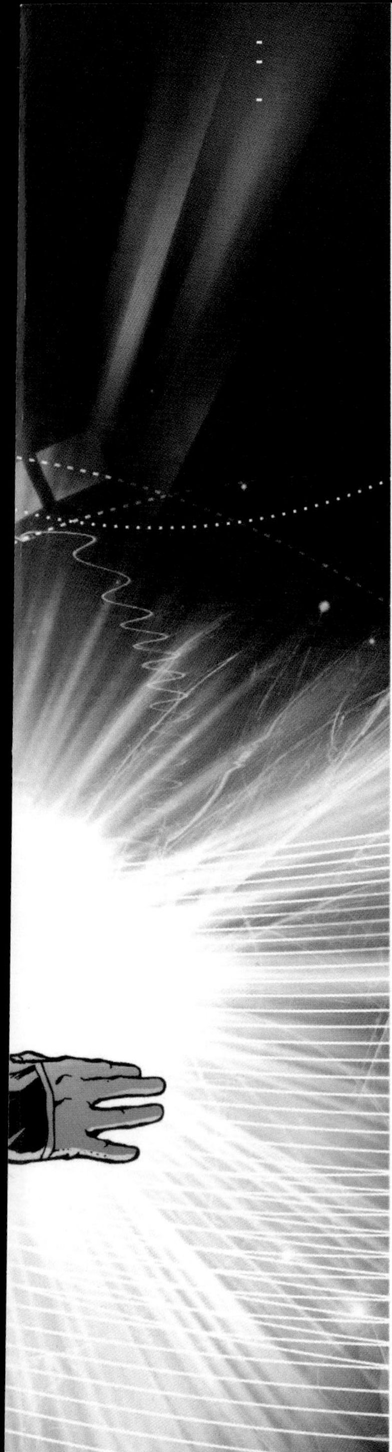

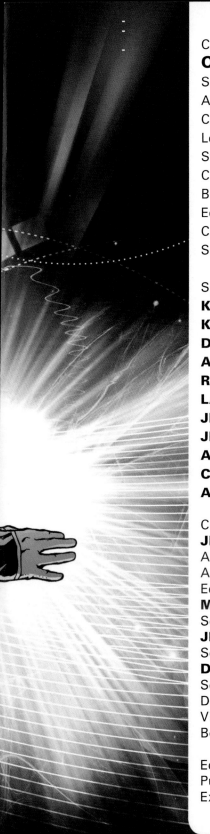

Creative Director & Executive Director:
ORSON SCOTT CARD
Script: **MIKE CAREY**
Art: **SEBASTIAN FIUMARA**
Color Art: **GIULIA BRUSCO**
Lettering: **VC'S CORY PETIT**
Story Consultant: **JAKE BLACK**
Cover Art: **TIMOTHY GREEN II**
Book Cover Art: **PASQUAL FERRY**
Editor: **JORDAN D. WHITE**
Consulting Editor: **NICK LOWE**
Senior Editor: **MARK PANICCIA**

Special thanks to
KRISTINE CARD,
KATHLEEN BELLAMY,
DARIAN ROBBINS,
ANDREW BAUGHAN,
RALPH MACCHIO,
LAUREN SANKOVITCH,
JIM NAUSEDAS,
JIM MCCANN,
ARUNE SINGH,
CHRIS ALLO
AND JEFF SUTER

Collection Editor:
JENNIFER GRÜNWALD
Assistant Editor: **ALEX STARBUCK**
Associate Editor: **JOHN DENNING**
Editor, Special Projects:
MARK D. BEAZLEY
Senior Editor, Special Projects:
JEFF YOUNGQUIST
Senior Vice President of Sales:
DAVID GABRIEL
Senior Vice President of Strategic
Development: **RUWAN JAYATILLEKE**
Vice President of Creative: **TOM MARVELLI**
Book designer: **RODOLFO MURAGUCHI**

Editor in Chief: **JOE QUESADA**
Publisher: **DAN BUCKLEY**
Executive Producer: **ALAN FINE**

ENDER'S SHADOW: COMMAND SCHOOL. Contains material originally published in magazine form as ENDER'S SHADOW: COMMAND SCHOOL #1-5. First printing 2010. ISBN# 978-0-7851-3598-2. Published by MARVEL WORLDWIDE, INC., a subsidiary of MARVEL ENTERTAINMENT, LLC. OFFICE OF PUBLICATION: 417 5th Avenue, New York, NY 10016. **Printed in the U.S.A**. ALAN FINE, EVP - Office of the President, Marvel Worldwide, Inc. and EVP & CMO Marvel Characters B.V.; DAN BUCKLEY, Chief Executive Officer and Publisher - Print, Animation & Digital Media; JIM SOKOLOWSKI, Chief Operating Officer; DAVID GABRIEL, SVP of Publishing Sales & Circulation; DAVID BOGART, SVP of Business Affairs & Talent Management; MICHAEL PASCIULLO, VP Merchandising & Communications; JIM O'KEEFE, VP of Operations & Logistics; DAN CARR, Executive Director of Publishing Technology; JUSTIN F. GABRIE, Director of Publishing & Editorial Operations; SUSAN CRESPI, Editorial Operations Manager; ALEX MORALES, Publishing Operations Manager; STAN LEE, Chairman Emeritus. For information regarding advertising in Marvel Comics or on Marvel.com, please contact Ron Stern, VP of Business Development, at rstern@marvel.com. For Marvel subscription inquiries, please call 800-217-9158. **Manufactured between 2/8/2010 and 3/10/2010 by R.R. DONNELLEY, INC., SALEM, VA, USA.**

10 9 8 7 6 5 4 3 2 1

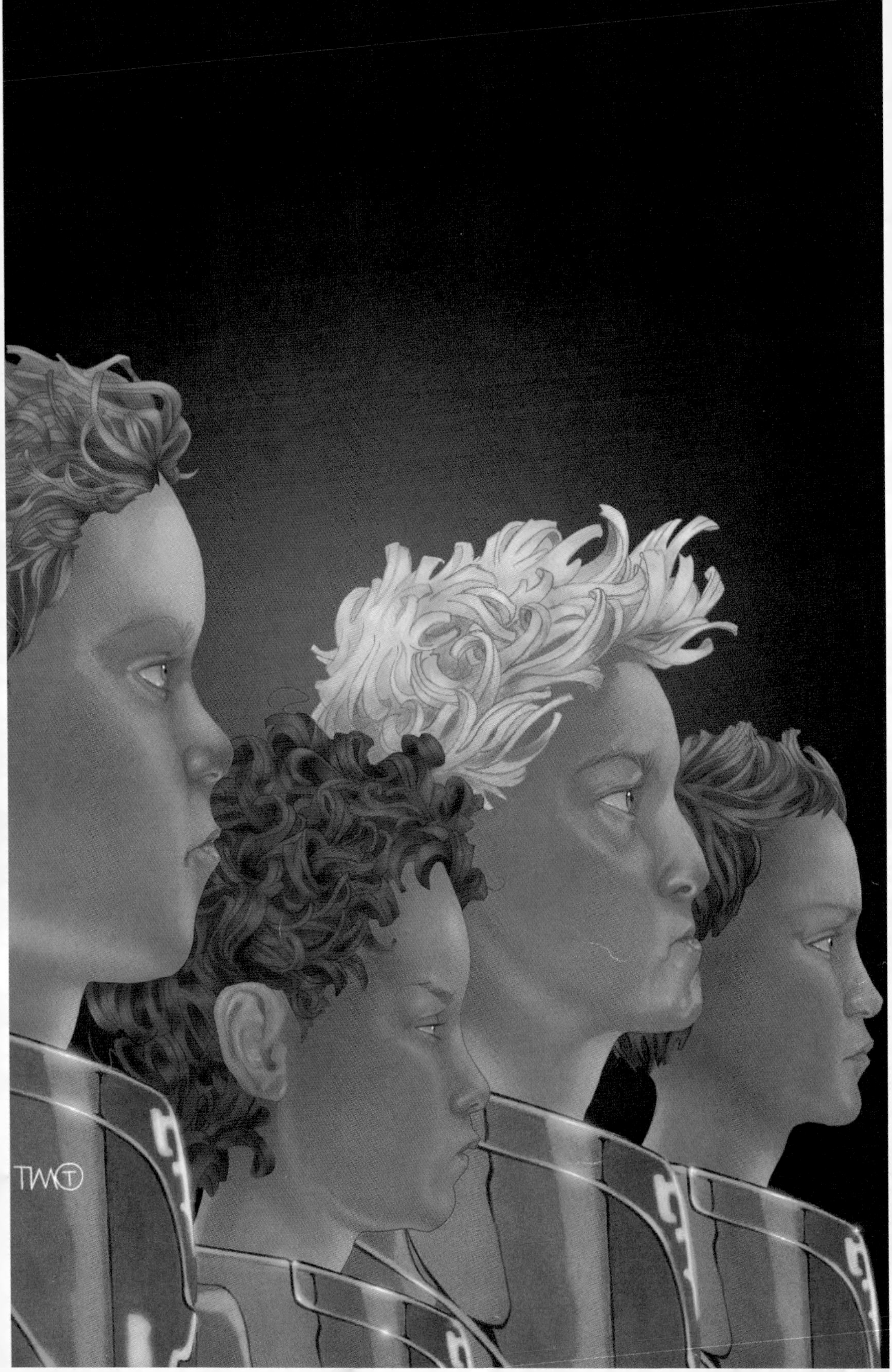

"If Wiggin's the one, then let's get him to Eros."

"He's not ready for command school yet. It's premature."

"Then we have to go with one of the alternates."

"That would be your call to make."

"Of course it would. But do we have all the information we need to make it? Full data on all the children scoring at Wiggin's level?"

"No."

"Why not?"

"Some of them are disqualified for various reasons."

"Let me be blunt. We hear rumors about a very young boy."

"They're all young."

"A boy who makes the Wiggin boy look slow."

"They all have their different strengths."

"Bean. The boy we refer to is named Bean."

"I know what his name is. General, I have to trust my instincts. You can't run this operation like a machine."

"And that's why you mistrust this child? Because he was made, like a machine?"

"I don't analyze myself. I analyze them."

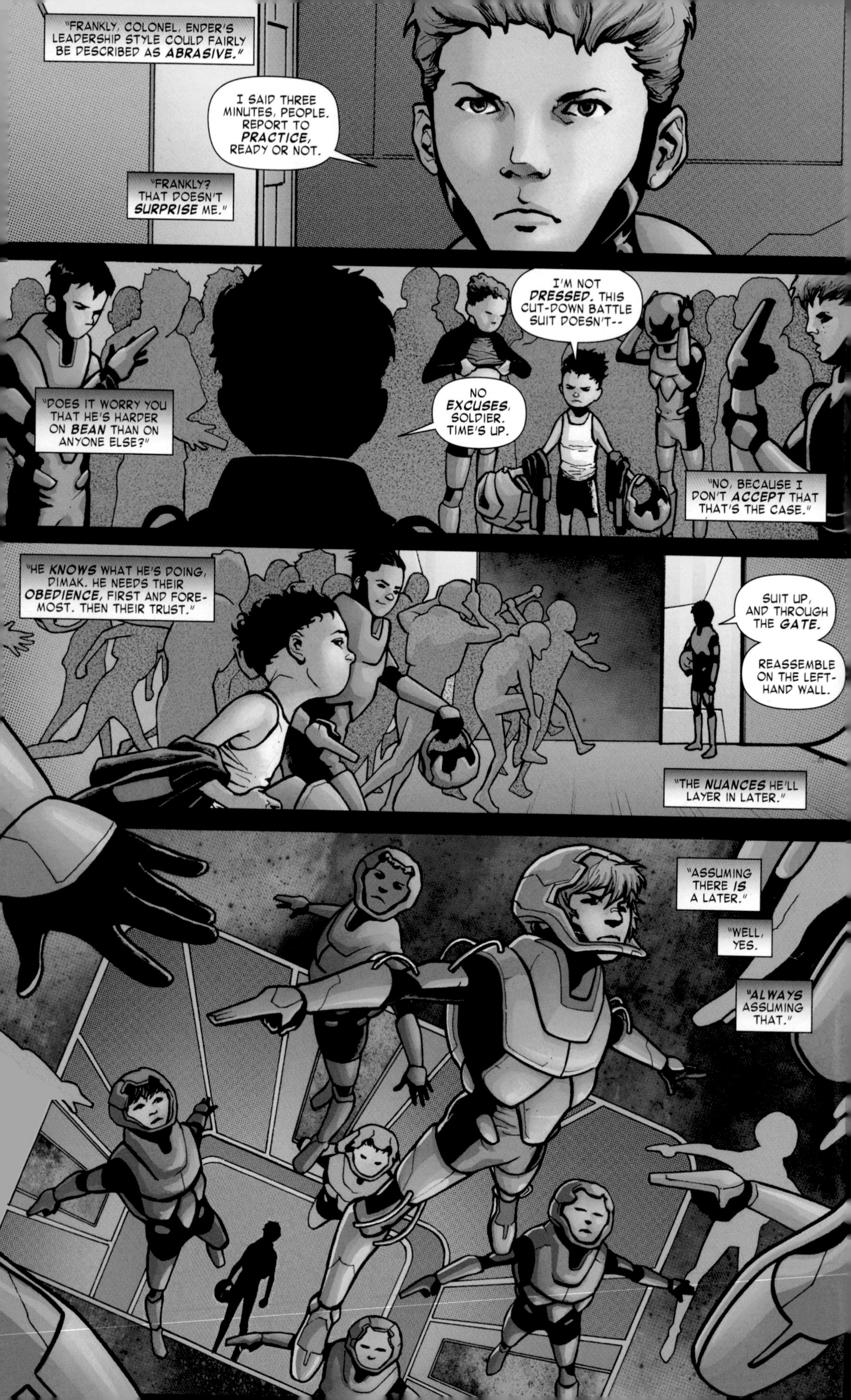
"FRANKLY, COLONEL, ENDER'S LEADERSHIP STYLE COULD FAIRLY BE DESCRIBED AS ABRASIVE."
I SAID THREE MINUTES, PEOPLE. REPORT TO PRACTICE, READY OR NOT.
"FRANKLY? THAT DOESN'T SURPRISE ME."
"DOES IT WORRY YOU THAT HE'S HARDER ON BEAN THAN ON ANYONE ELSE?"
I'M NOT DRESSED. THIS CUT-DOWN BATTLE SUIT DOESN'T--
NO EXCUSES, SOLDIER. TIME'S UP.
"NO, BECAUSE I DON'T ACCEPT THAT THAT'S THE CASE."
"HE KNOWS WHAT HE'S DOING, DIMAK. HE NEEDS THEIR OBEDIENCE, FIRST AND FOREMOST. THEN THEIR TRUST."
SUIT UP, AND THROUGH THE GATE.
REASSEMBLE ON THE LEFT-HAND WALL.
"THE NUANCES HE'LL LAYER IN LATER."
"ASSUMING THERE IS A LATER."
"WELL, YES.
"ALWAYS ASSUMING THAT."

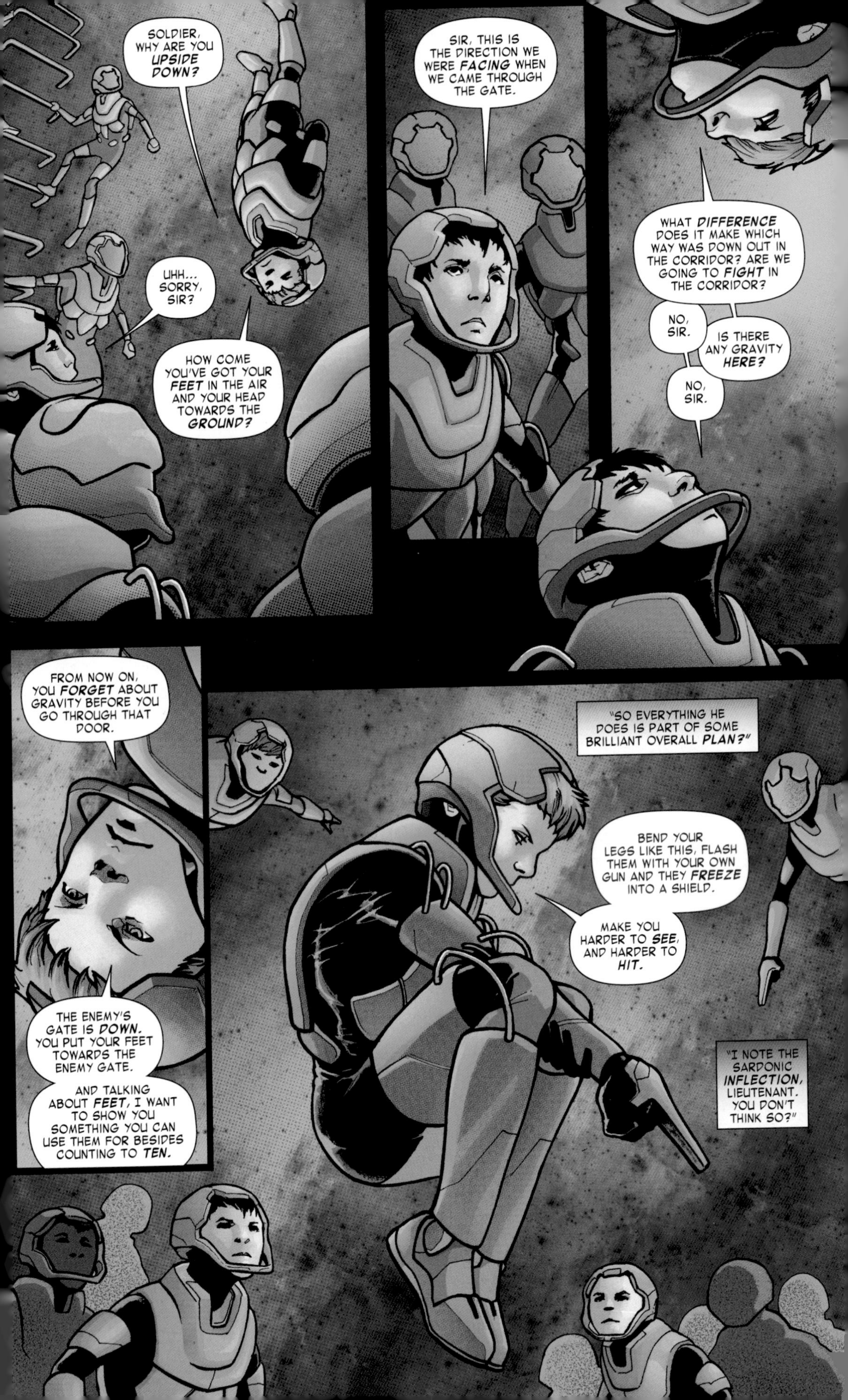
SOLDIER, WHY ARE YOU UPSIDE DOWN?
UHH... SORRY, SIR?
HOW COME YOU'VE GOT YOUR FEET IN THE AIR AND YOUR HEAD TOWARDS THE GROUND?
SIR, THIS IS THE DIRECTION WE WERE FACING WHEN WE CAME THROUGH THE GATE.
WHAT DIFFERENCE DOES IT MAKE WHICH WAY WAS DOWN OUT IN THE CORRIDOR? ARE WE GOING TO FIGHT IN THE CORRIDOR?
NO, SIR.
IS THERE ANY GRAVITY HERE?
NO, SIR.
FROM NOW ON, YOU FORGET ABOUT GRAVITY BEFORE YOU GO THROUGH THAT DOOR.
THE ENEMY'S GATE IS DOWN. YOU PUT YOUR FEET TOWARDS THE ENEMY GATE.
AND TALKING ABOUT FEET, I WANT TO SHOW YOU SOMETHING YOU CAN USE THEM FOR BESIDES COUNTING TO TEN.
"SO EVERYTHING HE DOES IS PART OF SOME BRILLIANT OVERALL PLAN?"
BEND YOUR LEGS LIKE THIS, FLASH THEM WITH YOUR OWN GUN AND THEY FREEZE INTO A SHIELD.
MAKE YOU HARDER TO SEE, AND HARDER TO HIT.
"I NOTE THE SARDONIC INFLECTION, LIEUTENANT. YOU DON'T THINK SO?"

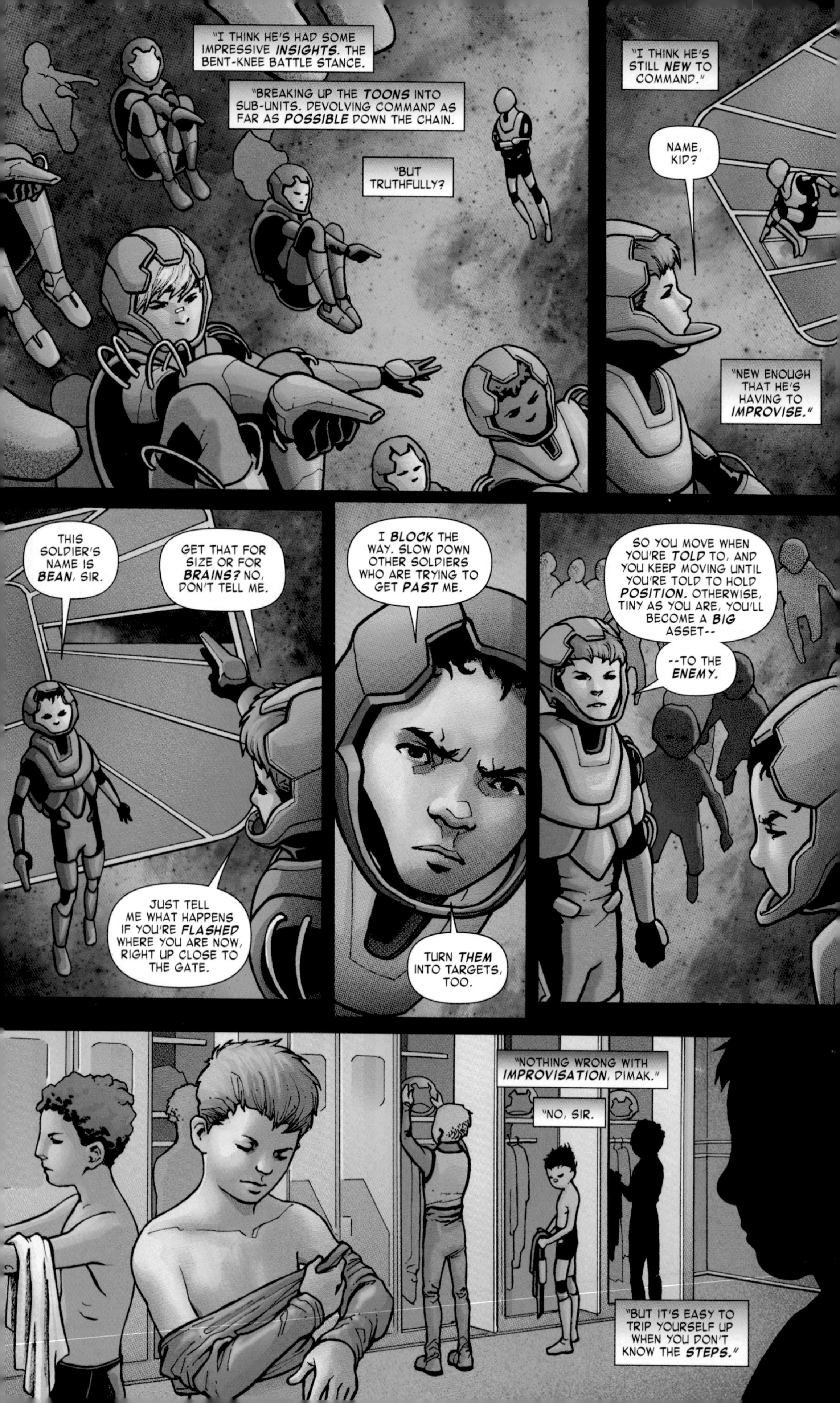
"I THINK HE'S HAD SOME IMPRESSIVE INSIGHTS. THE BENT-KNEE BATTLE STANCE.
"BREAKING UP THE TOONS INTO SUB-UNITS. DEVOLVING COMMAND AS FAR AS POSSIBLE DOWN THE CHAIN.
"BUT TRUTHFULLY?
"I THINK HE'S STILL NEW TO COMMAND."
NAME, KID?
"NEW ENOUGH THAT HE'S HAVING TO IMPROVISE."
THIS SOLDIER'S NAME IS BEAN, SIR.
GET THAT FOR SIZE OR FOR BRAINS? NO, DON'T TELL ME.
JUST TELL ME WHAT HAPPENS IF YOU'RE FLASHED WHERE YOU ARE NOW, RIGHT UP CLOSE TO THE GATE.
I BLOCK THE WAY. SLOW DOWN OTHER SOLDIERS WHO ARE TRYING TO GET PAST ME.
TURN THEM INTO TARGETS, TOO.
SO YOU MOVE WHEN YOU'RE TOLD TO, AND YOU KEEP MOVING UNTIL YOU'RE TOLD TO HOLD POSITION. OTHERWISE, TINY AS YOU ARE, YOU'LL BECOME A BIG ASSET--
--TO THE ENEMY.
"NOTHING WRONG WITH IMPROVISATION, DIMAK."
"NO, SIR.
"BUT IT'S EASY TO TRIP YOURSELF UP WHEN YOU DON'T KNOW THE STEPS."

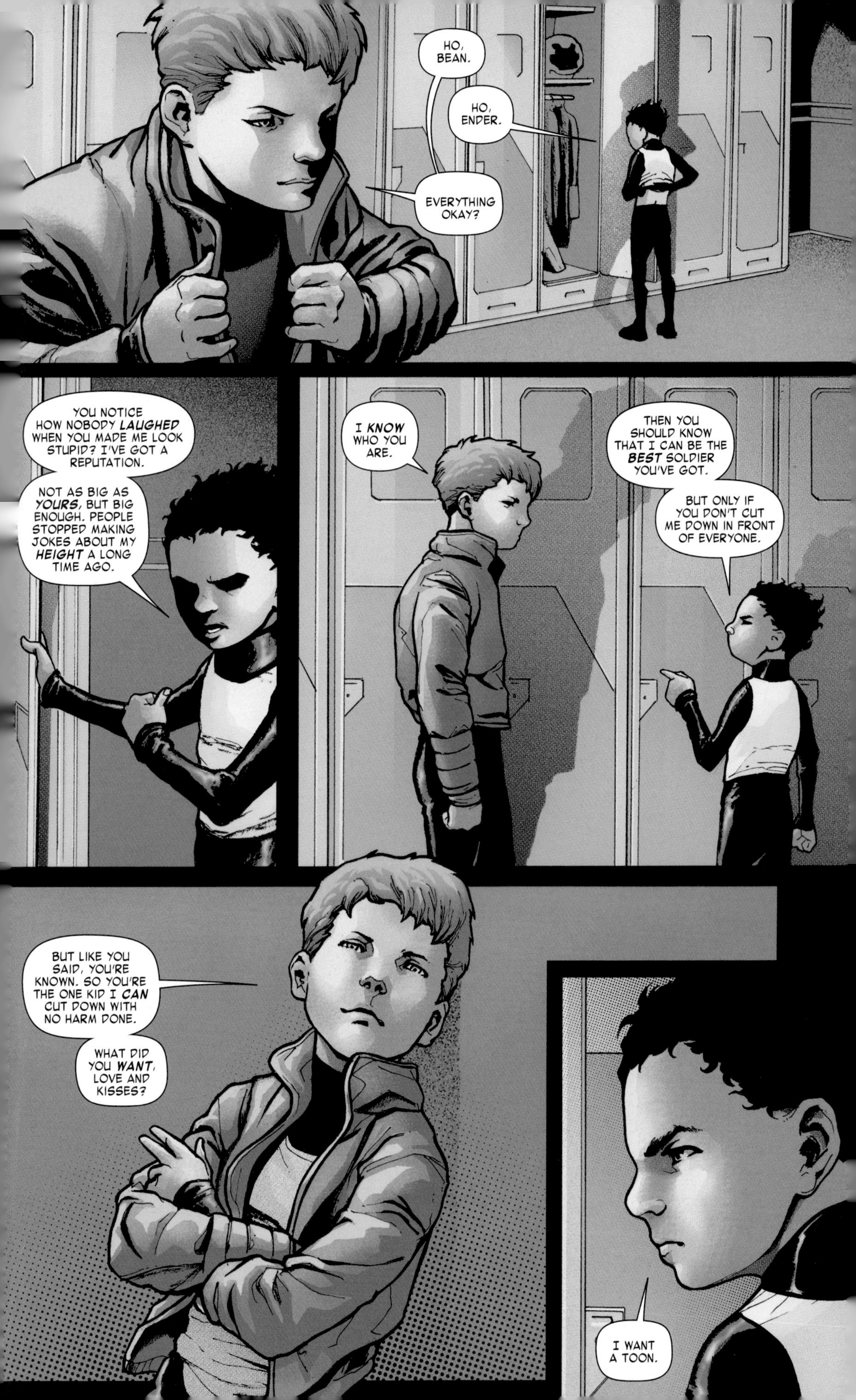
HO, BEAN.
HO, ENDER.
EVERYTHING OKAY?
YOU NOTICE HOW NOBODY LAUGHED WHEN YOU MADE ME LOOK STUPID? I'VE GOT A REPUTATION.
NOT AS BIG AS YOURS, BUT BIG ENOUGH. PEOPLE STOPPED MAKING JOKES ABOUT MY HEIGHT A LONG TIME AGO.
I KNOW WHO YOU ARE.
THEN YOU SHOULD KNOW THAT I CAN BE THE BEST SOLDIER YOU'VE GOT.
BUT ONLY IF YOU DON'T CUT ME DOWN IN FRONT OF EVERYONE.
BUT LIKE YOU SAID, YOU'RE KNOWN. SO YOU'RE THE ONE KID I CAN CUT DOWN WITH NO HARM DONE.
WHAT DID YOU WANT, LOVE AND KISSES?
I WANT A TOON.

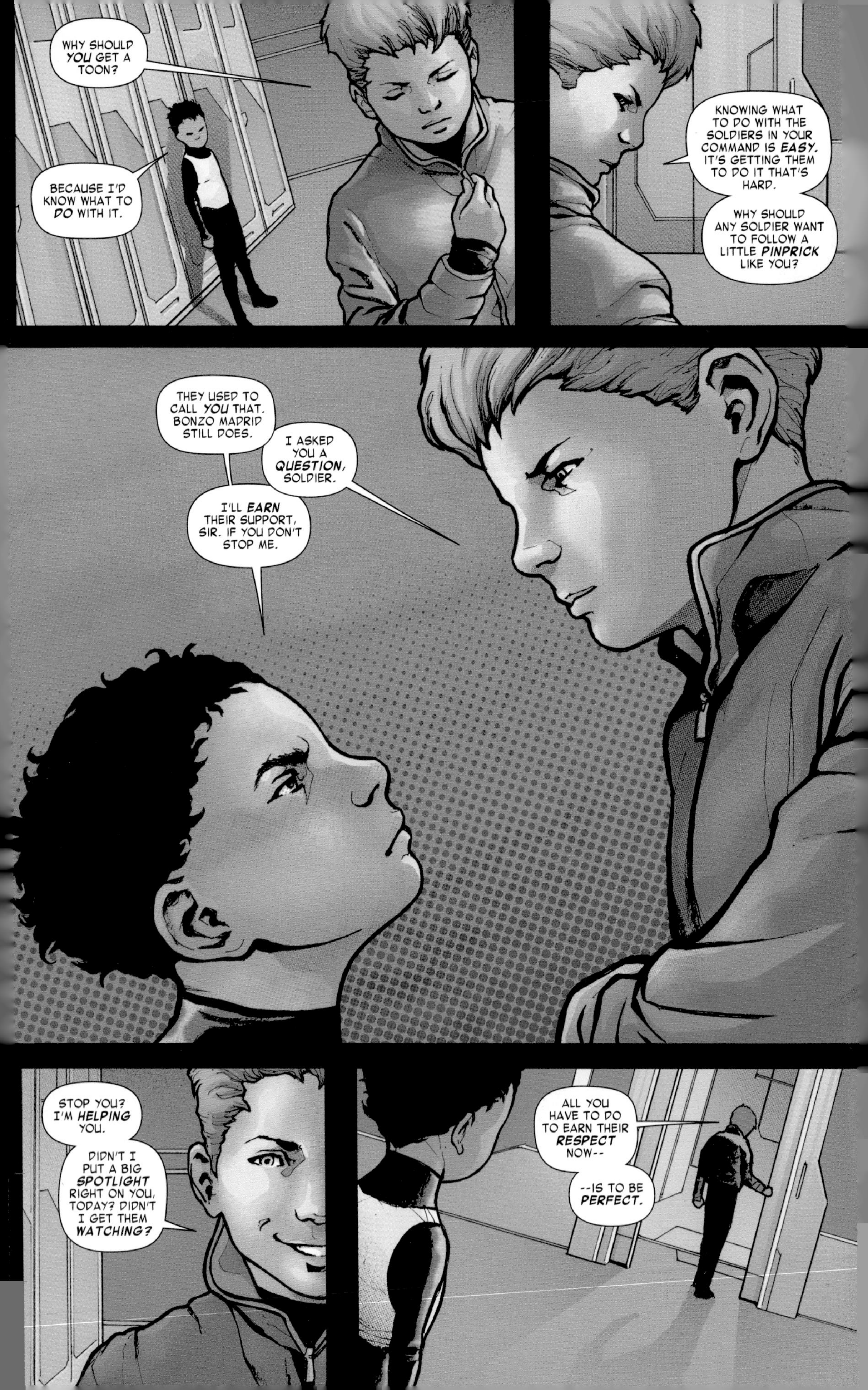
WHY SHOULD YOU GET A TOON?
BECAUSE I'D KNOW WHAT TO DO WITH IT.
KNOWING WHAT TO DO WITH THE SOLDIERS IN YOUR COMMAND IS EASY. IT'S GETTING THEM TO DO IT THAT'S HARD.
WHY SHOULD ANY SOLDIER WANT TO FOLLOW A LITTLE PINPRICK LIKE YOU?
THEY USED TO CALL YOU THAT. BONZO MADRID STILL DOES.
I ASKED YOU A QUESTION, SOLDIER.
I'LL EARN THEIR SUPPORT, SIR. IF YOU DON'T STOP ME.
STOP YOU? I'M HELPING YOU.
DIDN'T I PUT A BIG SPOTLIGHT RIGHT ON YOU, TODAY? DIDN'T I GET THEM WATCHING?
ALL YOU HAVE TO DO TO EARN THEIR RESPECT NOW--
--IS TO BE PERFECT.

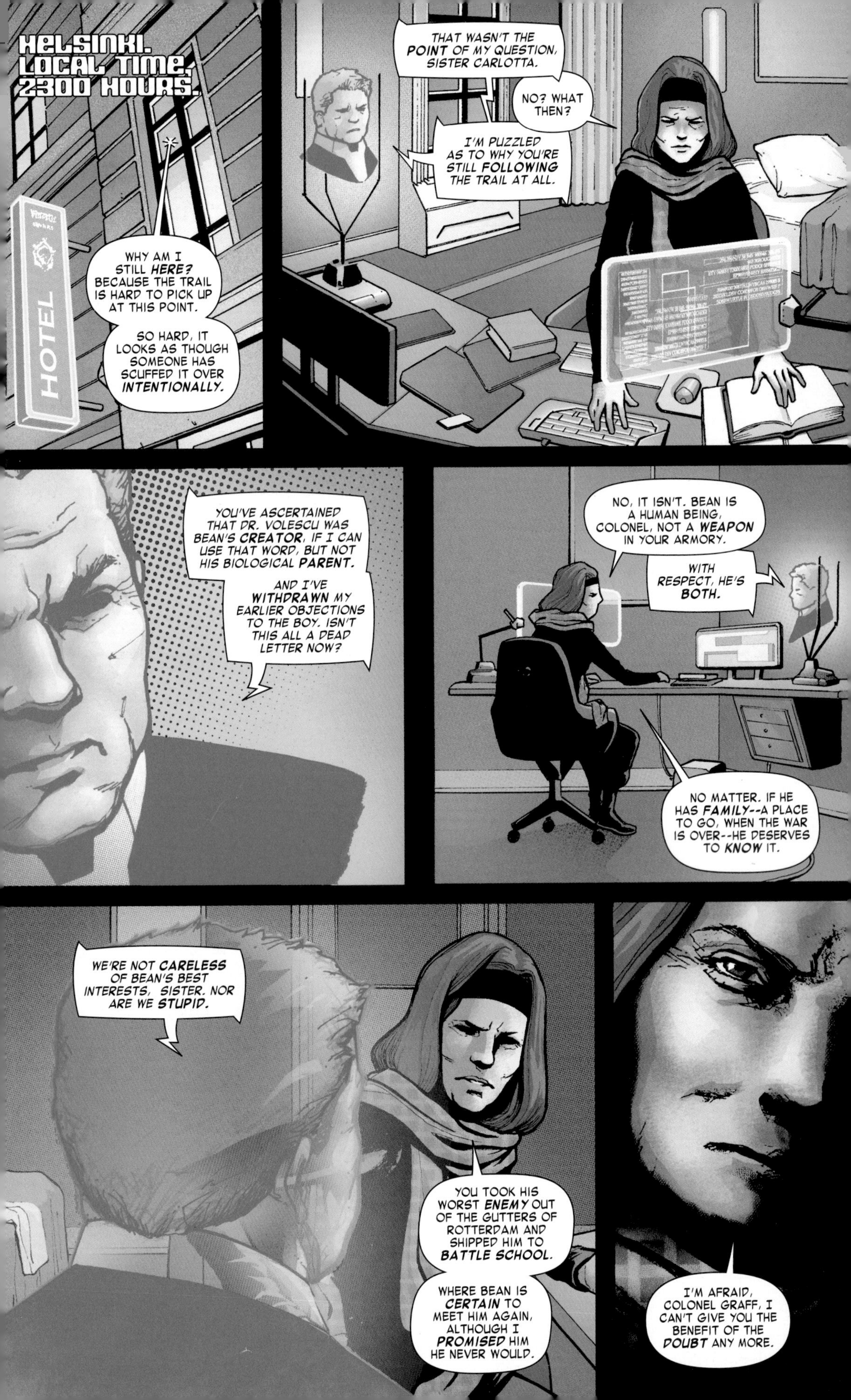
HELSINKI. LOCAL TIME, 2300 HOURS.
WHY AM I STILL HERE? BECAUSE THE TRAIL IS HARD TO PICK UP AT THIS POINT.
SO HARD, IT LOOKS AS THOUGH SOMEONE HAS SCUFFED IT OVER INTENTIONALLY.
HOTEL
THAT WASN'T THE POINT OF MY QUESTION, SISTER CARLOTTA.
NO? WHAT THEN?
I'M PUZZLED AS TO WHY YOU'RE STILL FOLLOWING THE TRAIL AT ALL.
YOU'VE ASCERTAINED THAT DR. VOLESCU WAS BEAN'S CREATOR, IF I CAN USE THAT WORD, BUT NOT HIS BIOLOGICAL PARENT.
AND I'VE WITHDRAWN MY EARLIER OBJECTIONS TO THE BOY. ISN'T THIS ALL A DEAD LETTER NOW?
NO, IT ISN'T. BEAN IS A HUMAN BEING, COLONEL, NOT A WEAPON IN YOUR ARMORY.
WITH RESPECT, HE'S BOTH.
NO MATTER. IF HE HAS FAMILY--A PLACE TO GO, WHEN THE WAR IS OVER--HE DESERVES TO KNOW IT.
WE'RE NOT CARELESS OF BEAN'S BEST INTERESTS, SISTER. NOR ARE WE STUPID.
YOU TOOK HIS WORST ENEMY OUT OF THE GUTTERS OF ROTTERDAM AND SHIPPED HIM TO BATTLE SCHOOL.
WHERE BEAN IS CERTAIN TO MEET HIM AGAIN, ALTHOUGH I PROMISED HIM HE NEVER WOULD.
I'M AFRAID, COLONEL GRAFF, I CAN'T GIVE YOU THE BENEFIT OF THE DOUBT ANY MORE.

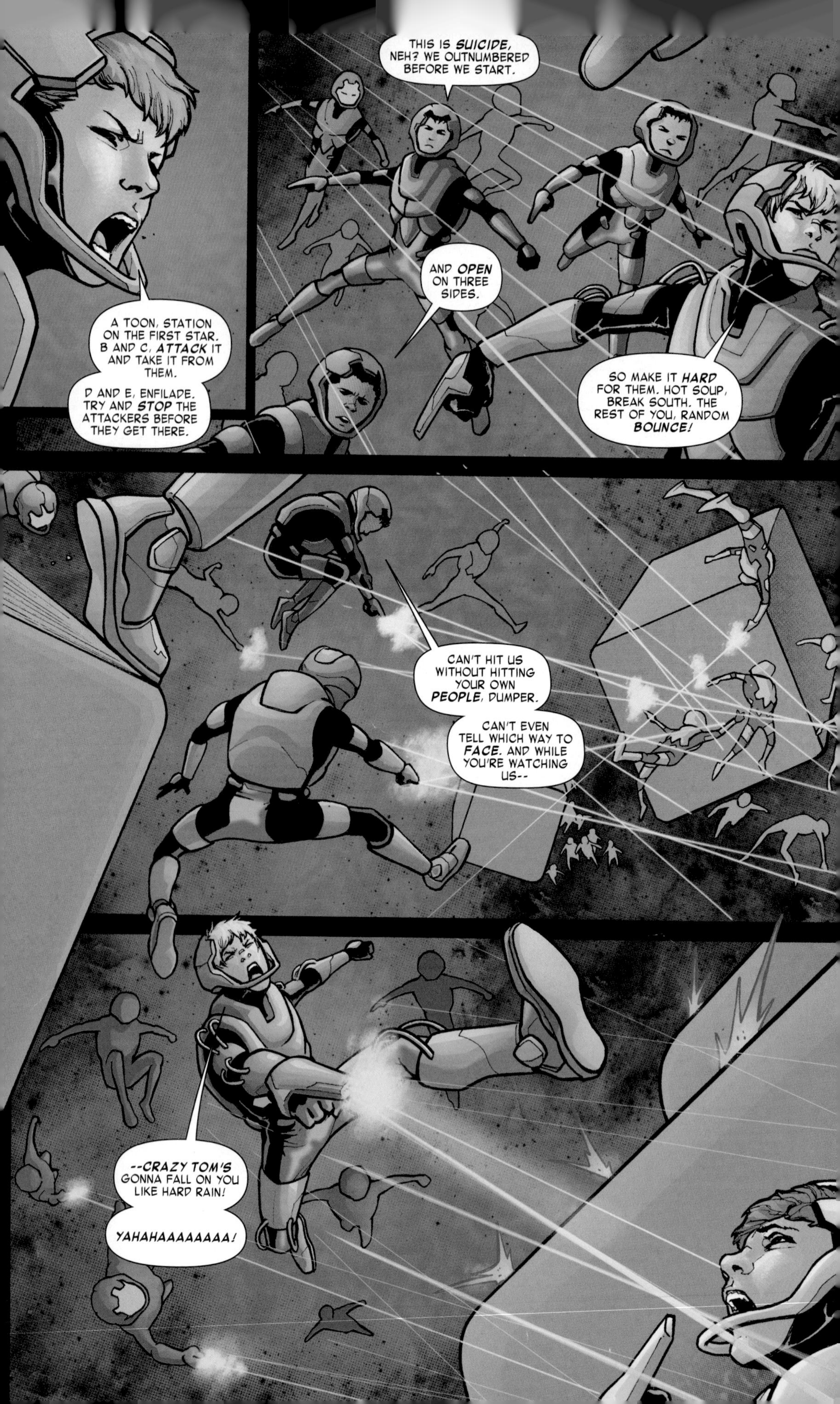
A TOON, STATION ON THE FIRST STAR. B AND C, ATTACK IT AND TAKE IT FROM THEM.
D AND E, ENFILADE. TRY AND STOP THE ATTACKERS BEFORE THEY GET THERE.
THIS IS SUICIDE, NEH? WE OUTNUMBERED BEFORE WE START.
AND OPEN ON THREE SIDES.
SO MAKE IT HARD FOR THEM. HOT SOUP, BREAK SOUTH. THE REST OF YOU, RANDOM BOUNCE!
CAN'T HIT US WITHOUT HITTING YOUR OWN PEOPLE, DUMPER.
CAN'T EVEN TELL WHICH WAY TO FACE. AND WHILE YOU'RE WATCHING US--
--CRAZY TOM'S GONNA FALL ON YOU LIKE HARD RAIN!
YAHAHAAAAAAAAA!

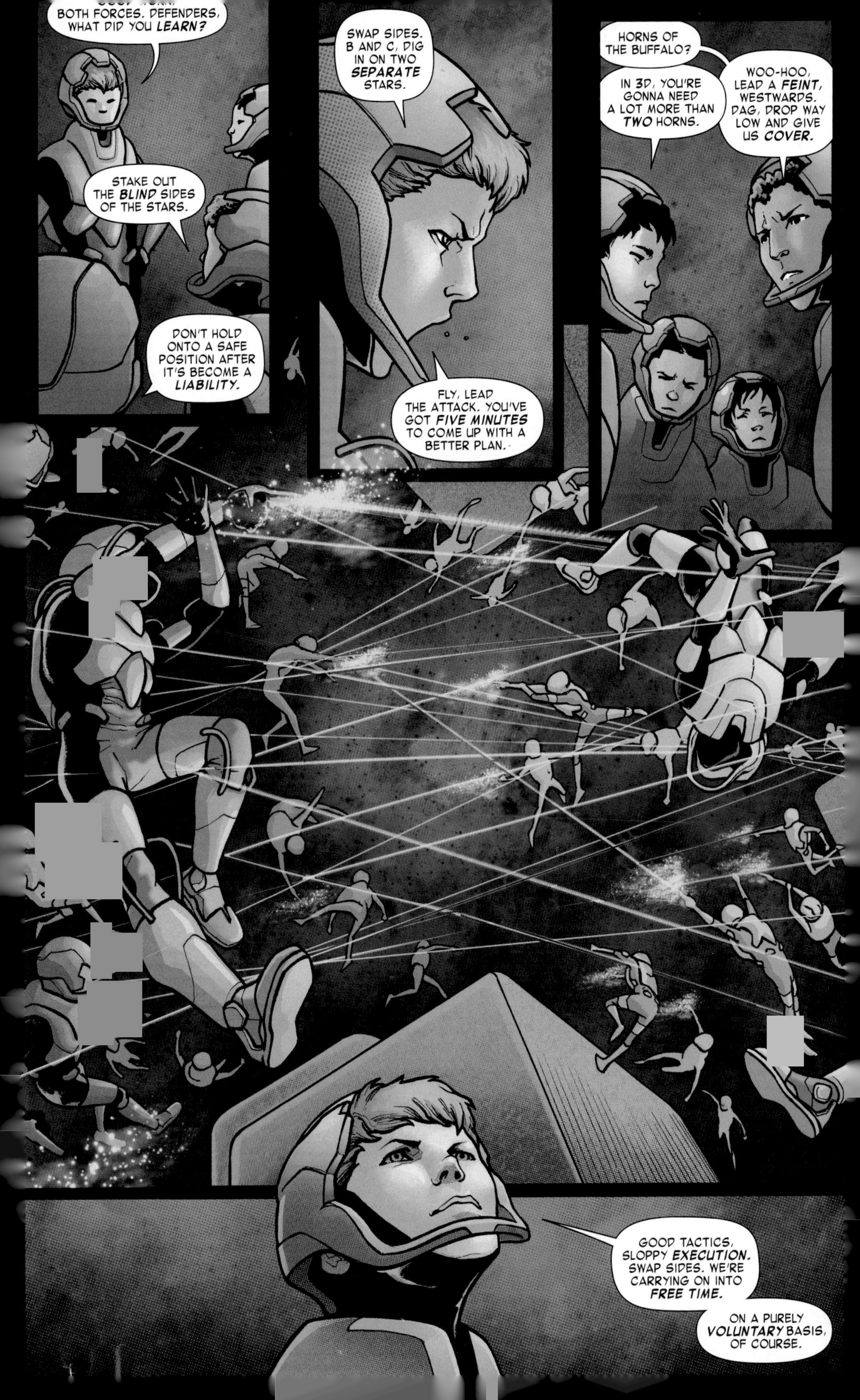
BOTH FORCES. DEFENDERS, WHAT DID YOU LEARN?
STAKE OUT THE BLIND SIDES OF THE STARS.
DON'T HOLD ONTO A SAFE POSITION AFTER IT'S BECOME A LIABILITY.
SWAP SIDES. B AND C, DIG IN ON TWO SEPARATE STARS.
FLY, LEAD THE ATTACK. YOU'VE GOT FIVE MINUTES TO COME UP WITH A BETTER PLAN.
HORNS OF THE BUFFALO?
IN 3D, YOU'RE GONNA NEED A LOT MORE THAN TWO HORNS.
WOO-HOO, LEAD A FEINT, WESTWARDS. DAG, DROP WAY LOW AND GIVE US COVER.
GOOD TACTICS, SLOPPY EXECUTION. SWAP SIDES. WE'RE CARRYING ON INTO FREE TIME.
ON A PURELY VOLUNTARY BASIS, OF COURSE.

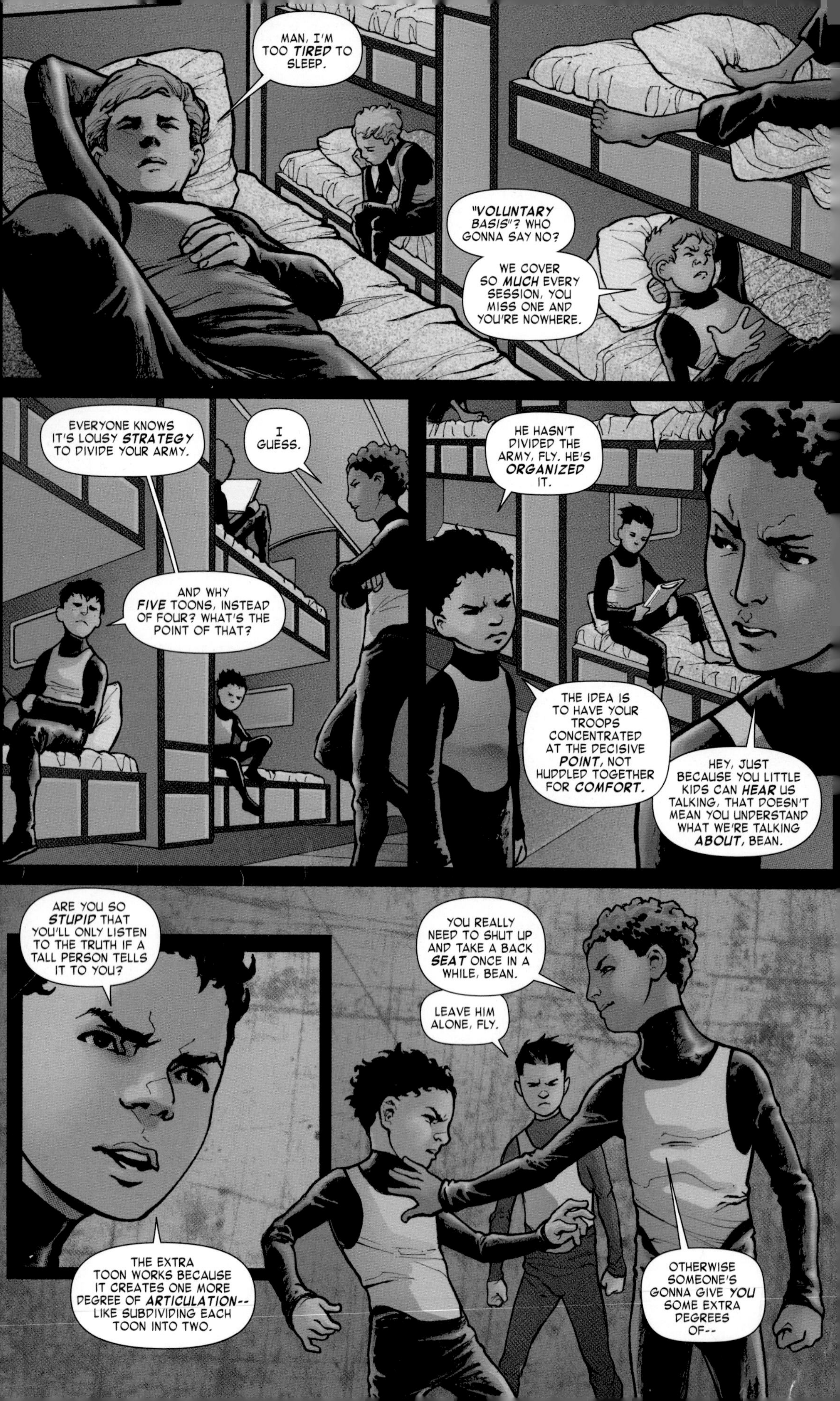
MAN, I'M TOO TIRED TO SLEEP.
"VOLUNTARY BASIS"? WHO GONNA SAY NO?
WE COVER SO MUCH EVERY SESSION, YOU MISS ONE AND YOU'RE NOWHERE.
EVERYONE KNOWS IT'S LOUSY STRATEGY TO DIVIDE YOUR ARMY.
I GUESS.
AND WHY FIVE TOONS, INSTEAD OF FOUR? WHAT'S THE POINT OF THAT?
HE HASN'T DIVIDED THE ARMY, FLY. HE'S ORGANIZED IT.
THE IDEA IS TO HAVE YOUR TROOPS CONCENTRATED AT THE DECISIVE POINT, NOT HUDDLED TOGETHER FOR COMFORT.
HEY, JUST BECAUSE YOU LITTLE KIDS CAN HEAR US TALKING, THAT DOESN'T MEAN YOU UNDERSTAND WHAT WE'RE TALKING ABOUT, BEAN.
ARE YOU SO STUPID THAT YOU'LL ONLY LISTEN TO THE TRUTH IF A TALL PERSON TELLS IT TO YOU?
THE EXTRA TOON WORKS BECAUSE IT CREATES ONE MORE DEGREE OF ARTICULATION-- LIKE SUBDIVIDING EACH TOON INTO TWO.
YOU REALLY NEED TO SHUT UP AND TAKE A BACK SEAT ONCE IN A WHILE, BEAN.
LEAVE HIM ALONE, FLY.
OTHERWISE SOMEONE'S GONNA GIVE YOU SOME EXTRA DEGREES OF--

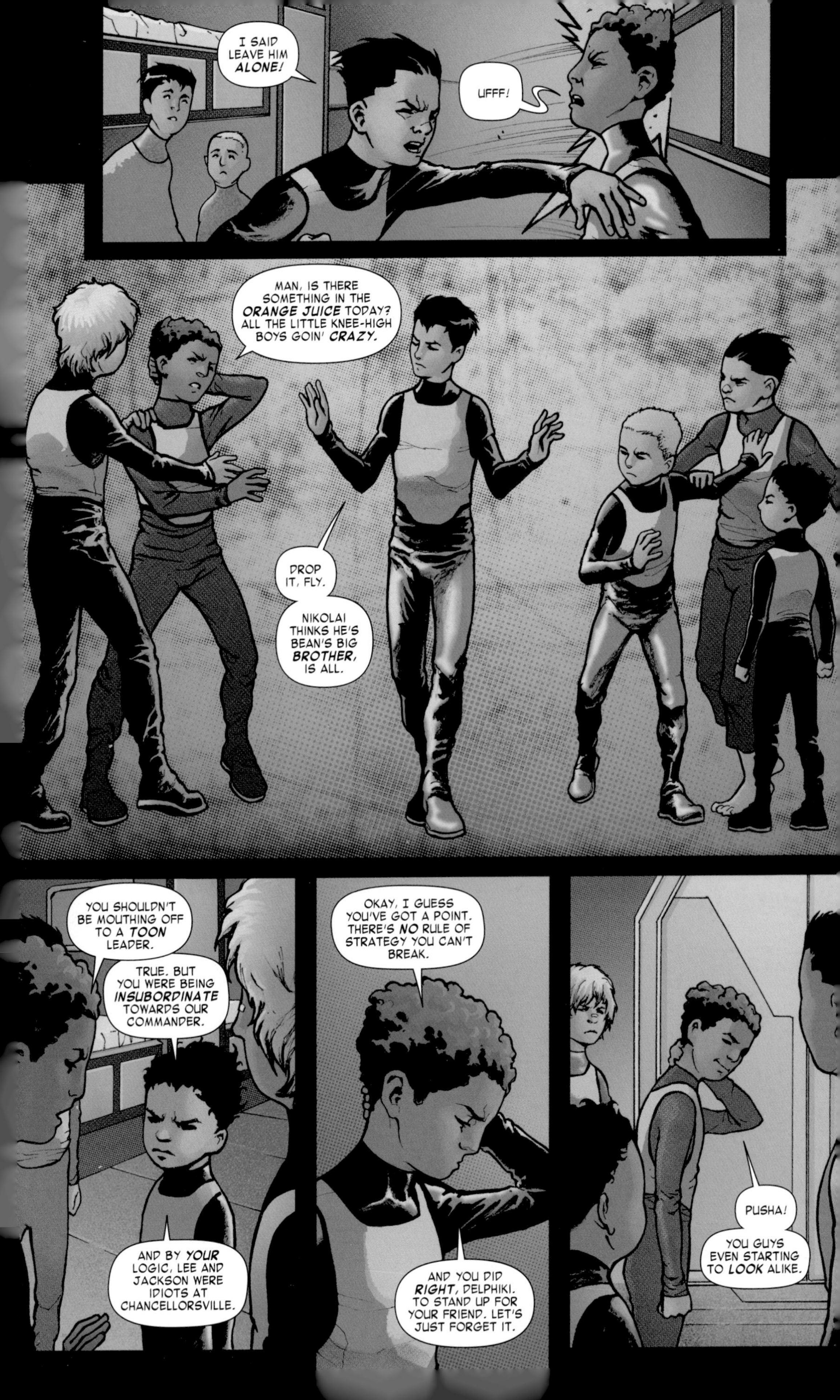
I SAID LEAVE HIM ALONE!
UFFF!
MAN, IS THERE SOMETHING IN THE ORANGE JUICE TODAY? ALL THE LITTLE KNEE-HIGH BOYS GOIN' CRAZY.
DROP IT, FLY.
NIKOLAI THINKS HE'S BEAN'S BIG BROTHER, IS ALL.
YOU SHOULDN'T BE MOUTHING OFF TO A TOON LEADER.
TRUE. BUT YOU WERE BEING INSUBORDINATE TOWARDS OUR COMMANDER.
AND BY YOUR LOGIC, LEE AND JACKSON WERE IDIOTS AT CHANCELLORSVILLE.
OKAY, I GUESS YOU'VE GOT A POINT. THERE'S NO RULE OF STRATEGY YOU CAN'T BREAK.
AND YOU DID RIGHT, DELPHIKI. TO STAND UP FOR YOUR FRIEND. LET'S JUST FORGET IT.
PUSHA!
YOU GUYS EVEN STARTING TO LOOK ALIKE.

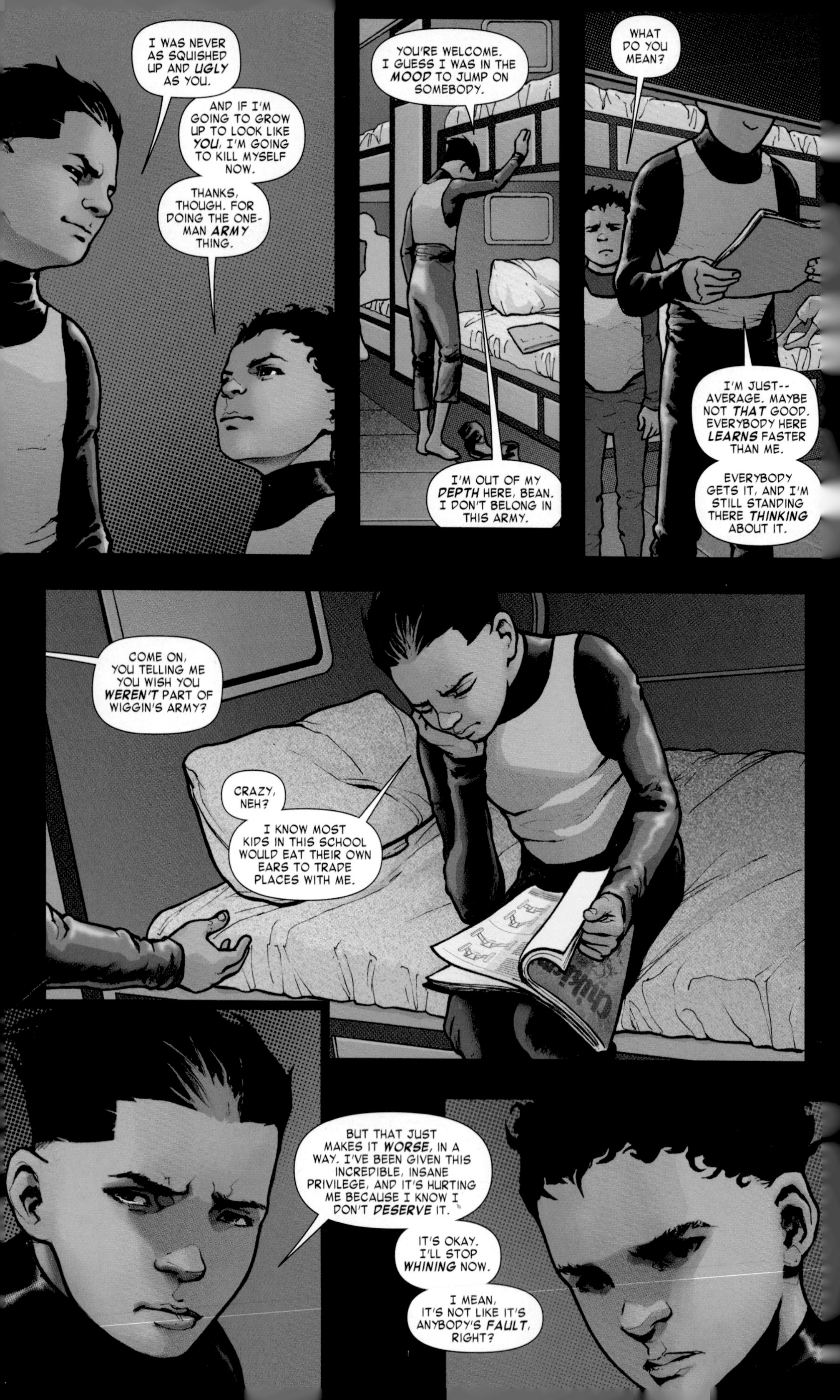
I WAS NEVER AS SQUISHED UP AND UGLY AS YOU.
AND IF I'M GOING TO GROW UP TO LOOK LIKE YOU, I'M GOING TO KILL MYSELF NOW.
THANKS, THOUGH. FOR DOING THE ONE-MAN ARMY THING.
YOU'RE WELCOME. I GUESS I WAS IN THE MOOD TO JUMP ON SOMEBODY.
I'M OUT OF MY DEPTH HERE, BEAN. I DON'T BELONG IN THIS ARMY.
WHAT DO YOU MEAN?
I'M JUST-- AVERAGE. MAYBE NOT THAT GOOD. EVERYBODY HERE LEARNS FASTER THAN ME.
EVERYBODY GETS IT, AND I'M STILL STANDING THERE THINKING ABOUT IT.
COME ON, YOU TELLING ME YOU WISH YOU WEREN'T PART OF WIGGIN'S ARMY?
CRAZY, NEH?
I KNOW MOST KIDS IN THIS SCHOOL WOULD EAT THEIR OWN EARS TO TRADE PLACES WITH ME.
BUT THAT JUST MAKES IT WORSE, IN A WAY. I'VE BEEN GIVEN THIS INCREDIBLE, INSANE PRIVILEGE, AND IT'S HURTING ME BECAUSE I KNOW I DON'T DESERVE IT.
IT'S OKAY. I'LL STOP WHINING NOW.
I MEAN, IT'S NOT LIKE IT'S ANYBODY'S FAULT, RIGHT?

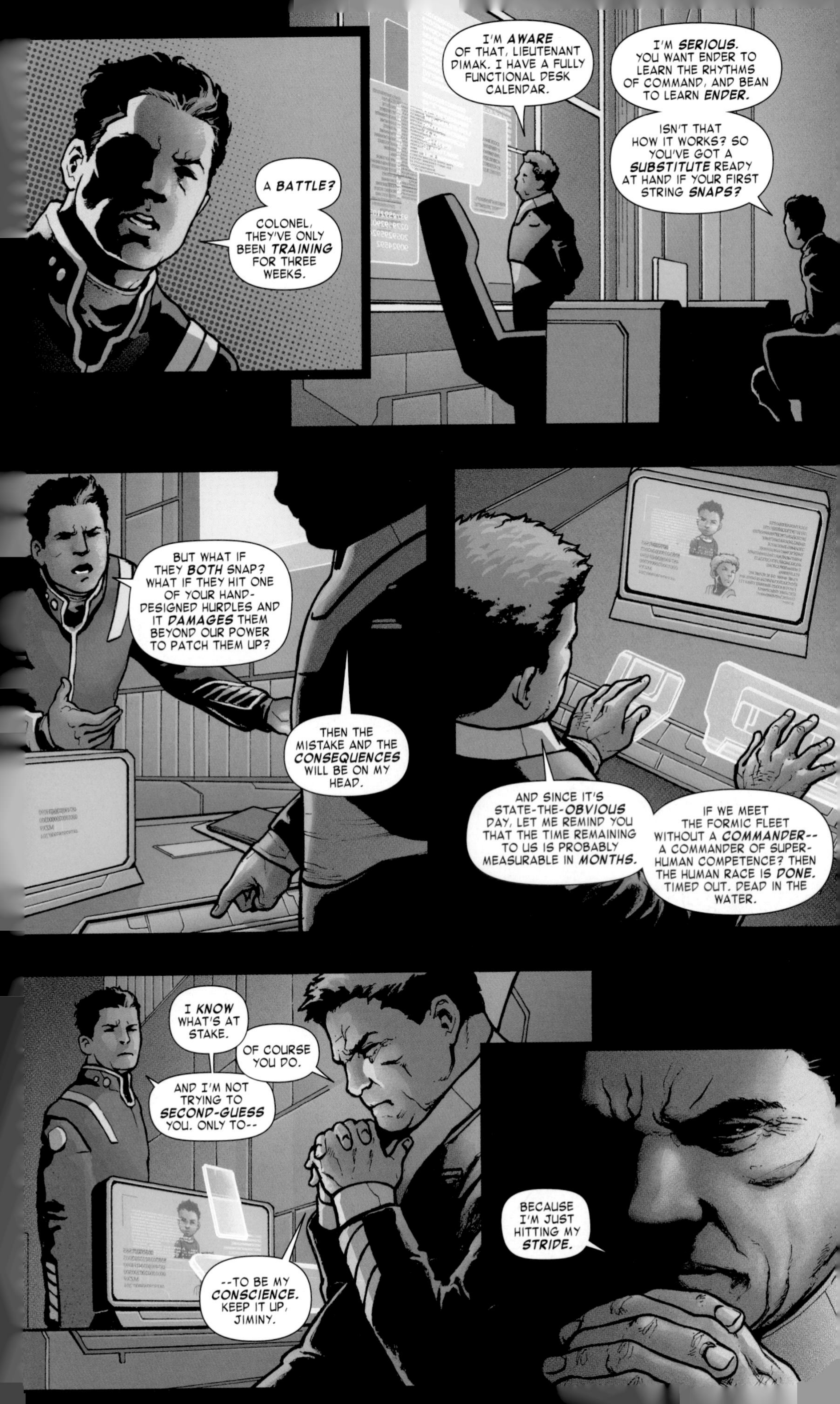
A BATTLE?
COLONEL, THEY'VE ONLY BEEN TRAINING FOR THREE WEEKS.
I'M AWARE OF THAT, LIEUTENANT DIMAK. I HAVE A FULLY FUNCTIONAL DESK CALENDAR.
I'M SERIOUS. YOU WANT ENDER TO LEARN THE RHYTHMS OF COMMAND, AND BEAN TO LEARN ENDER.
ISN'T THAT HOW IT WORKS? SO YOU'VE GOT A SUBSTITUTE READY AT HAND IF YOUR FIRST STRING SNAPS?
BUT WHAT IF THEY BOTH SNAP? WHAT IF THEY HIT ONE OF YOUR HAND-DESIGNED HURDLES AND IT DAMAGES THEM BEYOND OUR POWER TO PATCH THEM UP?
THEN THE MISTAKE AND THE CONSEQUENCES WILL BE ON MY HEAD.
AND SINCE IT'S STATE-THE-OBVIOUS DAY, LET ME REMIND YOU THAT THE TIME REMAINING TO US IS PROBABLY MEASURABLE IN MONTHS.
IF WE MEET THE FORMIC FLEET WITHOUT A COMMANDER-- A COMMANDER OF SUPER-HUMAN COMPETENCE? THEN THE HUMAN RACE IS DONE. TIMED OUT. DEAD IN THE WATER.
I KNOW WHAT'S AT STAKE.
OF COURSE YOU DO.
AND I'M NOT TRYING TO SECOND-GUESS YOU. ONLY TO--
--TO BE MY CONSCIENCE. KEEP IT UP, JIMINY.
BECAUSE I'M JUST HITTING MY STRIDE.

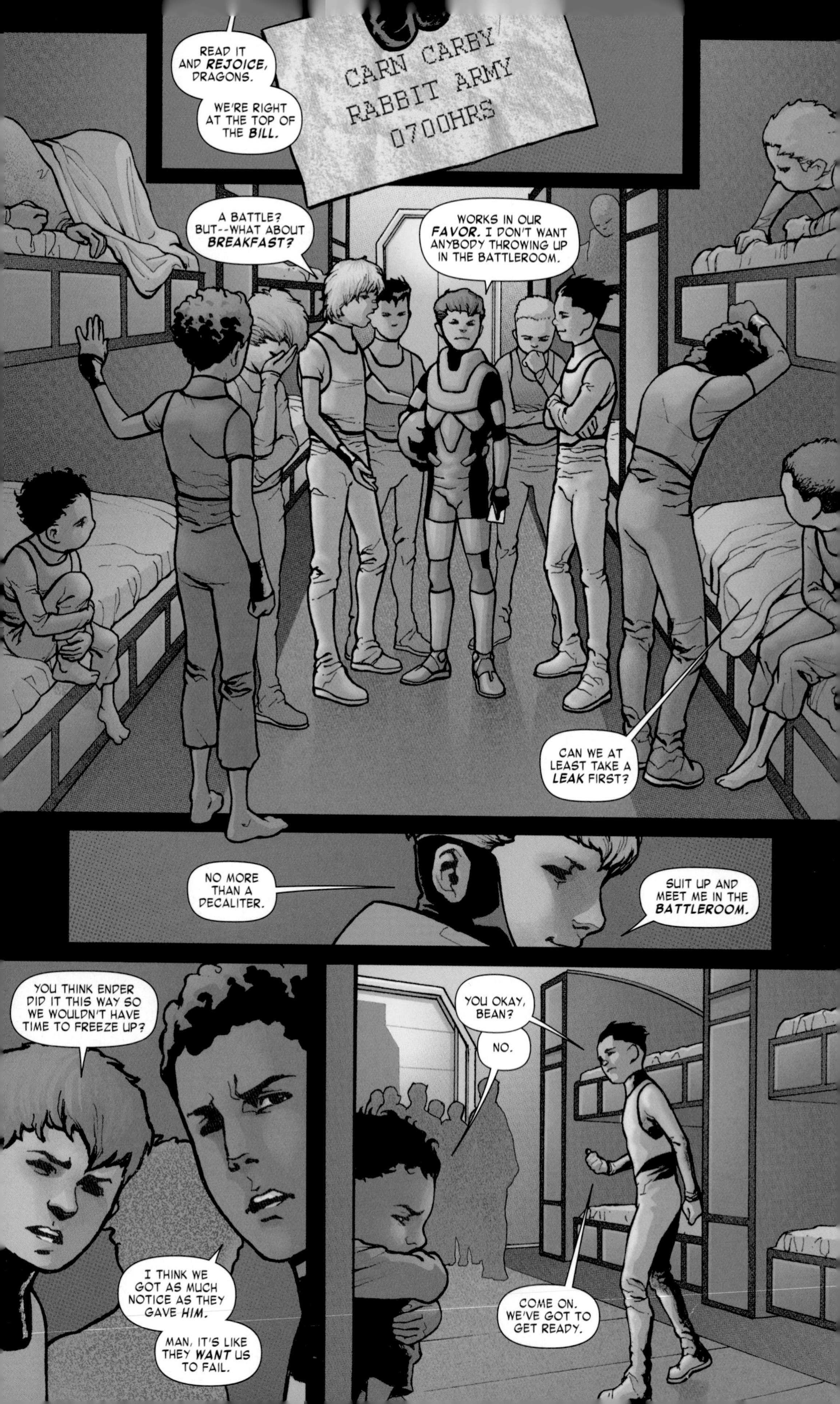
READ IT AND REJOICE, DRAGONS.
WE'RE RIGHT AT THE TOP OF THE BILL.
CARN CARBY
RABBIT ARMY
0700HRS
A BATTLE? BUT--WHAT ABOUT BREAKFAST?
WORKS IN OUR FAVOR. I DON'T WANT ANYBODY THROWING UP IN THE BATTLEROOM.
CAN WE AT LEAST TAKE A LEAK FIRST?
NO MORE THAN A DECALITER.
SUIT UP AND MEET ME IN THE BATTLEROOM.
YOU THINK ENDER DID IT THIS WAY SO WE WOULDN'T HAVE TIME TO FREEZE UP?
I THINK WE GOT AS MUCH NOTICE AS THEY GAVE HIM.
MAN, IT'S LIKE THEY WANT US TO FAIL.
YOU OKAY, BEAN?
NO.
COME ON. WE'VE GOT TO GET READY.

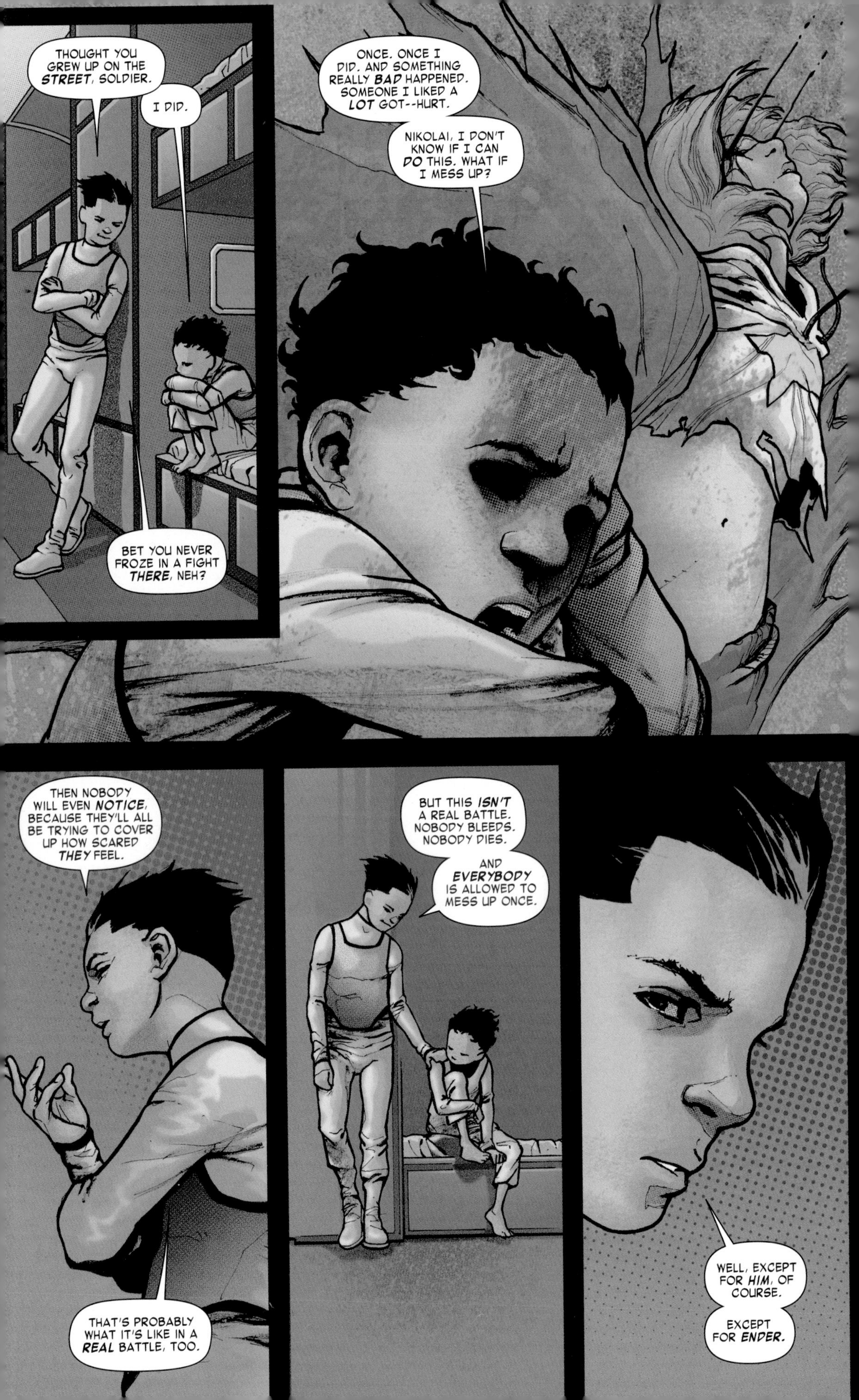
THOUGHT YOU GREW UP ON THE STREET, SOLDIER.
I DID.
BET YOU NEVER FROZE IN A FIGHT THERE, NEH?
ONCE. ONCE I DID. AND SOMETHING REALLY BAD HAPPENED. SOMEONE I LIKED A LOT GOT--HURT.
NIKOLAI, I DON'T KNOW IF I CAN DO THIS. WHAT IF I MESS UP?
THEN NOBODY WILL EVEN NOTICE, BECAUSE THEY'LL ALL BE TRYING TO COVER UP HOW SCARED THEY FEEL.
THAT'S PROBABLY WHAT IT'S LIKE IN A REAL BATTLE, TOO.
BUT THIS ISN'T A REAL BATTLE. NOBODY BLEEDS. NOBODY DIES.
AND EVERYBODY IS ALLOWED TO MESS UP ONCE.
WELL, EXCEPT FOR HIM, OF COURSE.
EXCEPT FOR ENDER.

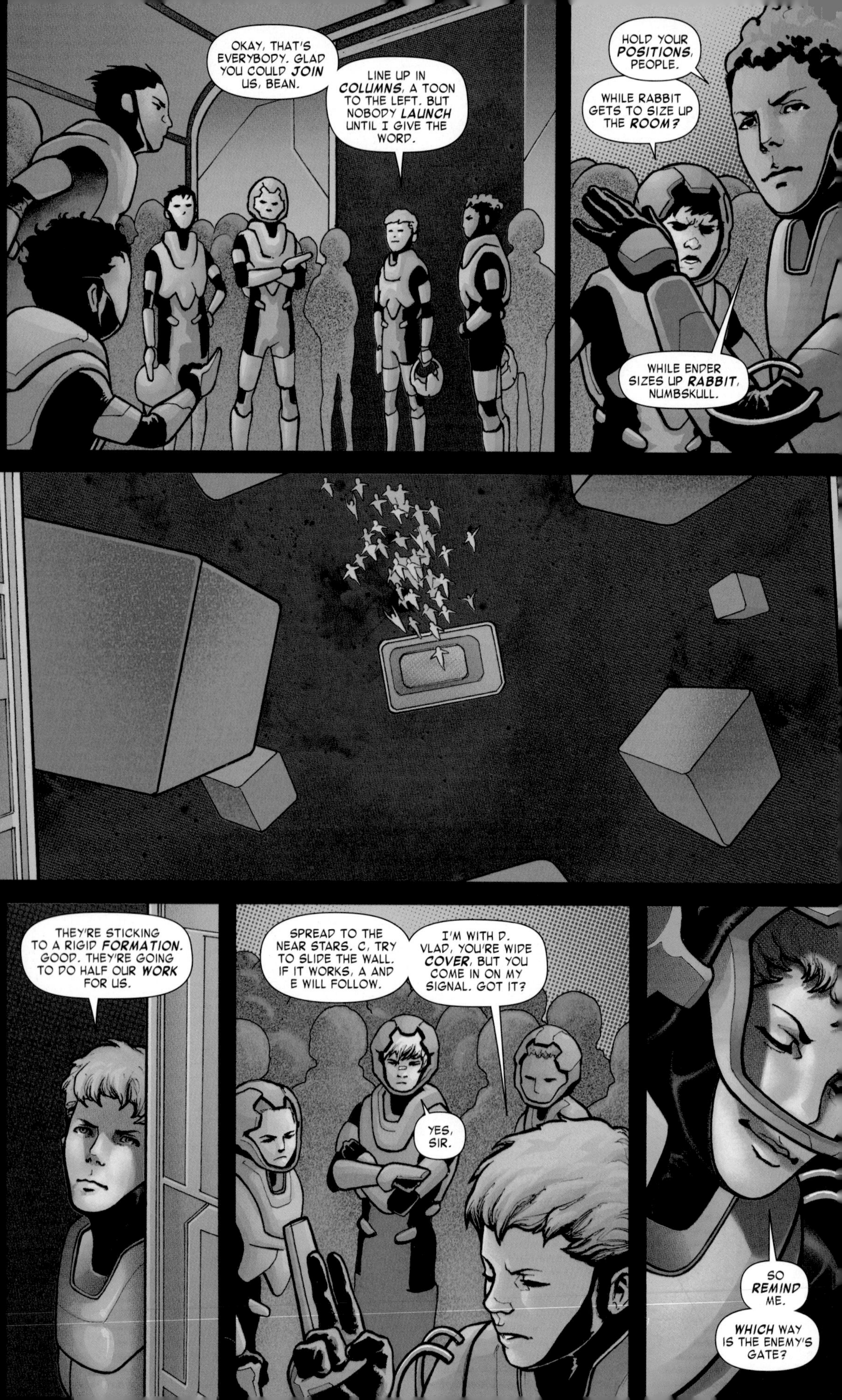
OKAY, THAT'S EVERYBODY. GLAD YOU COULD JOIN US, BEAN.
LINE UP IN COLUMNS, A TOON TO THE LEFT. BUT NOBODY LAUNCH UNTIL I GIVE THE WORD.
HOLD YOUR POSITIONS, PEOPLE.
WHILE RABBIT GETS TO SIZE UP THE ROOM?
WHILE ENDER SIZES UP RABBIT, NUMBSKULL.
THEY'RE STICKING TO A RIGID FORMATION. GOOD. THEY'RE GOING TO DO HALF OUR WORK FOR US.
SPREAD TO THE NEAR STARS. C, TRY TO SLIDE THE WALL. IF IT WORKS, A AND E WILL FOLLOW.
I'M WITH D. VLAD, YOU'RE WIDE COVER, BUT YOU COME IN ON MY SIGNAL. GOT IT?
YES, SIR.
SO REMIND ME.
WHICH WAY IS THE ENEMY'S GATE?

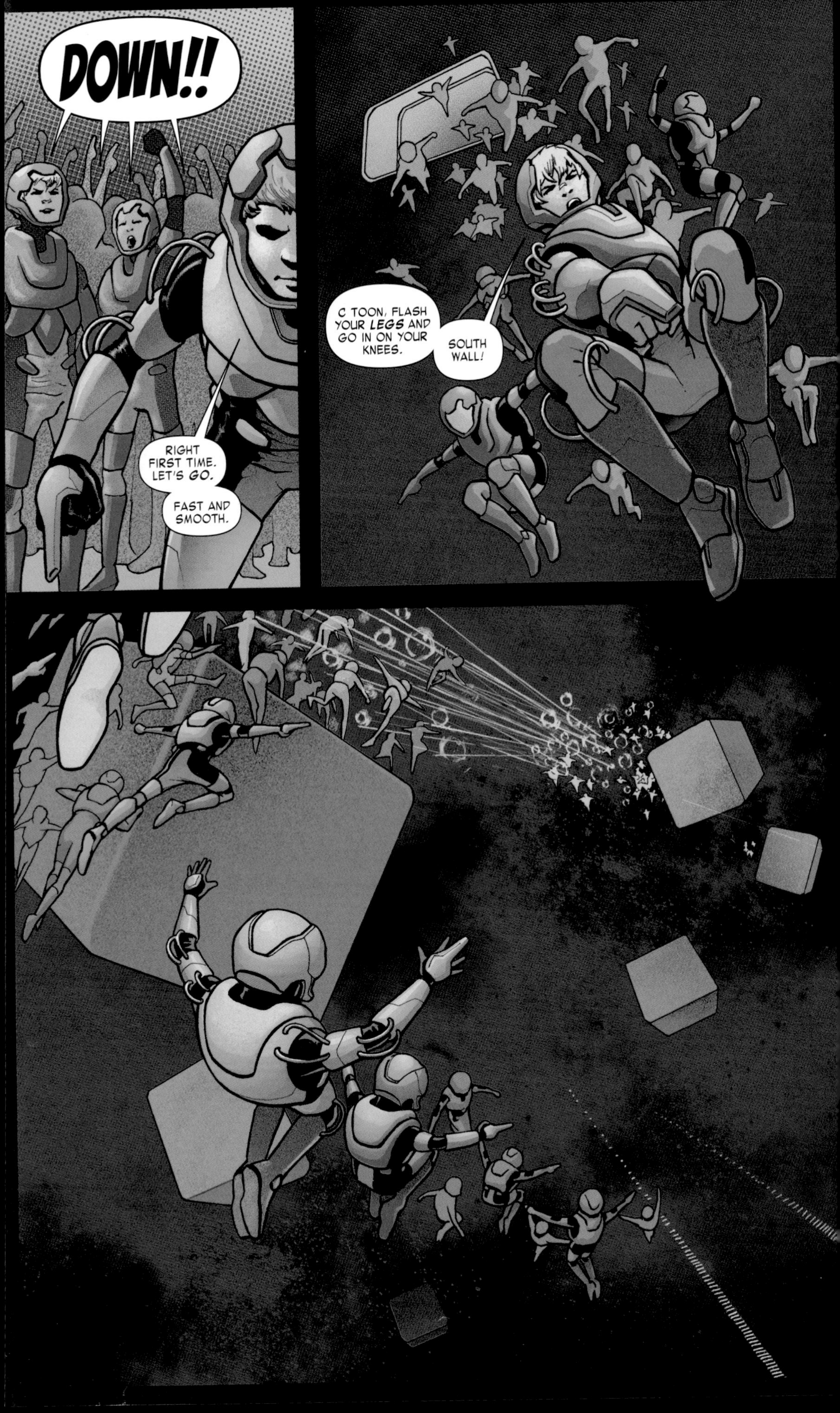
DOWN!!
RIGHT FIRST TIME. LET'S GO.
FAST AND SMOOTH.
C TOON, FLASH YOUR LEGS AND GO IN ON YOUR KNEES.
SOUTH WALL!

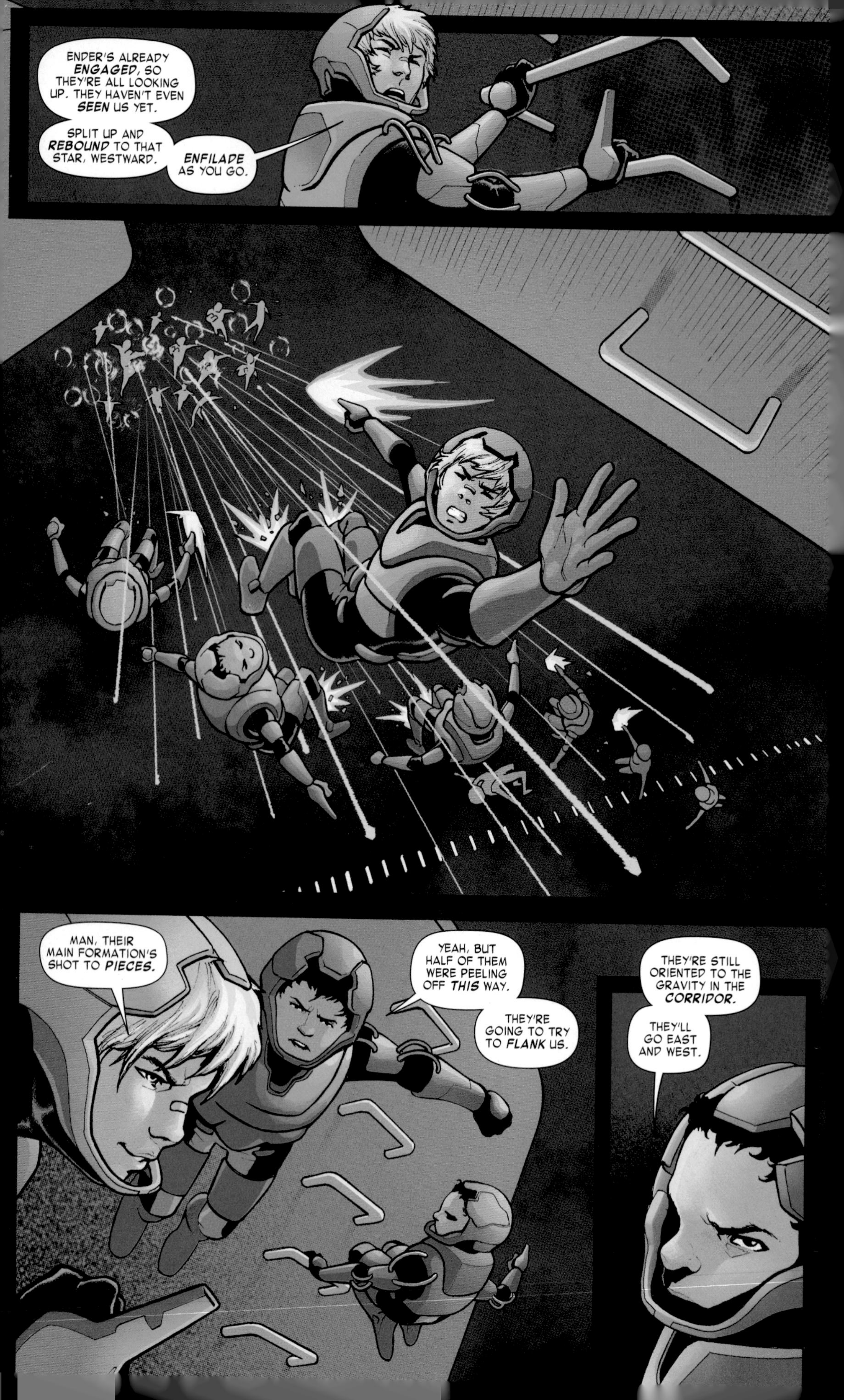
ENDER'S ALREADY ENGAGED, SO THEY'RE ALL LOOKING UP. THEY HAVEN'T EVEN SEEN US YET.
SPLIT UP AND REBOUND TO THAT STAR, WESTWARD.
ENFILADE AS YOU GO.
MAN, THEIR MAIN FORMATION'S SHOT TO PIECES.
YEAH, BUT HALF OF THEM WERE PEELING OFF THIS WAY.
THEY'RE GOING TO TRY TO FLANK US.
THEY'RE STILL ORIENTED TO THE GRAVITY IN THE CORRIDOR.
THEY'LL GO EAST AND WEST.

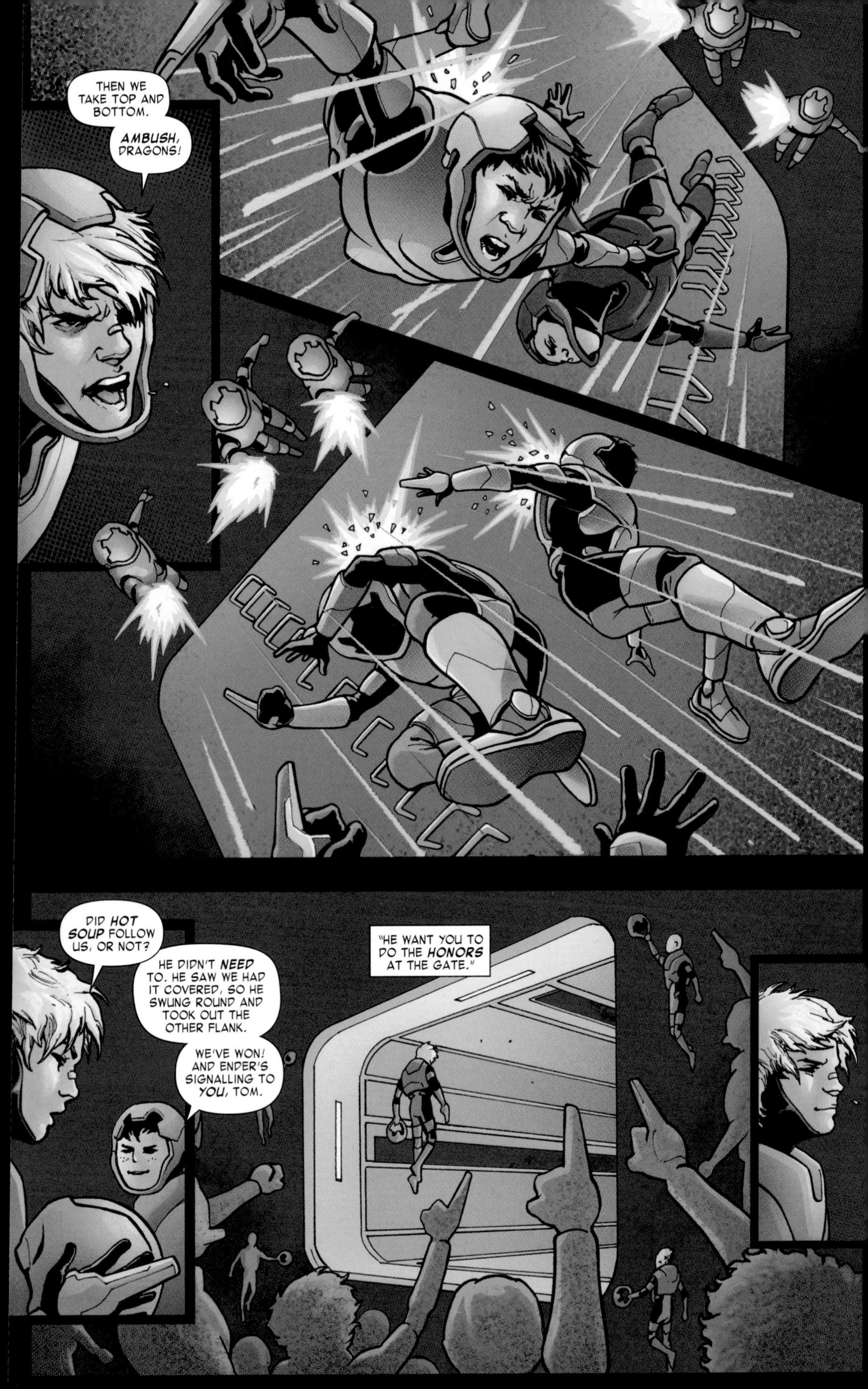
THEN WE TAKE TOP AND BOTTOM.
AMBUSH, DRAGONS!
DID HOT SOUP FOLLOW US, OR NOT?
HE DIDN'T NEED TO. HE SAW WE HAD IT COVERED, SO HE SWUNG ROUND AND TOOK OUT THE OTHER FLANK.
WE'VE WON! AND ENDER'S SIGNALLING TO YOU, TOM.
"HE WANT YOU TO DO THE HONORS AT THE GATE."

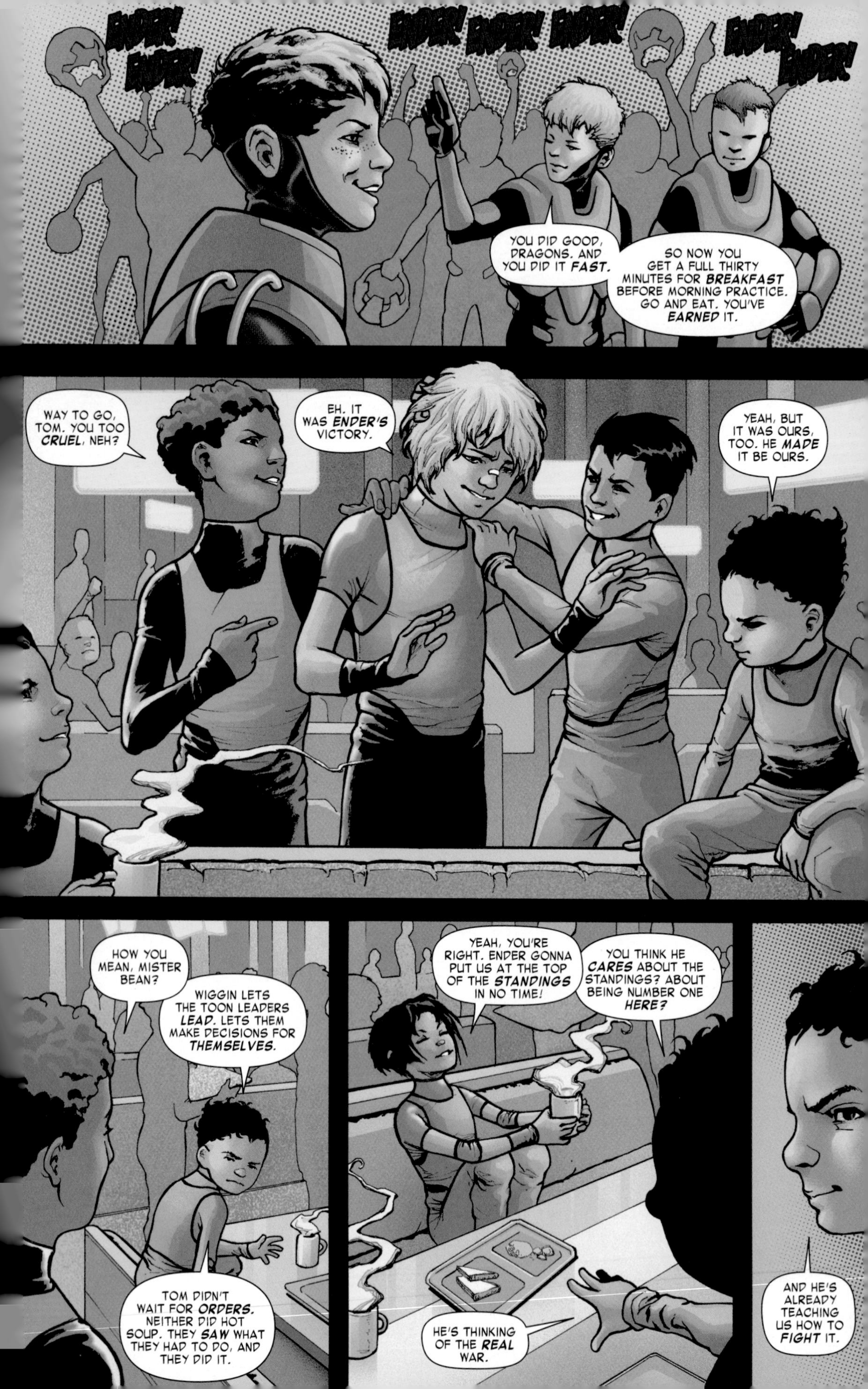
ENDER! ENDER!
ENDER! ENDER! ENDER!
ENDER! ENDER!
YOU DID GOOD, DRAGONS. AND YOU DID IT FAST.
SO NOW YOU GET A FULL THIRTY MINUTES FOR BREAKFAST BEFORE MORNING PRACTICE. GO AND EAT. YOU'VE EARNED IT.
WAY TO GO, TOM. YOU TOO CRUEL, NEH?
EH. IT WAS ENDER'S VICTORY.
YEAH, BUT IT WAS OURS, TOO. HE MADE IT BE OURS.
HOW YOU MEAN, MISTER BEAN?
WIGGIN LETS THE TOON LEADERS LEAD. LETS THEM MAKE DECISIONS FOR THEMSELVES.
TOM DIDN'T WAIT FOR ORDERS. NEITHER DID HOT SOUP. THEY SAW WHAT THEY HAD TO DO, AND THEY DID IT.
YEAH, YOU'RE RIGHT. ENDER GONNA PUT US AT THE TOP OF THE STANDINGS IN NO TIME!
YOU THINK HE CARES ABOUT THE STANDINGS? ABOUT BEING NUMBER ONE HERE?
HE'S THINKING OF THE REAL WAR.
AND HE'S ALREADY TEACHING US HOW TO FIGHT IT.

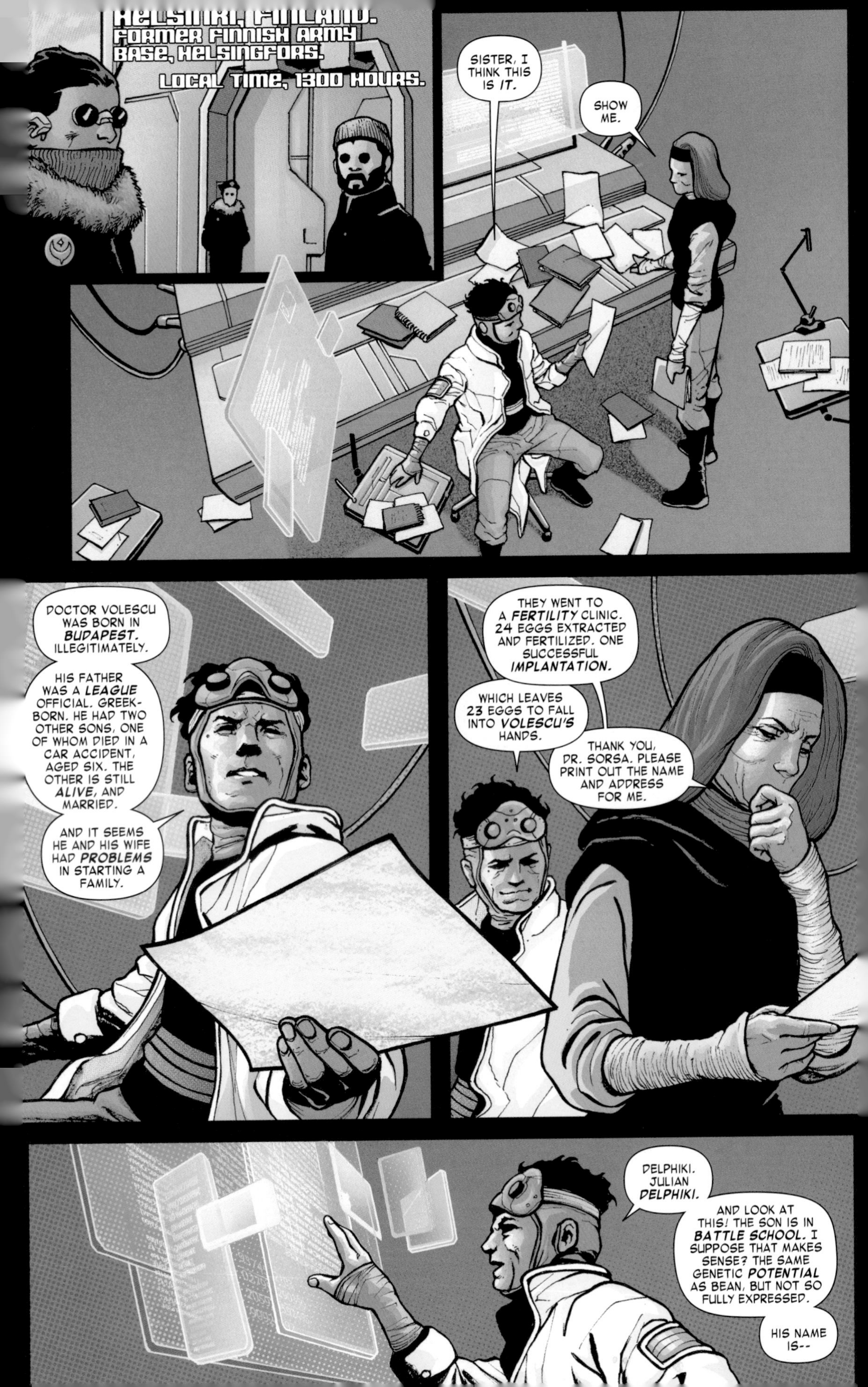
HELSINKI, FINLAND.
FORMER FINNISH ARMY BASE, HELSINGFORS.
LOCAL TIME, 1300 HOURS.
SISTER, I THINK THIS IS *IT*.
SHOW ME.
DOCTOR VOLESCU WAS BORN IN ***BUDAPEST.*** ILLEGITIMATELY.
HIS FATHER WAS A ***LEAGUE*** OFFICIAL. GREEK-BORN. HE HAD TWO OTHER SONS, ONE OF WHOM DIED IN A CAR ACCIDENT, AGED SIX. THE OTHER IS STILL ***ALIVE,*** AND MARRIED.
AND IT SEEMS HE AND HIS WIFE HAD ***PROBLEMS*** IN STARTING A FAMILY.
THEY WENT TO A ***FERTILITY*** CLINIC. 24 EGGS EXTRACTED AND FERTILIZED. ONE SUCCESSFUL ***IMPLANTATION.***
WHICH LEAVES 23 EGGS TO FALL INTO ***VOLESCU'S*** HANDS.
THANK YOU, DR. SORSA. PLEASE PRINT OUT THE NAME AND ADDRESS FOR ME.
DELPHIKI. JULIAN ***DELPHIKI.***
AND LOOK AT THIS! THE SON IS IN ***BATTLE SCHOOL.*** I SUPPOSE THAT MAKES SENSE? THE SAME GENETIC ***POTENTIAL*** AS BEAN, BUT NOT SO FULLY EXPRESSED.
HIS NAME IS--

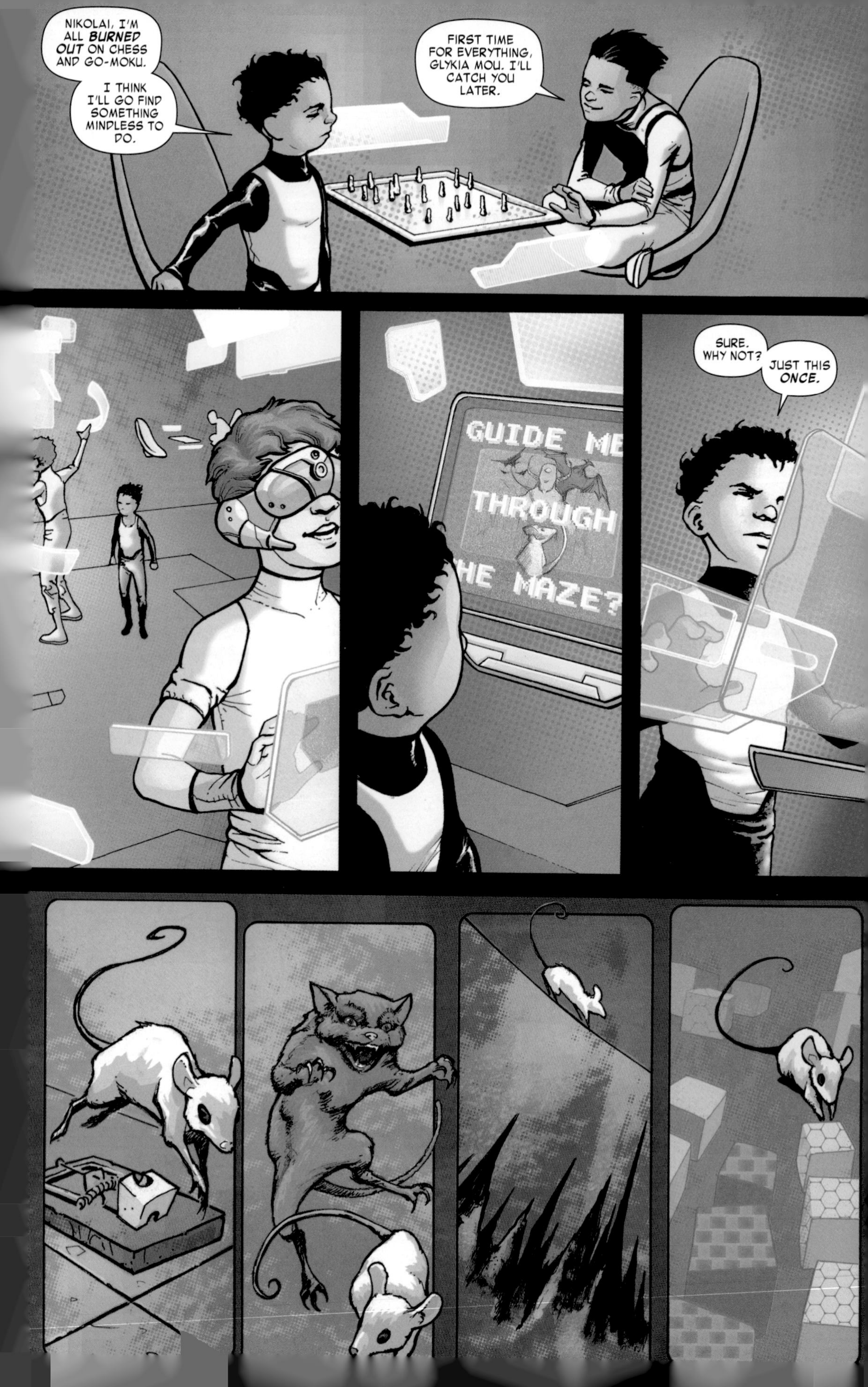
NIKOLAI, I'M ALL *BURNED OUT* ON CHESS AND GO-MOKU.
I THINK I'LL GO FIND SOMETHING MINDLESS TO DO.
FIRST TIME FOR EVERYTHING, GLYKIA MOU. I'LL CATCH YOU LATER.
GUIDE ME THROUGH THE MAZE?
SURE. WHY NOT?
JUST THIS *ONCE.*

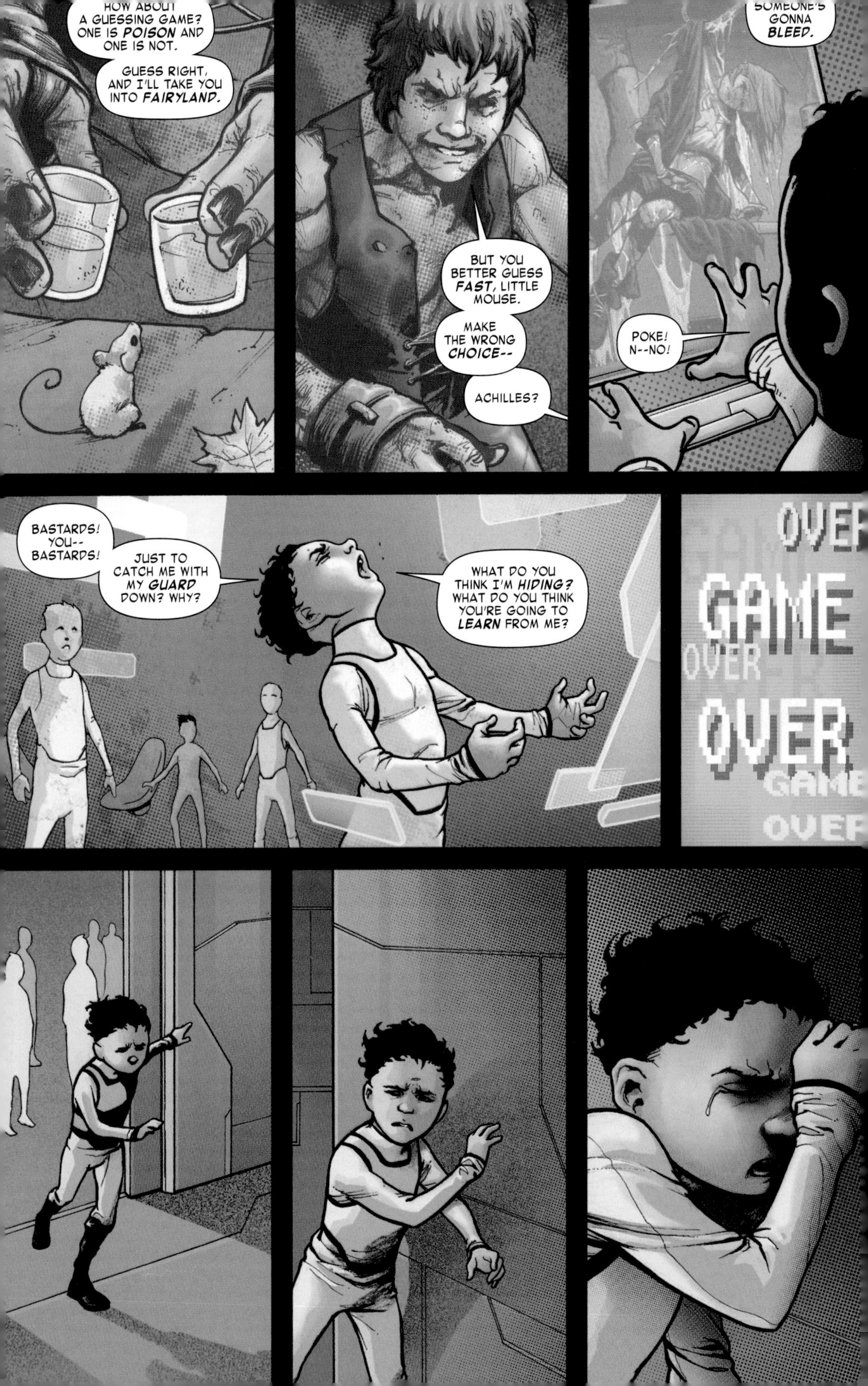
HOW ABOUT A GUESSING GAME? ONE IS POISON AND ONE IS NOT.
GUESS RIGHT, AND I'LL TAKE YOU INTO FAIRYLAND.
BUT YOU BETTER GUESS FAST, LITTLE MOUSE.
MAKE THE WRONG CHOICE--
ACHILLES?
SOMEONE'S GONNA BLEED.
POKE! N--NO!
BASTARDS! YOU-- BASTARDS!
JUST TO CATCH ME WITH MY GUARD DOWN? WHY?
WHAT DO YOU THINK I'M HIDING? WHAT DO YOU THINK YOU'RE GOING TO LEARN FROM ME?
GAME
OVER
GAME
OVER

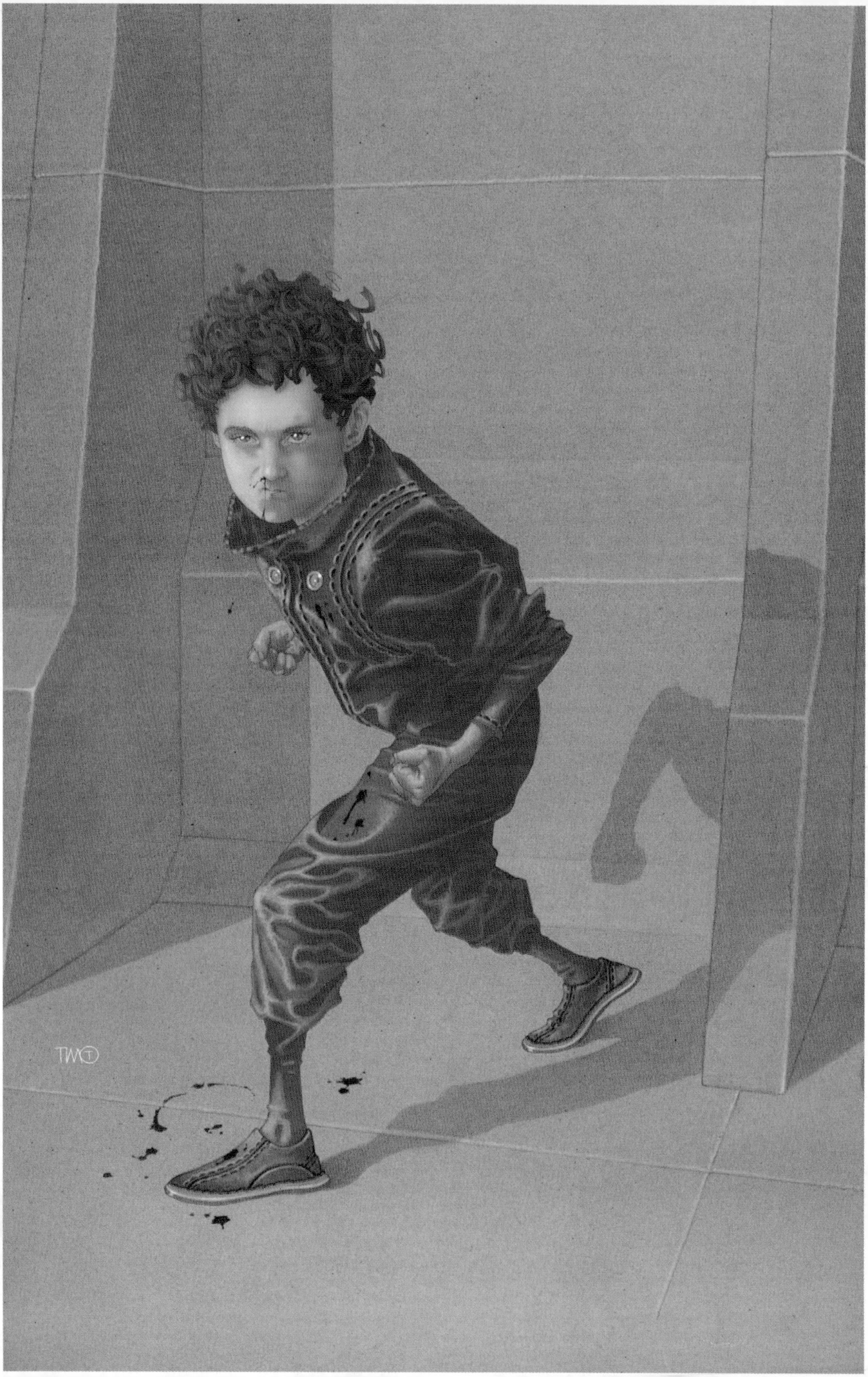

"I don't even know how to interpret this. The mind game had only one shot at Bean, and it puts up the face of this kid – Achilles. And Bean goes off the charts with – what? Fear? Rage? Isn't there anyone who knows how this so-called game works?"

"Was that a rant, or is there any particular one of those questions you want answered?"

"What I want you to answer is this: how the hell can you tell me that something was 'very significant' if you have no idea what it signifies?"

"The image of Achilles was very important to Bean. We know that much."

"Important positive, or important negative?"

"That's too cut-and-dried, sir. The whole purpose of the game, the way it works, is that the computer makes connections we would never think of, and gets responses we weren't looking for."

"Like screaming hysteria."

"Bean wept. He showed emotion. He didn't become hysterical."

"It's the most we've ever got from him. And I repeat, I'd like your best guess as to what it means."

"We're working on it. But Colonel, didn't you say you had an alternative source of information on this? One of your Earthside civilian liaisons?"

"Let's just say she's not likely to be particularly forthcoming right now. Keep working, and get me an answer. Or I might go for a more empirical approach."

"Meaning..."

"Meaning that when the messenger won't tell me what the hell the message is, my trigger finger gets itchy. Dismissed."

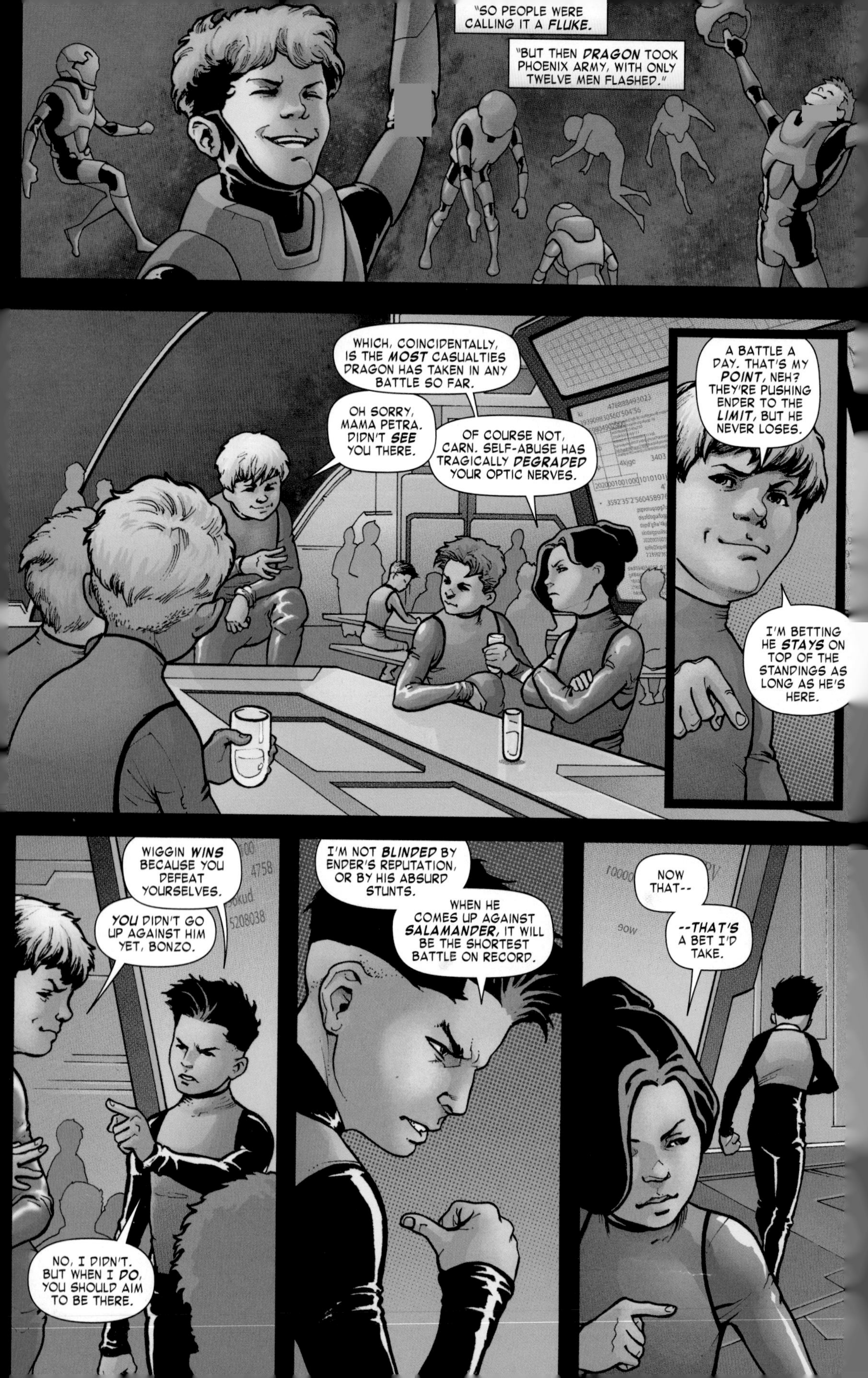
"SO PEOPLE WERE CALLING IT A FLUKE.
"BUT THEN DRAGON TOOK PHOENIX ARMY, WITH ONLY TWELVE MEN FLASHED."
WHICH, COINCIDENTALLY, IS THE MOST CASUALTIES DRAGON HAS TAKEN IN ANY BATTLE SO FAR.
OH SORRY, MAMA PETRA. DIDN'T SEE YOU THERE.
OF COURSE NOT, CARN. SELF-ABUSE HAS TRAGICALLY DEGRADED YOUR OPTIC NERVES.
A BATTLE A DAY. THAT'S MY POINT, NEH? THEY'RE PUSHING ENDER TO THE LIMIT, BUT HE NEVER LOSES.
I'M BETTING HE STAYS ON TOP OF THE STANDINGS AS LONG AS HE'S HERE.
WIGGIN WINS BECAUSE YOU DEFEAT YOURSELVES.
YOU DIDN'T GO UP AGAINST HIM YET, BONZO.
NO, I DIDN'T. BUT WHEN I DO, YOU SHOULD AIM TO BE THERE.
I'M NOT BLINDED BY ENDER'S REPUTATION, OR BY HIS ABSURD STUNTS.
WHEN HE COMES UP AGAINST SALAMANDER, IT WILL BE THE SHORTEST BATTLE ON RECORD.
NOW THAT--
--THAT'S A BET I'D TAKE.

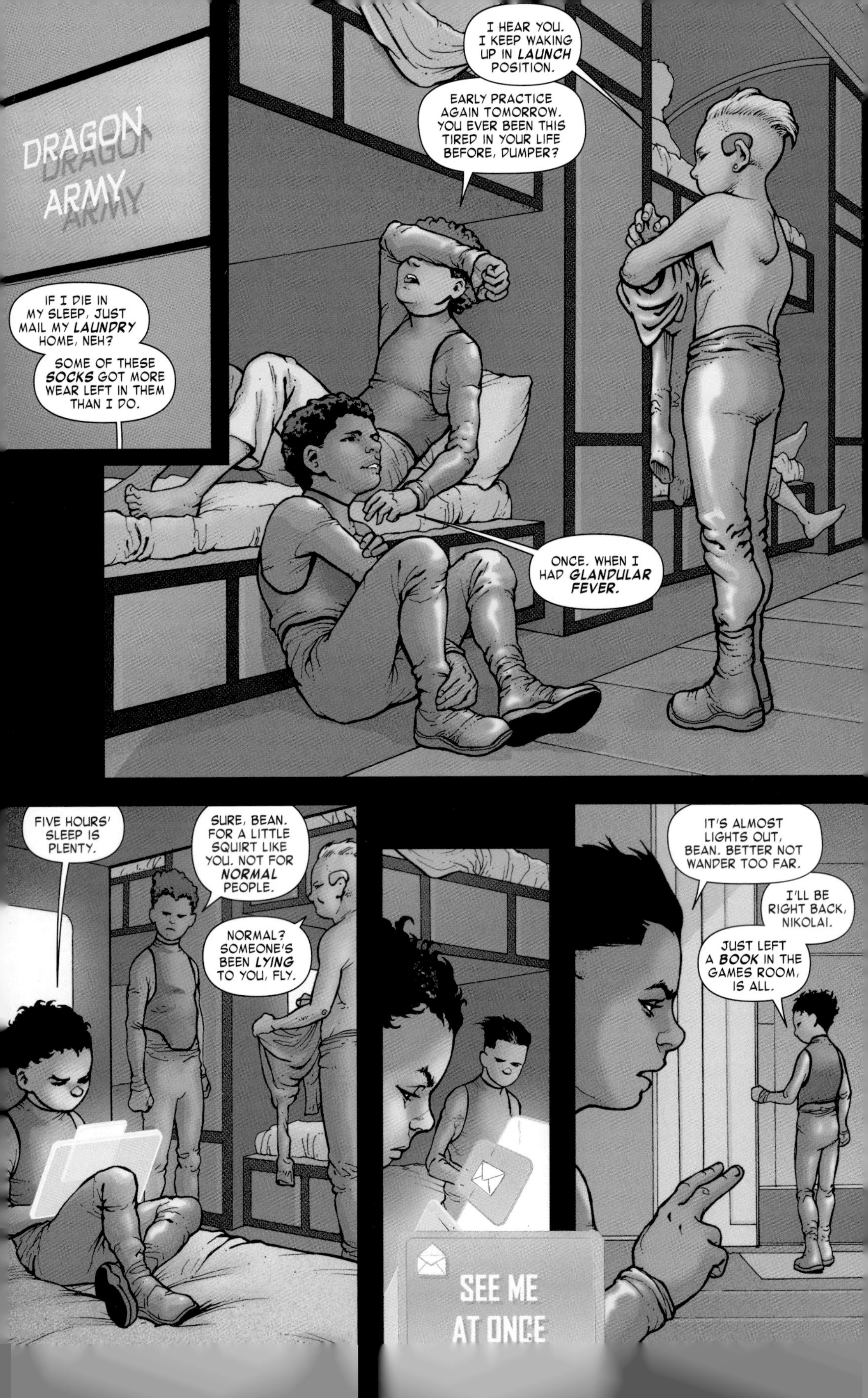
DRAGON ARMY
IF I DIE IN MY SLEEP, JUST MAIL MY *LAUNDRY* HOME, NEH?
SOME OF THESE *SOCKS* GOT MORE WEAR LEFT IN THEM THAN I DO.
I HEAR YOU. I KEEP WAKING UP IN *LAUNCH* POSITION.
EARLY PRACTICE AGAIN TOMORROW. YOU EVER BEEN THIS TIRED IN YOUR LIFE BEFORE, DUMPER?
ONCE. WHEN I HAD *GLANDULAR FEVER.*
FIVE HOURS' SLEEP IS PLENTY.
SURE, BEAN. FOR A LITTLE SQUIRT LIKE YOU. NOT FOR *NORMAL* PEOPLE.
NORMAL? SOMEONE'S BEEN *LYING* TO YOU, FLY.
SEE ME AT ONCE
IT'S ALMOST LIGHTS OUT, BEAN. BETTER NOT WANDER TOO FAR.
I'LL BE RIGHT BACK, NIKOLAI.
JUST LEFT A *BOOK* IN THE GAMES ROOM, IS ALL.

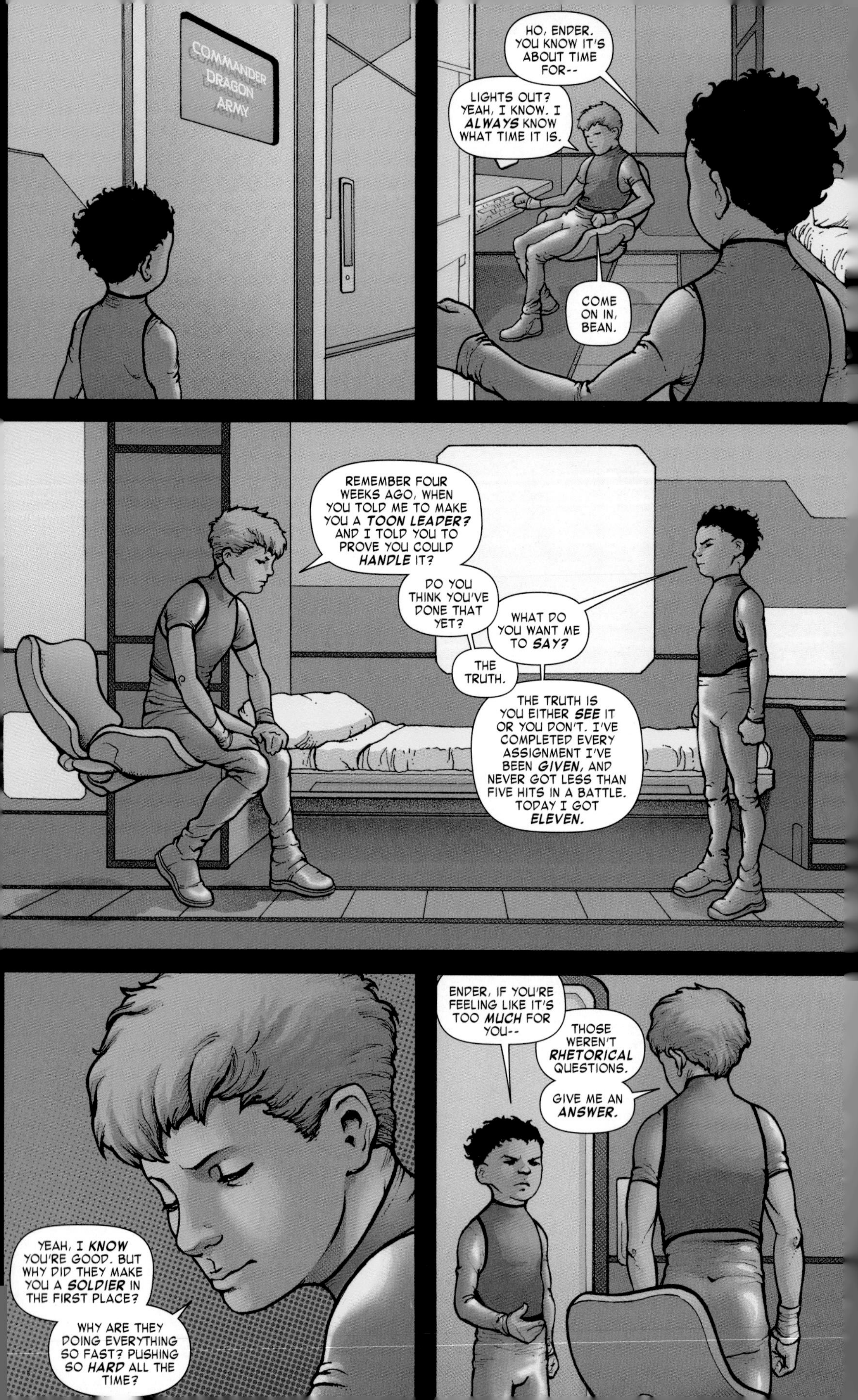
COMMANDER DRAGON ARMY
HO, ENDER. YOU KNOW IT'S ABOUT TIME FOR--
LIGHTS OUT? YEAH, I KNOW. I ALWAYS KNOW WHAT TIME IT IS.
COME ON IN, BEAN.
REMEMBER FOUR WEEKS AGO, WHEN YOU TOLD ME TO MAKE YOU A TOON LEADER? AND I TOLD YOU TO PROVE YOU COULD HANDLE IT?
DO YOU THINK YOU'VE DONE THAT YET?
WHAT DO YOU WANT ME TO SAY?
THE TRUTH.
THE TRUTH IS YOU EITHER SEE IT OR YOU DON'T. I'VE COMPLETED EVERY ASSIGNMENT I'VE BEEN GIVEN, AND NEVER GOT LESS THAN FIVE HITS IN A BATTLE. TODAY I GOT ELEVEN.
YEAH, I KNOW YOU'RE GOOD. BUT WHY DID THEY MAKE YOU A SOLDIER IN THE FIRST PLACE?
WHY ARE THEY DOING EVERYTHING SO FAST? PUSHING SO HARD ALL THE TIME?
ENDER, IF YOU'RE FEELING LIKE IT'S TOO MUCH FOR YOU--
THOSE WEREN'T RHETORICAL QUESTIONS.
GIVE ME AN ANSWER.

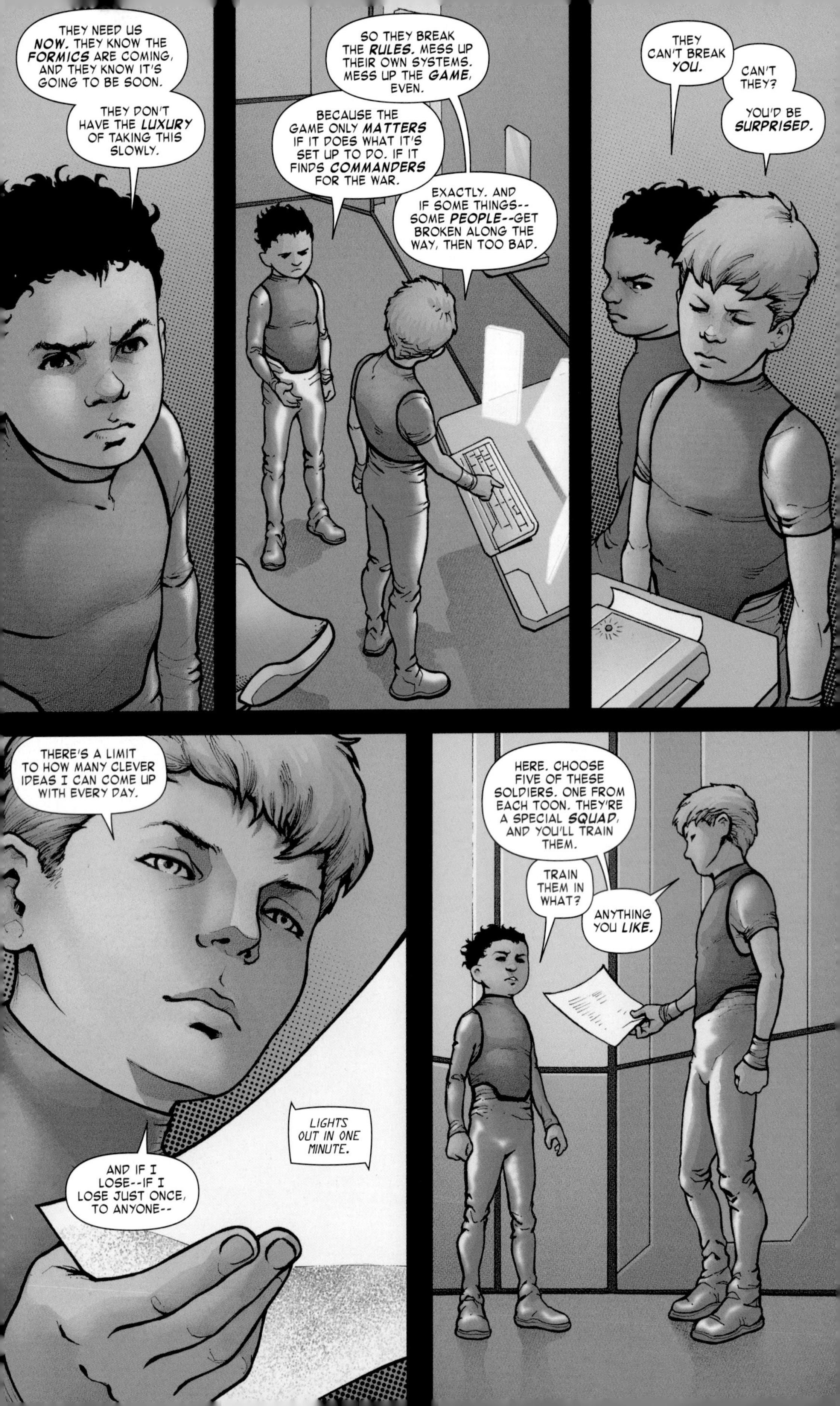
THEY NEED US NOW. THEY KNOW THE FORMICS ARE COMING, AND THEY KNOW IT'S GOING TO BE SOON.
THEY DON'T HAVE THE LUXURY OF TAKING THIS SLOWLY.
SO THEY BREAK THE RULES. MESS UP THEIR OWN SYSTEMS. MESS UP THE GAME, EVEN.
BECAUSE THE GAME ONLY MATTERS IF IT DOES WHAT IT'S SET UP TO DO. IF IT FINDS COMMANDERS FOR THE WAR.
EXACTLY. AND IF SOME THINGS--SOME PEOPLE--GET BROKEN ALONG THE WAY, THEN TOO BAD.
THEY CAN'T BREAK YOU.
CAN'T THEY?
YOU'D BE SURPRISED.
THERE'S A LIMIT TO HOW MANY CLEVER IDEAS I CAN COME UP WITH EVERY DAY.
AND IF I LOSE--IF I LOSE JUST ONCE, TO ANYONE--
LIGHTS OUT IN ONE MINUTE.
HERE. CHOOSE FIVE OF THESE SOLDIERS. ONE FROM EACH TOON. THEY'RE A SPECIAL SQUAD, AND YOU'LL TRAIN THEM.
TRAIN THEM IN WHAT?
ANYTHING YOU LIKE.

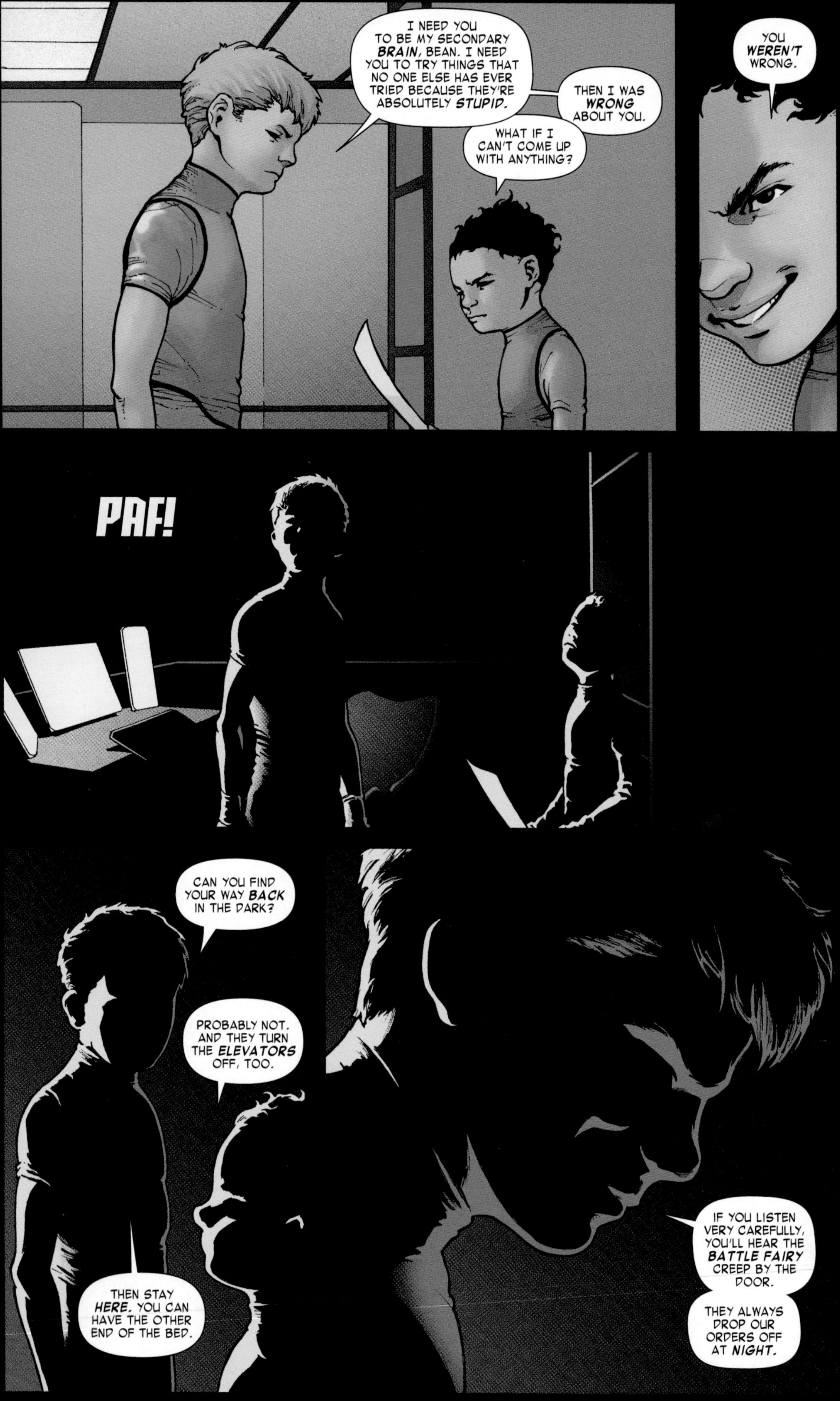
I NEED YOU TO BE MY SECONDARY BRAIN, BEAN. I NEED YOU TO TRY THINGS THAT NO ONE ELSE HAS EVER TRIED BECAUSE THEY'RE ABSOLUTELY STUPID.
WHAT IF I CAN'T COME UP WITH ANYTHING?
THEN I WAS WRONG ABOUT YOU.
YOU WEREN'T WRONG.
PAF!
CAN YOU FIND YOUR WAY BACK IN THE DARK?
PROBABLY NOT. AND THEY TURN THE ELEVATORS OFF, TOO.
THEN STAY HERE. YOU CAN HAVE THE OTHER END OF THE BED.
IF YOU LISTEN VERY CAREFULLY, YOU'LL HEAR THE BATTLE FAIRY CREEP BY THE DOOR.
THEY ALWAYS DROP OUR ORDERS OFF AT NIGHT.

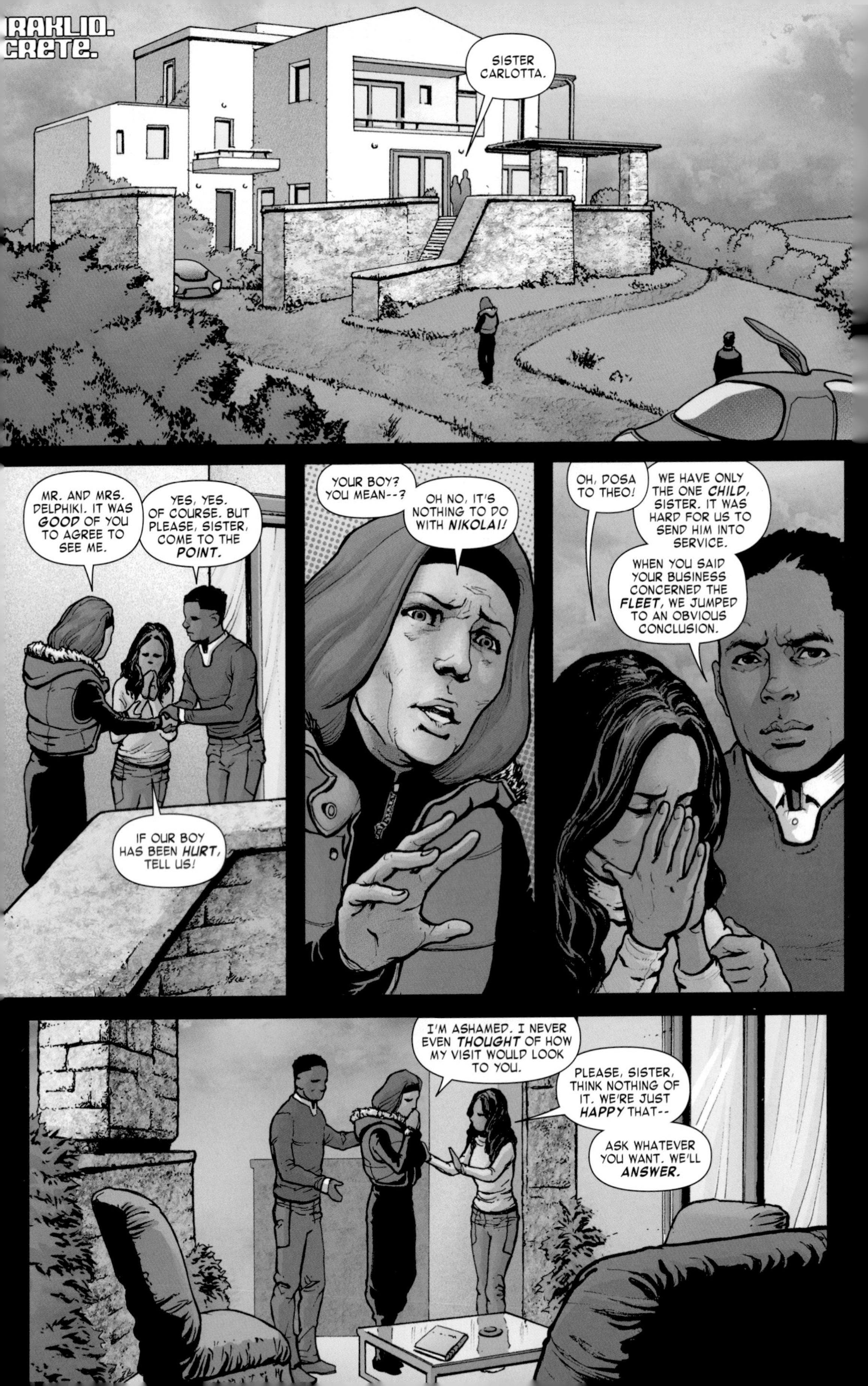
RAKLIO. CRETE.
SISTER CARLOTTA.
MR. AND MRS. DELPHIKI. IT WAS GOOD OF YOU TO AGREE TO SEE ME.
YES, YES. OF COURSE. BUT PLEASE, SISTER, COME TO THE POINT.
IF OUR BOY HAS BEEN HURT, TELL US!
YOUR BOY? YOU MEAN--?
OH NO, IT'S NOTHING TO DO WITH NIKOLAI!
OH, DOSA TO THEO!
WE HAVE ONLY THE ONE CHILD, SISTER. IT WAS HARD FOR US TO SEND HIM INTO SERVICE.
WHEN YOU SAID YOUR BUSINESS CONCERNED THE FLEET, WE JUMPED TO AN OBVIOUS CONCLUSION.
I'M ASHAMED. I NEVER EVEN THOUGHT OF HOW MY VISIT WOULD LOOK TO YOU.
PLEASE, SISTER, THINK NOTHING OF IT. WE'RE JUST HAPPY THAT--
ASK WHATEVER YOU WANT. WE'LL ANSWER.

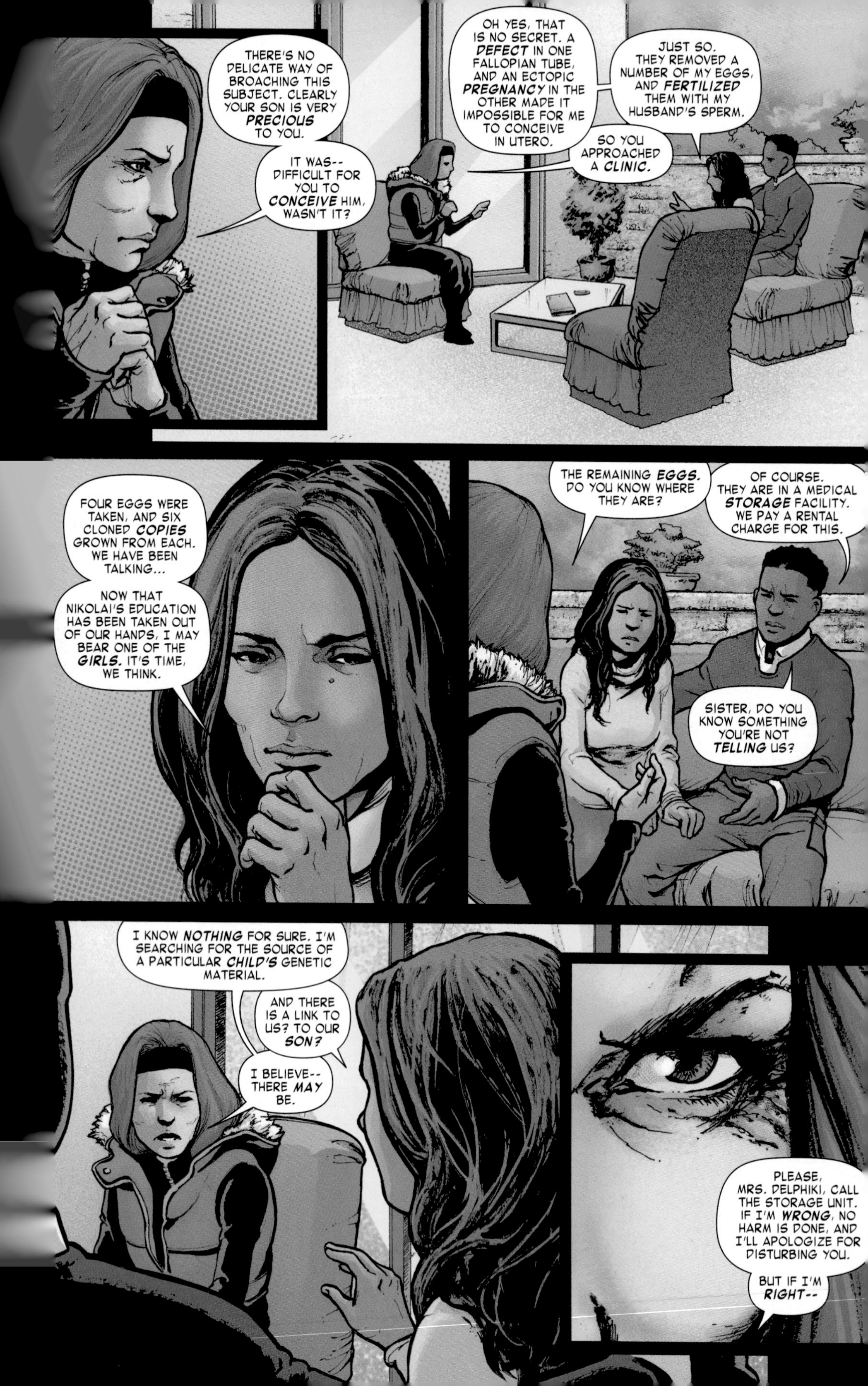
THERE'S NO DELICATE WAY OF BROACHING THIS SUBJECT. CLEARLY YOUR SON IS VERY PRECIOUS TO YOU.
IT WAS-- DIFFICULT FOR YOU TO CONCEIVE HIM, WASN'T IT?
OH YES, THAT IS NO SECRET. A DEFECT IN ONE FALLOPIAN TUBE, AND AN ECTOPIC PREGNANCY IN THE OTHER MADE IT IMPOSSIBLE FOR ME TO CONCEIVE IN UTERO.
SO YOU APPROACHED A CLINIC.
JUST SO. THEY REMOVED A NUMBER OF MY EGGS, AND FERTILIZED THEM WITH MY HUSBAND'S SPERM.
FOUR EGGS WERE TAKEN, AND SIX CLONED COPIES GROWN FROM EACH. WE HAVE BEEN TALKING...
NOW THAT NIKOLAI'S EDUCATION HAS BEEN TAKEN OUT OF OUR HANDS, I MAY BEAR ONE OF THE GIRLS. IT'S TIME, WE THINK.
THE REMAINING EGGS. DO YOU KNOW WHERE THEY ARE?
OF COURSE. THEY ARE IN A MEDICAL STORAGE FACILITY. WE PAY A RENTAL CHARGE FOR THIS.
SISTER, DO YOU KNOW SOMETHING YOU'RE NOT TELLING US?
I KNOW NOTHING FOR SURE. I'M SEARCHING FOR THE SOURCE OF A PARTICULAR CHILD'S GENETIC MATERIAL.
AND THERE IS A LINK TO US? TO OUR SON?
I BELIEVE-- THERE MAY BE.
PLEASE, MRS. DELPHIKI, CALL THE STORAGE UNIT. IF I'M WRONG, NO HARM IS DONE, AND I'LL APOLOGIZE FOR DISTURBING YOU.
BUT IF I'M RIGHT--

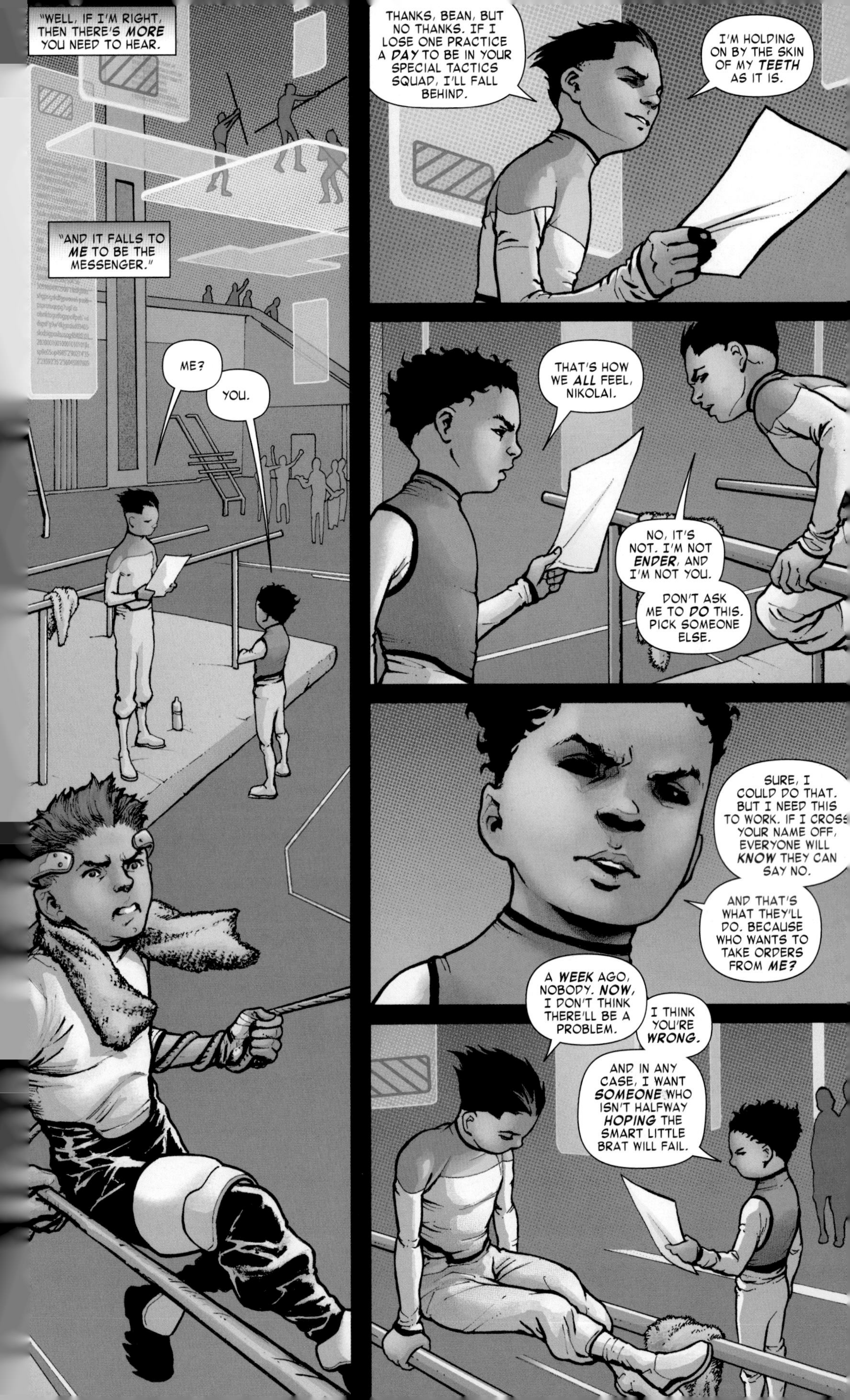
"WELL, IF I'M RIGHT, THEN THERE'S MORE YOU NEED TO HEAR.
"AND IT FALLS TO ME TO BE THE MESSENGER."
ME?
YOU.
THANKS, BEAN, BUT NO THANKS. IF I LOSE ONE PRACTICE A DAY TO BE IN YOUR SPECIAL TACTICS SQUAD, I'LL FALL BEHIND.
I'M HOLDING ON BY THE SKIN OF MY TEETH AS IT IS.
THAT'S HOW WE ALL FEEL, NIKOLAI.
NO, IT'S NOT. I'M NOT ENDER, AND I'M NOT YOU.
DON'T ASK ME TO DO THIS. PICK SOMEONE ELSE.
SURE, I COULD DO THAT. BUT I NEED THIS TO WORK. IF I CROSS YOUR NAME OFF, EVERYONE WILL KNOW THEY CAN SAY NO.
AND THAT'S WHAT THEY'LL DO. BECAUSE WHO WANTS TO TAKE ORDERS FROM ME?
A WEEK AGO, NOBODY. NOW, I DON'T THINK THERE'LL BE A PROBLEM.
I THINK YOU'RE WRONG.
AND IN ANY CASE, I WANT SOMEONE WHO ISN'T HALFWAY HOPING THE SMART LITTLE BRAT WILL FAIL.

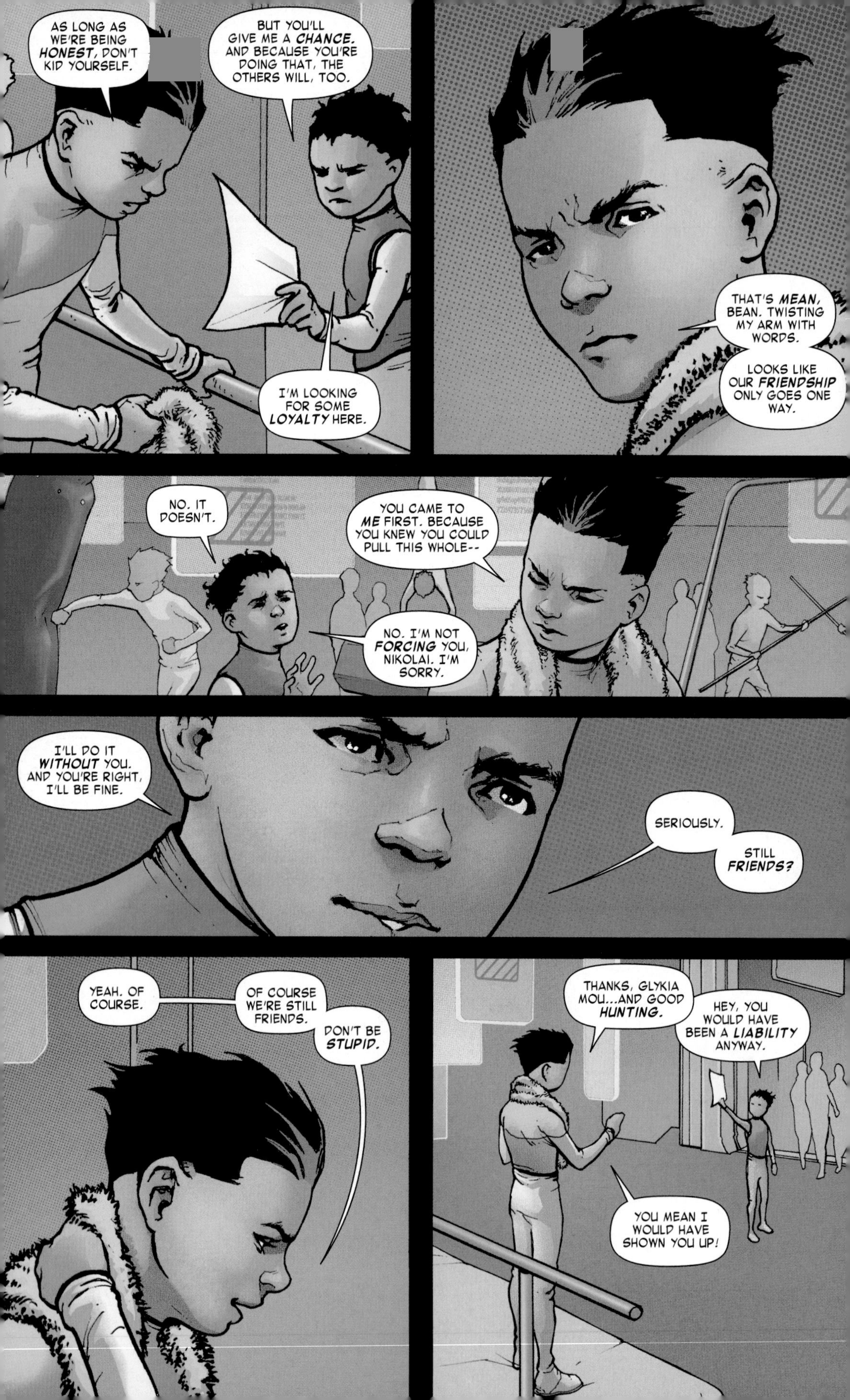
AS LONG AS WE'RE BEING HONEST, DON'T KID YOURSELF.
BUT YOU'LL GIVE ME A CHANCE. AND BECAUSE YOU'RE DOING THAT, THE OTHERS WILL, TOO.
I'M LOOKING FOR SOME LOYALTY HERE.
THAT'S MEAN, BEAN. TWISTING MY ARM WITH WORDS.
LOOKS LIKE OUR FRIENDSHIP ONLY GOES ONE WAY.
NO. IT DOESN'T.
YOU CAME TO ME FIRST. BECAUSE YOU KNEW YOU COULD PULL THIS WHOLE--
NO. I'M NOT FORCING YOU, NIKOLAI. I'M SORRY.
I'LL DO IT WITHOUT YOU. AND YOU'RE RIGHT, I'LL BE FINE.
SERIOUSLY.
STILL FRIENDS?
YEAH. OF COURSE.
OF COURSE WE'RE STILL FRIENDS.
DON'T BE STUPID.
THANKS, GLYKIA MOU...AND GOOD HUNTING.
HEY, YOU WOULD HAVE BEEN A LIABILITY ANYWAY.
YOU MEAN I WOULD HAVE SHOWN YOU UP!

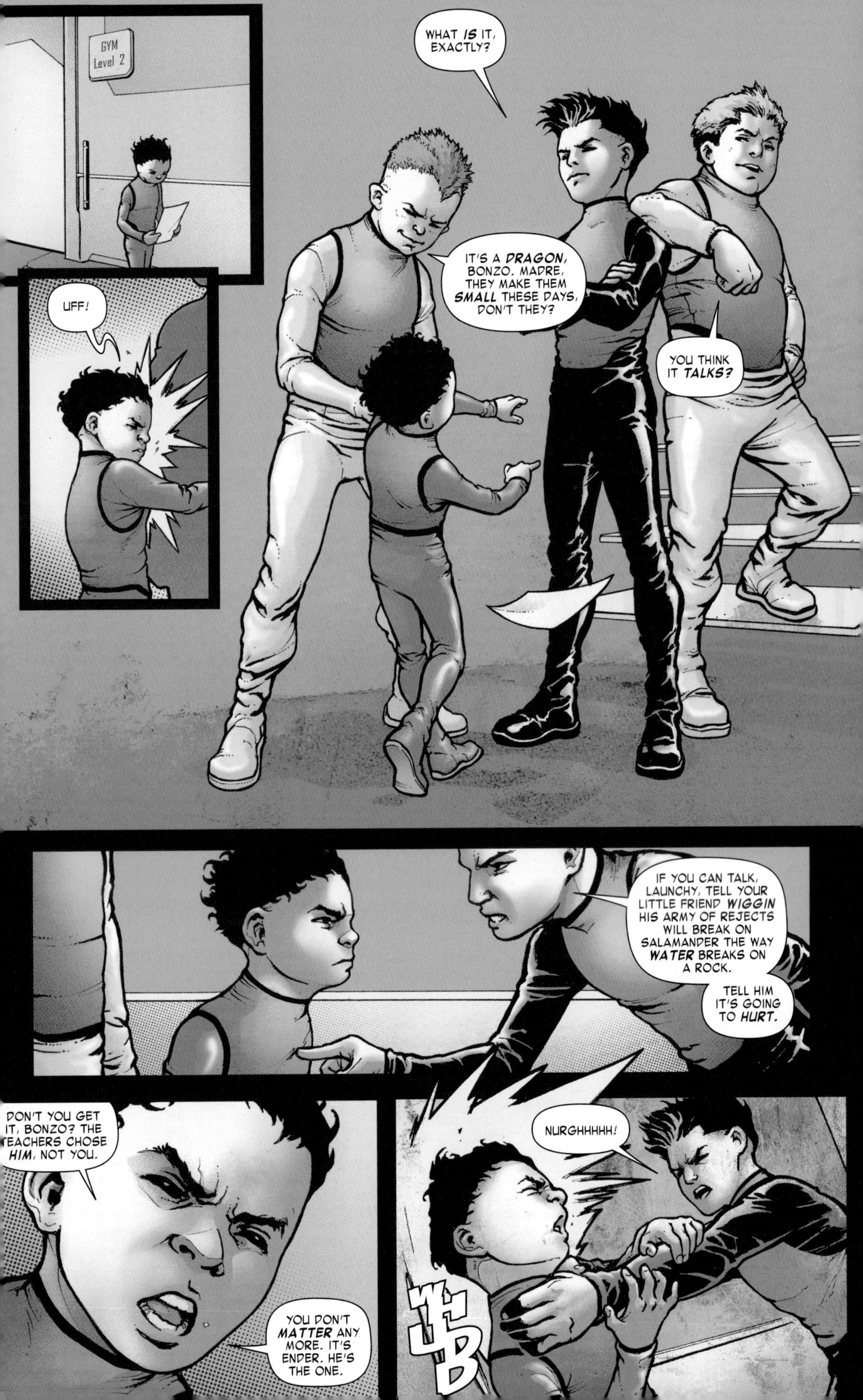
GYM
Level 2
UFF!
WHAT IS IT, EXACTLY?
IT'S A DRAGON, BONZO. MADRE, THEY MAKE THEM SMALL THESE DAYS, DON'T THEY?
YOU THINK IT TALKS?
IF YOU CAN TALK, LAUNCHY, TELL YOUR LITTLE FRIEND WIGGIN HIS ARMY OF REJECTS WILL BREAK ON SALAMANDER THE WAY WATER BREAKS ON A ROCK.
TELL HIM IT'S GOING TO HURT.
DON'T YOU GET IT, BONZO? THE TEACHERS CHOSE HIM, NOT YOU.
YOU DON'T MATTER ANY MORE. IT'S ENDER. HE'S THE ONE.
NURGHHHHH!
WHUB

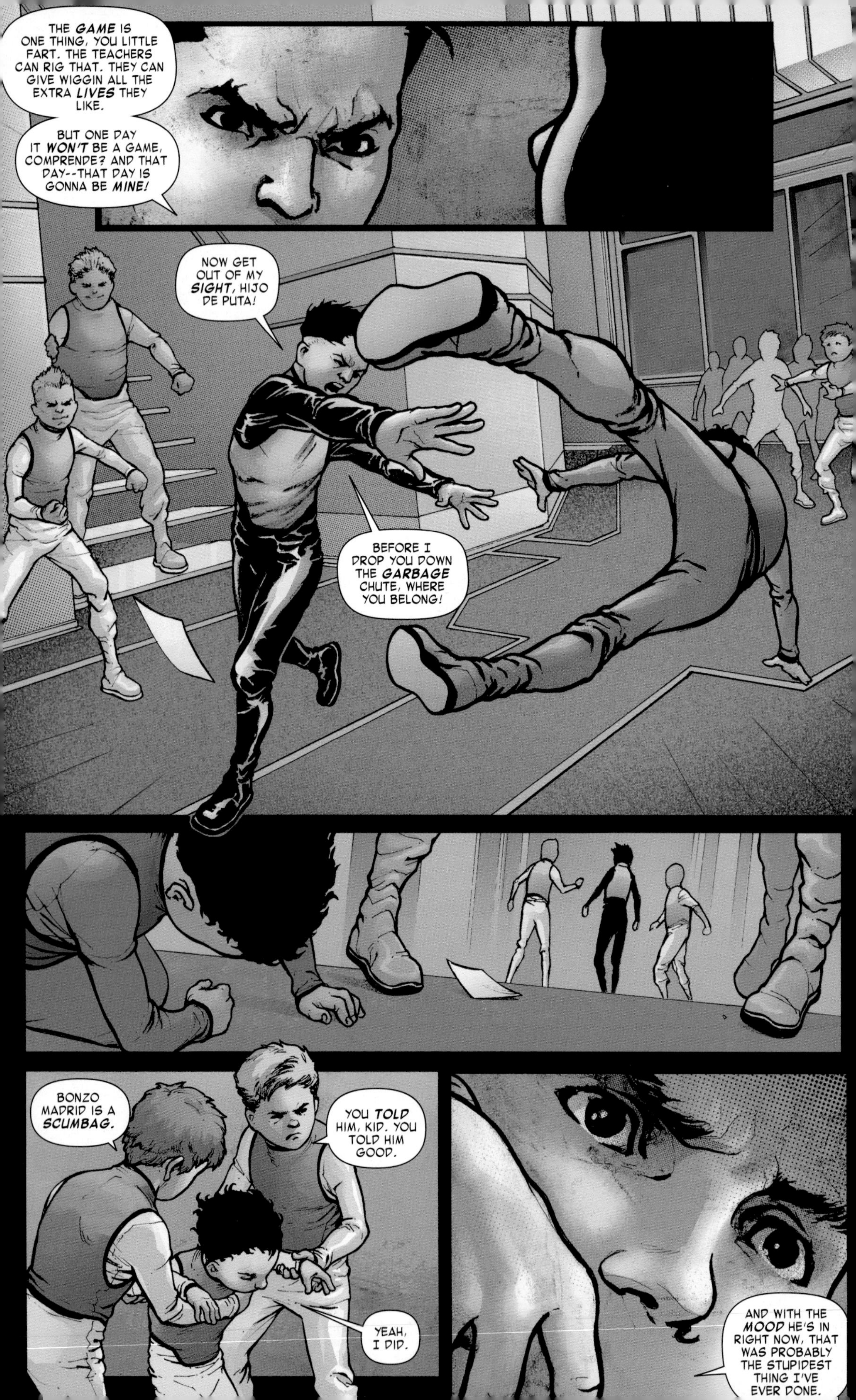
THE GAME IS ONE THING, YOU LITTLE FART. THE TEACHERS CAN RIG THAT. THEY CAN GIVE WIGGIN ALL THE EXTRA LIVES THEY LIKE.
BUT ONE DAY IT WON'T BE A GAME, COMPRENDE? AND THAT DAY--THAT DAY IS GONNA BE MINE!
NOW GET OUT OF MY SIGHT, HIJO DE PUTA!
BEFORE I DROP YOU DOWN THE GARBAGE CHUTE, WHERE YOU BELONG!
BONZO MADRID IS A SCUMBAG.
YOU TOLD HIM, KID. YOU TOLD HIM GOOD.
YEAH, I DID.
AND WITH THE MOOD HE'S IN RIGHT NOW, THAT WAS PROBABLY THE STUPIDEST THING I'VE EVER DONE.

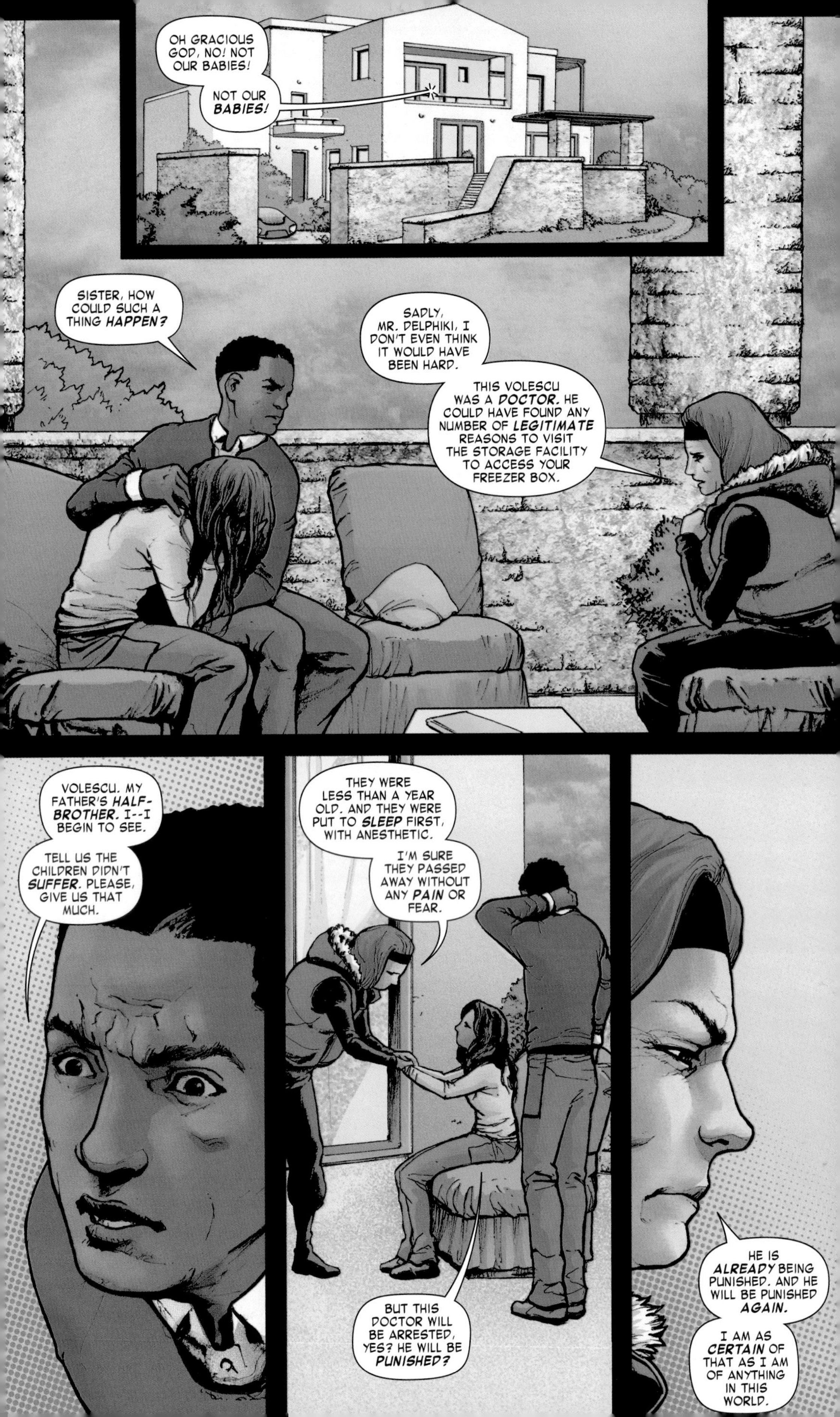
OH GRACIOUS GOD, NO! NOT OUR BABIES!
NOT OUR BABIES!
SISTER, HOW COULD SUCH A THING HAPPEN?
SADLY, MR. DELPHIKI, I DON'T EVEN THINK IT WOULD HAVE BEEN HARD.
THIS VOLESCU WAS A DOCTOR. HE COULD HAVE FOUND ANY NUMBER OF LEGITIMATE REASONS TO VISIT THE STORAGE FACILITY TO ACCESS YOUR FREEZER BOX.
VOLESCU. MY FATHER'S HALF-BROTHER. I--I BEGIN TO SEE.
TELL US THE CHILDREN DIDN'T SUFFER. PLEASE, GIVE US THAT MUCH.
THEY WERE LESS THAN A YEAR OLD. AND THEY WERE PUT TO SLEEP FIRST, WITH ANESTHETIC.
I'M SURE THEY PASSED AWAY WITHOUT ANY PAIN OR FEAR.
BUT THIS DOCTOR WILL BE ARRESTED, YES? HE WILL BE PUNISHED?
HE IS ALREADY BEING PUNISHED. AND HE WILL BE PUNISHED AGAIN.
I AM AS CERTAIN OF THAT AS I AM OF ANYTHING IN THIS WORLD.

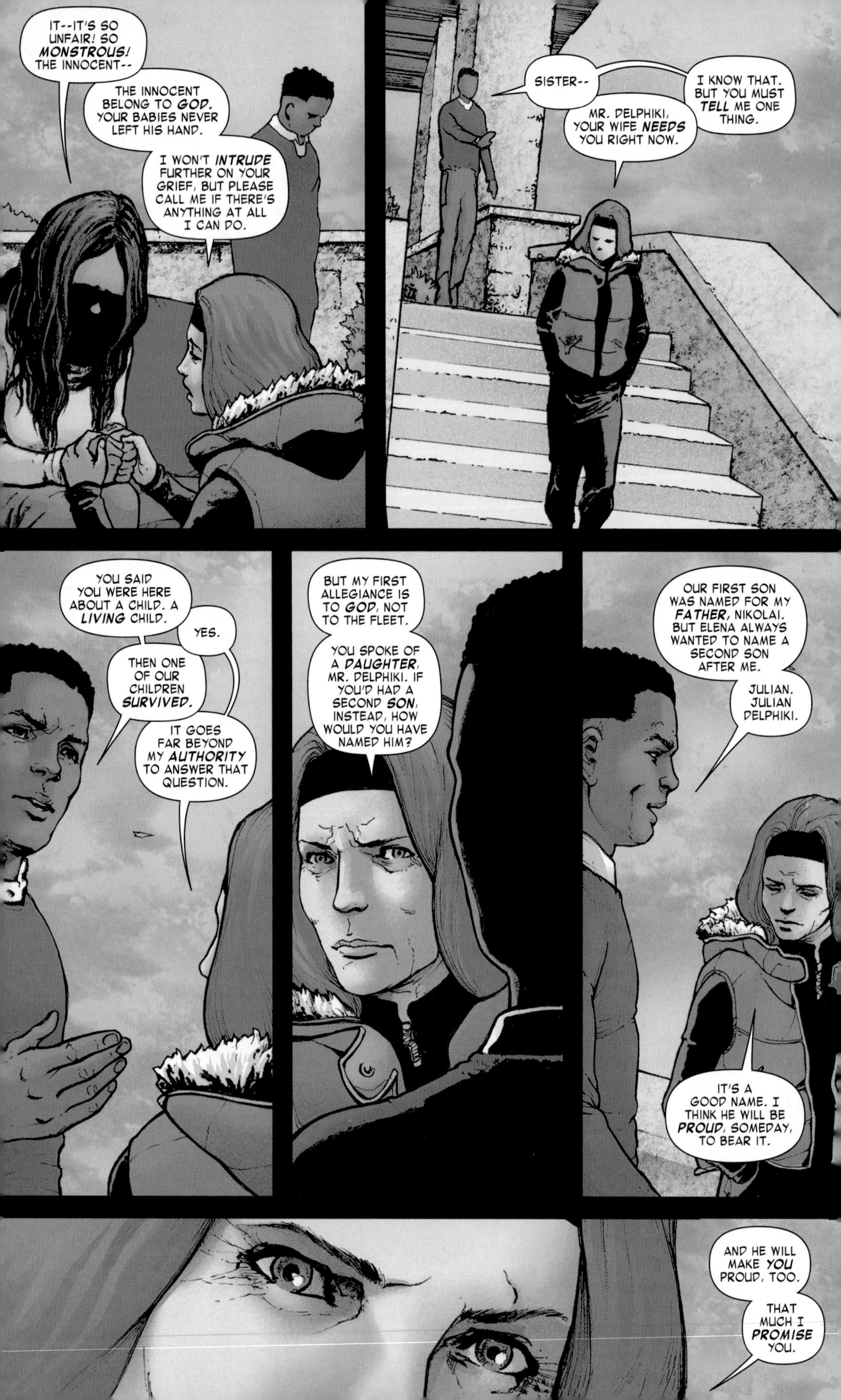

IT--IT'S SO UNFAIR! SO MONSTROUS! THE INNOCENT--
THE INNOCENT BELONG TO GOD. YOUR BABIES NEVER LEFT HIS HAND.
I WON'T INTRUDE FURTHER ON YOUR GRIEF, BUT PLEASE CALL ME IF THERE'S ANYTHING AT ALL I CAN DO.
SISTER--
I KNOW THAT. BUT YOU MUST TELL ME ONE THING.
MR. DELPHIKI, YOUR WIFE NEEDS YOU RIGHT NOW.
YOU SAID YOU WERE HERE ABOUT A CHILD. A LIVING CHILD.
YES.
THEN ONE OF OUR CHILDREN SURVIVED.
IT GOES FAR BEYOND MY AUTHORITY TO ANSWER THAT QUESTION.
BUT MY FIRST ALLEGIANCE IS TO GOD, NOT TO THE FLEET.
YOU SPOKE OF A DAUGHTER, MR. DELPHIKI. IF YOU'D HAD A SECOND SON, INSTEAD, HOW WOULD YOU HAVE NAMED HIM?
OUR FIRST SON WAS NAMED FOR MY FATHER, NIKOLAI. BUT ELENA ALWAYS WANTED TO NAME A SECOND SON AFTER ME.
JULIAN. JULIAN DELPHIKI.
IT'S A GOOD NAME. I THINK HE WILL BE PROUD, SOMEDAY, TO BEAR IT.
AND HE WILL MAKE YOU PROUD, TOO.
THAT MUCH I PROMISE YOU.

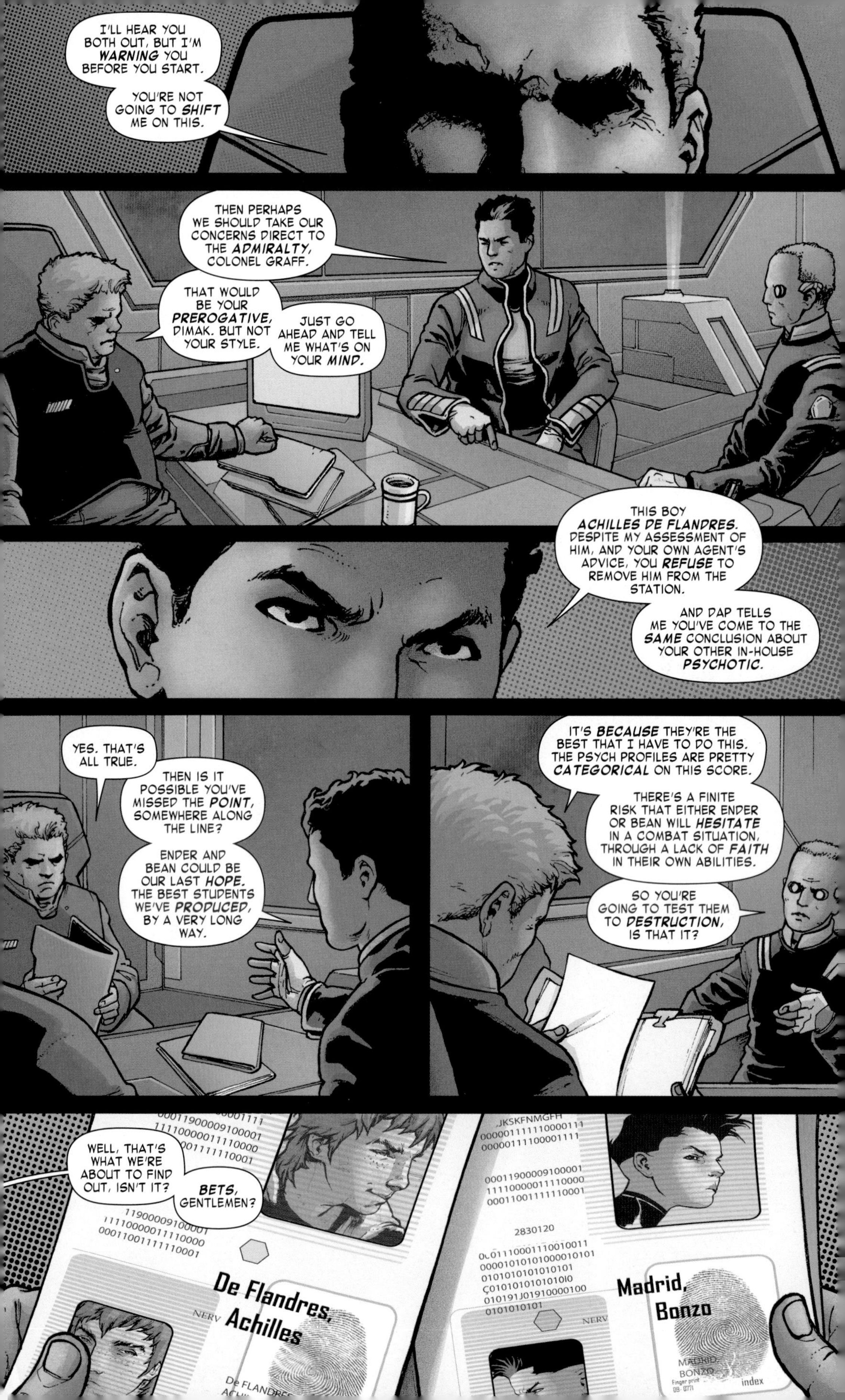

I'LL HEAR YOU BOTH OUT, BUT I'M WARNING YOU BEFORE YOU START.
YOU'RE NOT GOING TO SHIFT ME ON THIS.
THEN PERHAPS WE SHOULD TAKE OUR CONCERNS DIRECT TO THE ADMIRALTY, COLONEL GRAFF.
THAT WOULD BE YOUR PREROGATIVE, DIMAK. BUT NOT YOUR STYLE.
JUST GO AHEAD AND TELL ME WHAT'S ON YOUR MIND.
THIS BOY ACHILLES DE FLANDRES. DESPITE MY ASSESSMENT OF HIM, AND YOUR OWN AGENT'S ADVICE, YOU REFUSE TO REMOVE HIM FROM THE STATION.
AND DAP TELLS ME YOU'VE COME TO THE SAME CONCLUSION ABOUT YOUR OTHER IN-HOUSE PSYCHOTIC.
YES. THAT'S ALL TRUE.
THEN IS IT POSSIBLE YOU'VE MISSED THE POINT, SOMEWHERE ALONG THE LINE?
ENDER AND BEAN COULD BE OUR LAST HOPE. THE BEST STUDENTS WE'VE PRODUCED, BY A VERY LONG WAY.
IT'S BECAUSE THEY'RE THE BEST THAT I HAVE TO DO THIS. THE PSYCH PROFILES ARE PRETTY CATEGORICAL ON THIS SCORE.
THERE'S A FINITE RISK THAT EITHER ENDER OR BEAN WILL HESITATE IN A COMBAT SITUATION, THROUGH A LACK OF FAITH IN THEIR OWN ABILITIES.
SO YOU'RE GOING TO TEST THEM TO DESTRUCTION, IS THAT IT?
WELL, THAT'S WHAT WE'RE ABOUT TO FIND OUT, ISN'T IT?
BETS, GENTLEMEN?
De Flandres, Achilles
NERV
2830120
Madrid, Bonzo
NERV
index

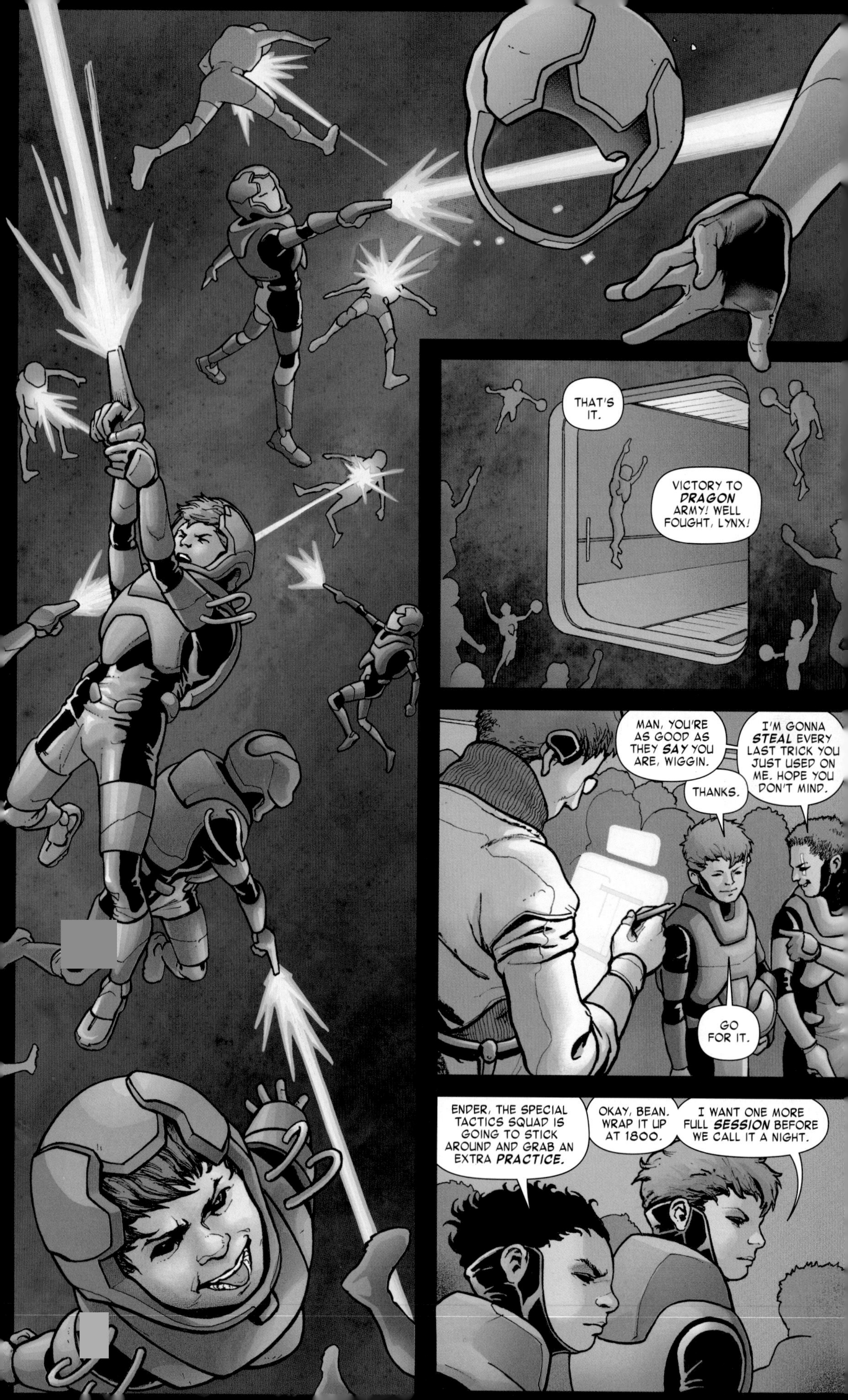
THAT'S IT.
VICTORY TO DRAGON ARMY! WELL FOUGHT, LYNX!
MAN, YOU'RE AS GOOD AS THEY SAY YOU ARE, WIGGIN.
THANKS.
I'M GONNA STEAL EVERY LAST TRICK YOU JUST USED ON ME. HOPE YOU DON'T MIND.
GO FOR IT.
ENDER, THE SPECIAL TACTICS SQUAD IS GOING TO STICK AROUND AND GRAB AN EXTRA PRACTICE.
OKAY, BEAN. WRAP IT UP AT 1800.
I WANT ONE MORE FULL SESSION BEFORE WE CALL IT A NIGHT.

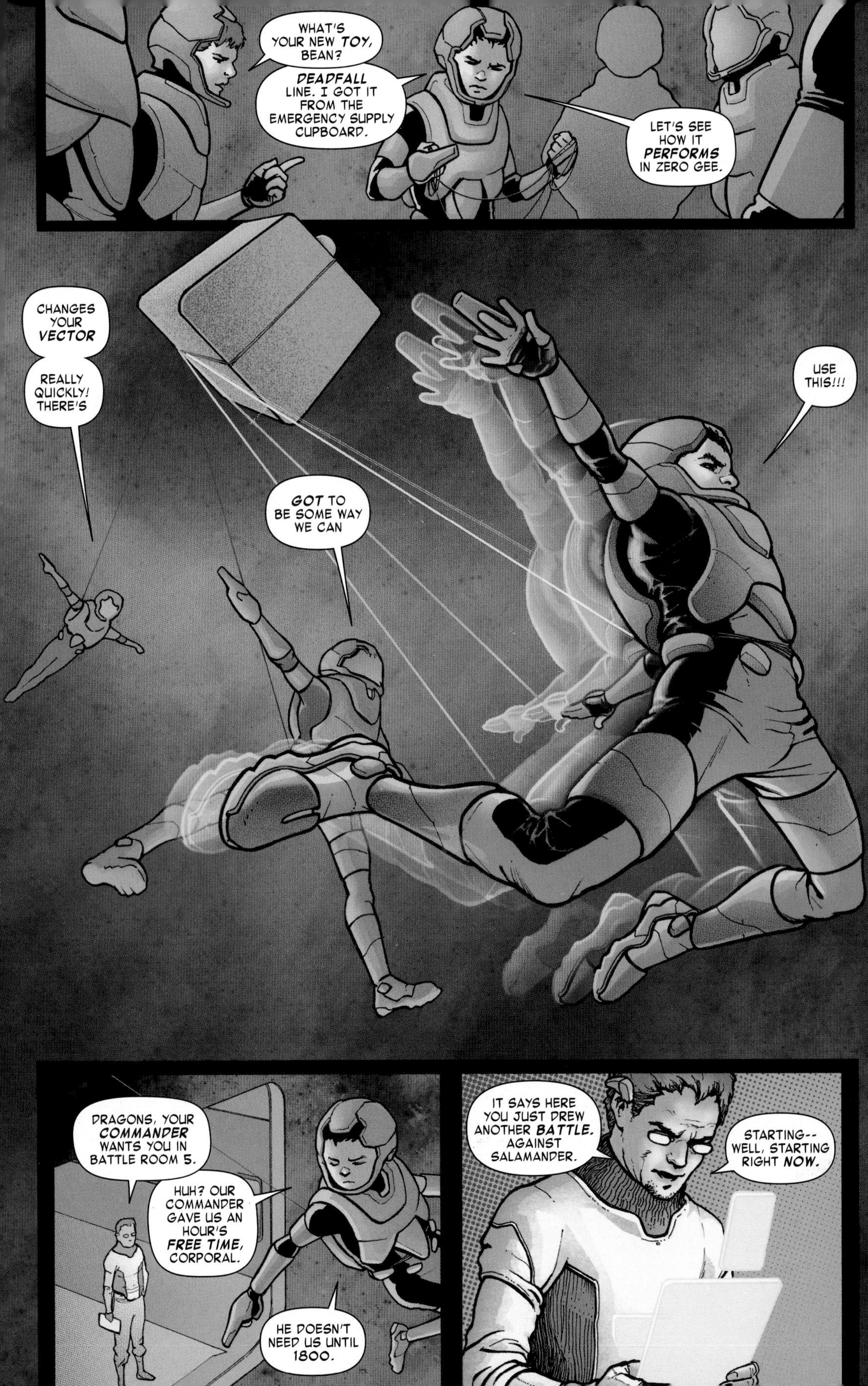
WHAT'S YOUR NEW TOY, BEAN?
DEADFALL LINE. I GOT IT FROM THE EMERGENCY SUPPLY CUPBOARD.
LET'S SEE HOW IT PERFORMS IN ZERO GEE.
USE THIS!!!
CHANGES YOUR VECTOR
REALLY QUICKLY! THERE'S
GOT TO BE SOME WAY WE CAN
DRAGONS, YOUR COMMANDER WANTS YOU IN BATTLE ROOM 5.
HUH? OUR COMMANDER GAVE US AN HOUR'S FREE TIME, CORPORAL.
HE DOESN'T NEED US UNTIL 1800.
IT SAYS HERE YOU JUST DREW ANOTHER BATTLE. AGAINST SALAMANDER.
STARTING-- WELL, STARTING RIGHT NOW.

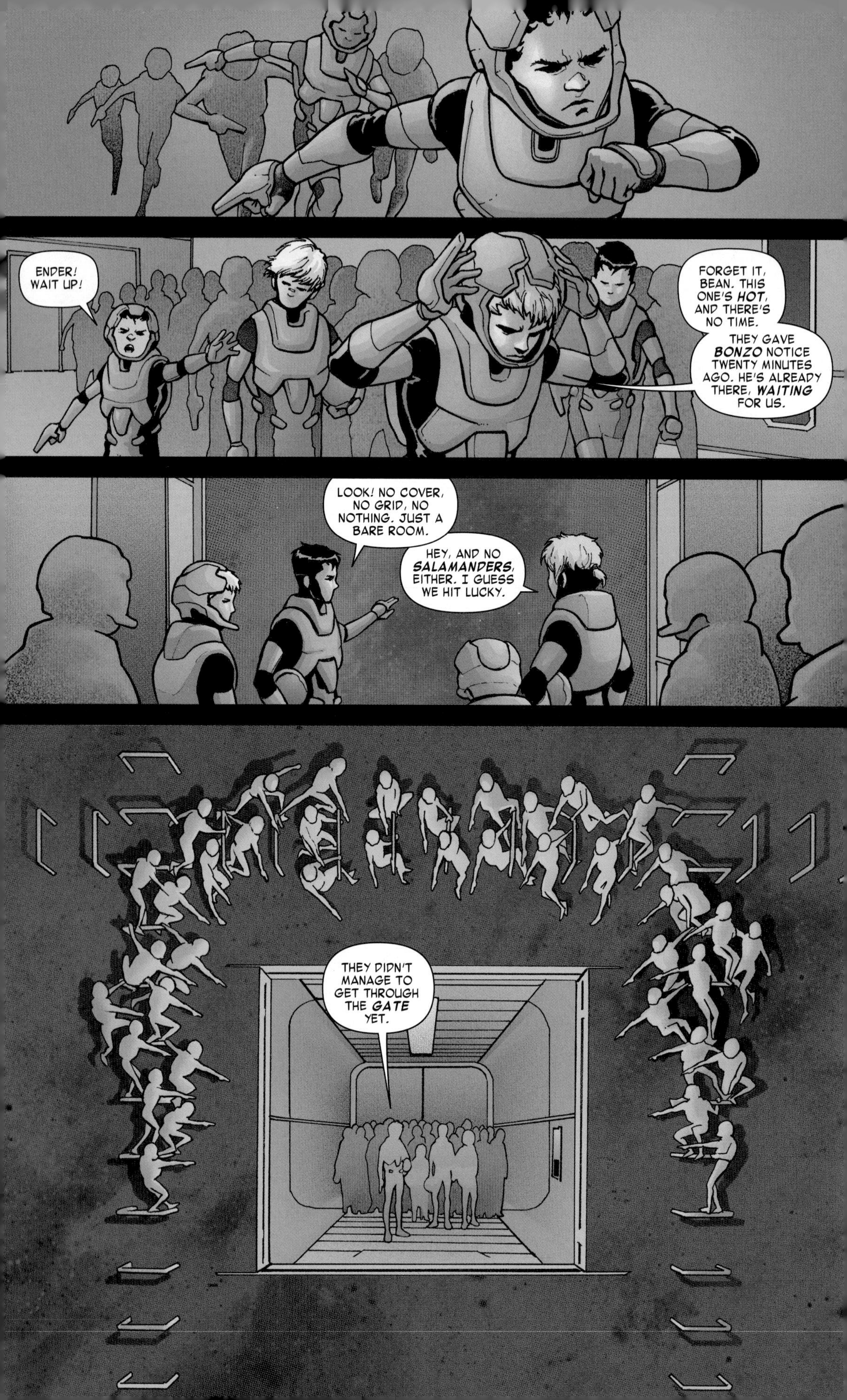
ENDER! WAIT UP!
FORGET IT, BEAN. THIS ONE'S HOT, AND THERE'S NO TIME.
THEY GAVE BONZO NOTICE TWENTY MINUTES AGO. HE'S ALREADY THERE, WAITING FOR US.
LOOK! NO COVER, NO GRID, NO NOTHING. JUST A BARE ROOM.
HEY, AND NO SALAMANDERS, EITHER. I GUESS WE HIT LUCKY.
THEY DIDN'T MANAGE TO GET THROUGH THE GATE YET.

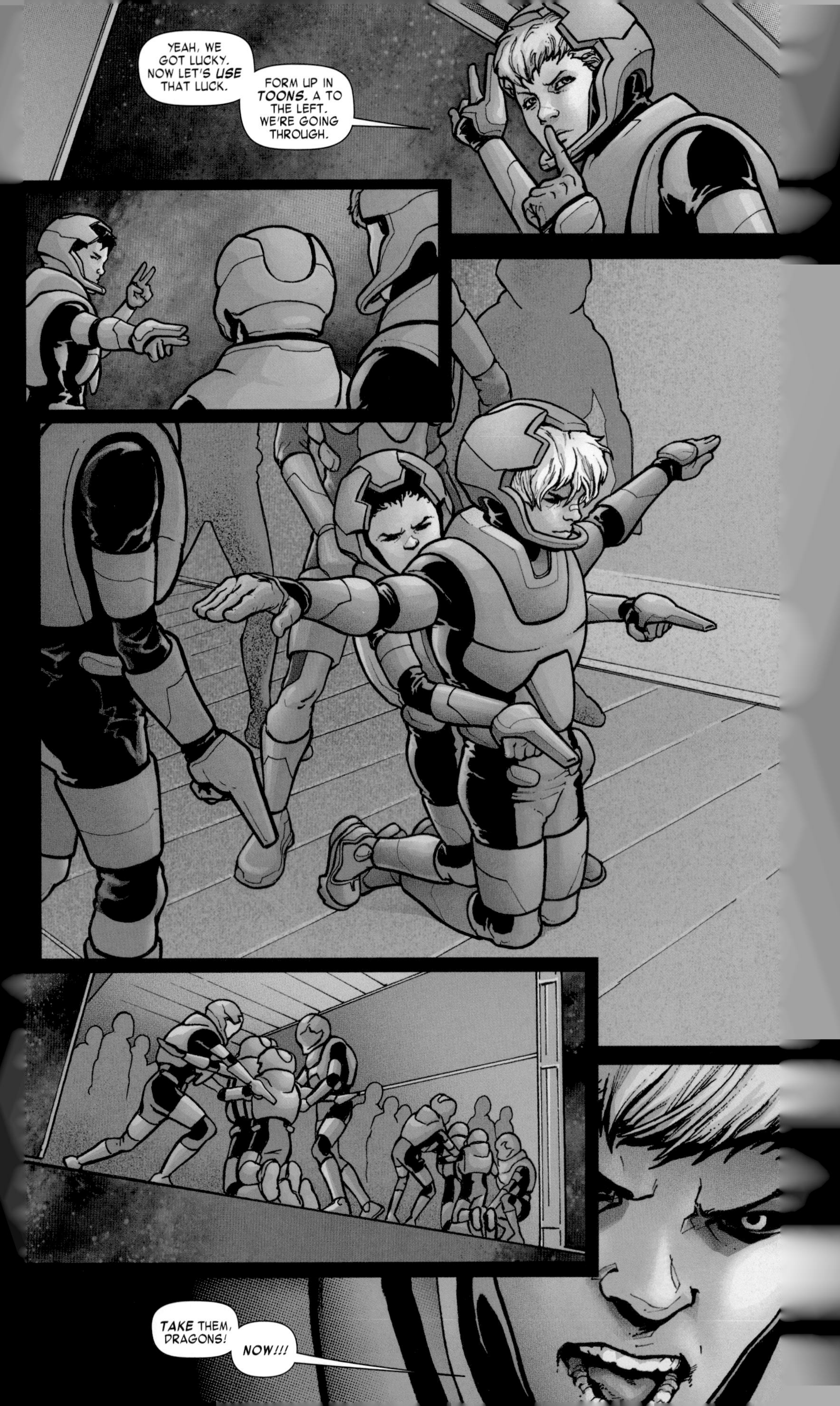
YEAH, WE GOT LUCKY. NOW LET'S *USE* THAT LUCK.
FORM UP IN *TOONS.* A TO THE LEFT. WE'RE GOING THROUGH.
TAKE THEM, DRAGONS!
NOW!!!

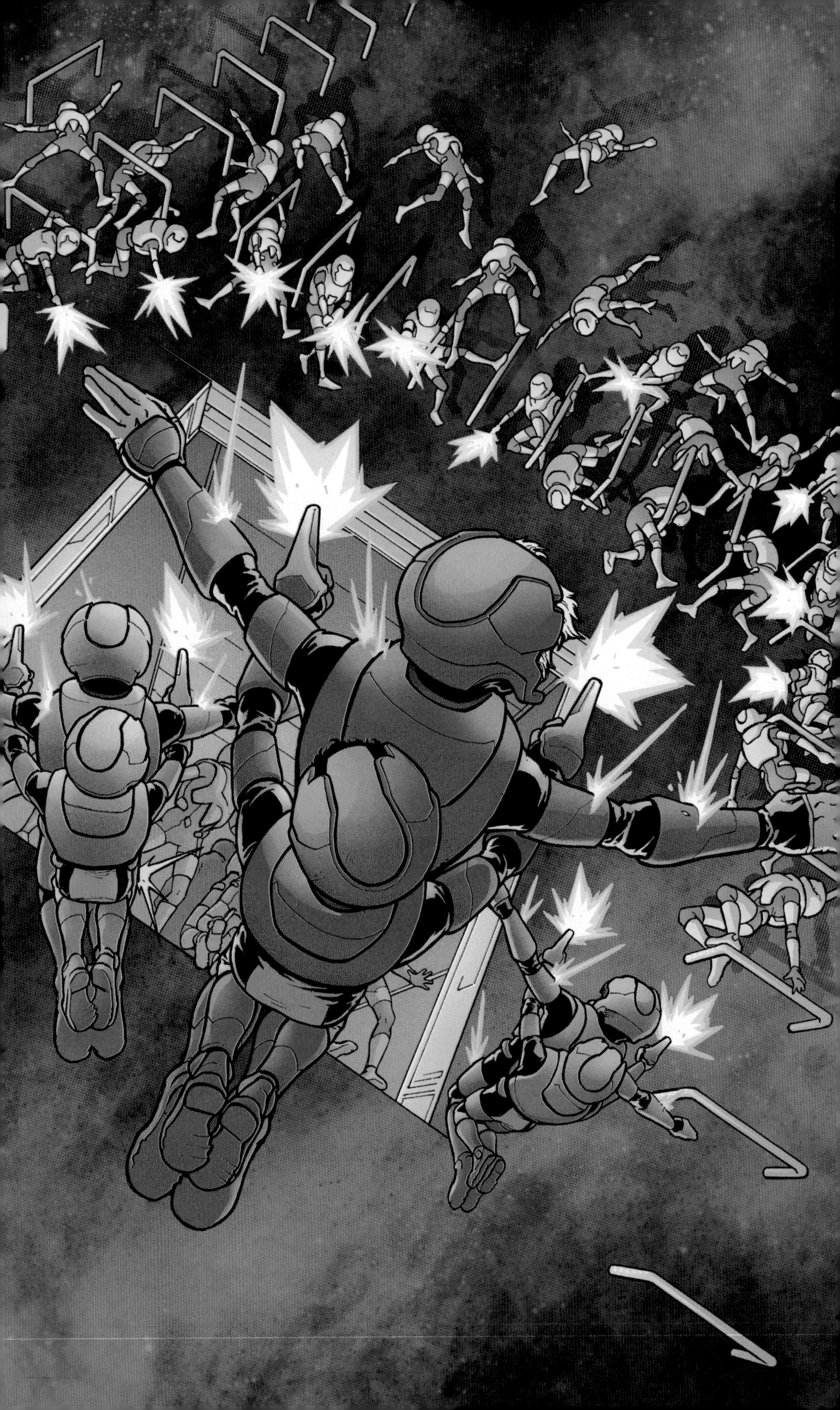

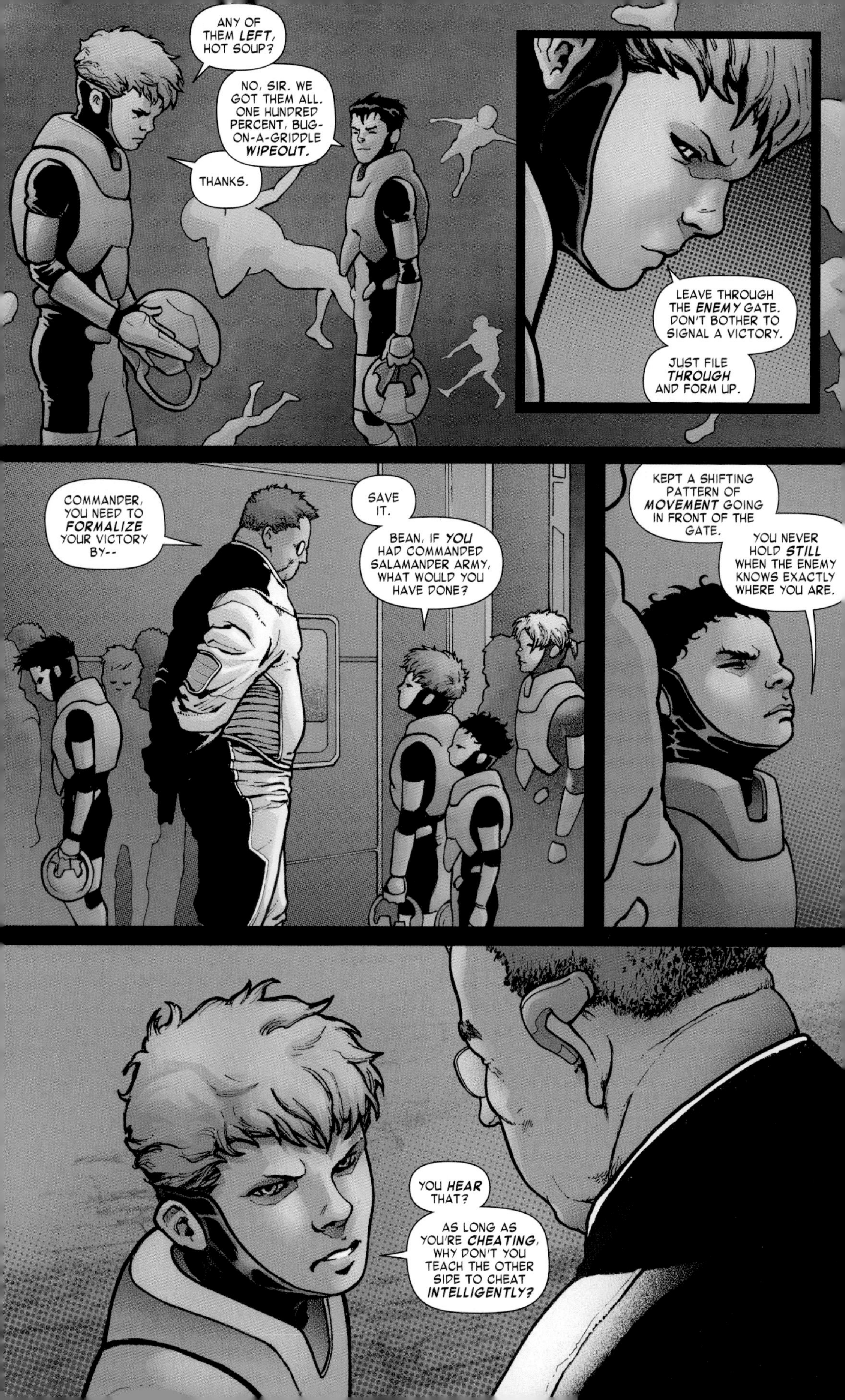
ANY OF THEM LEFT, HOT SOUP?
NO, SIR. WE GOT THEM ALL. ONE HUNDRED PERCENT, BUG-ON-A-GRIDDLE WIPEOUT.
THANKS.
LEAVE THROUGH THE ENEMY GATE. DON'T BOTHER TO SIGNAL A VICTORY.
JUST FILE THROUGH AND FORM UP.
COMMANDER, YOU NEED TO FORMALIZE YOUR VICTORY BY--
SAVE IT.
BEAN, IF YOU HAD COMMANDED SALAMANDER ARMY, WHAT WOULD YOU HAVE DONE?
KEPT A SHIFTING PATTERN OF MOVEMENT GOING IN FRONT OF THE GATE.
YOU NEVER HOLD STILL WHEN THE ENEMY KNOWS EXACTLY WHERE YOU ARE.
YOU HEAR THAT?
AS LONG AS YOU'RE CHEATING, WHY DON'T YOU TEACH THE OTHER SIDE TO CHEAT INTELLIGENTLY?

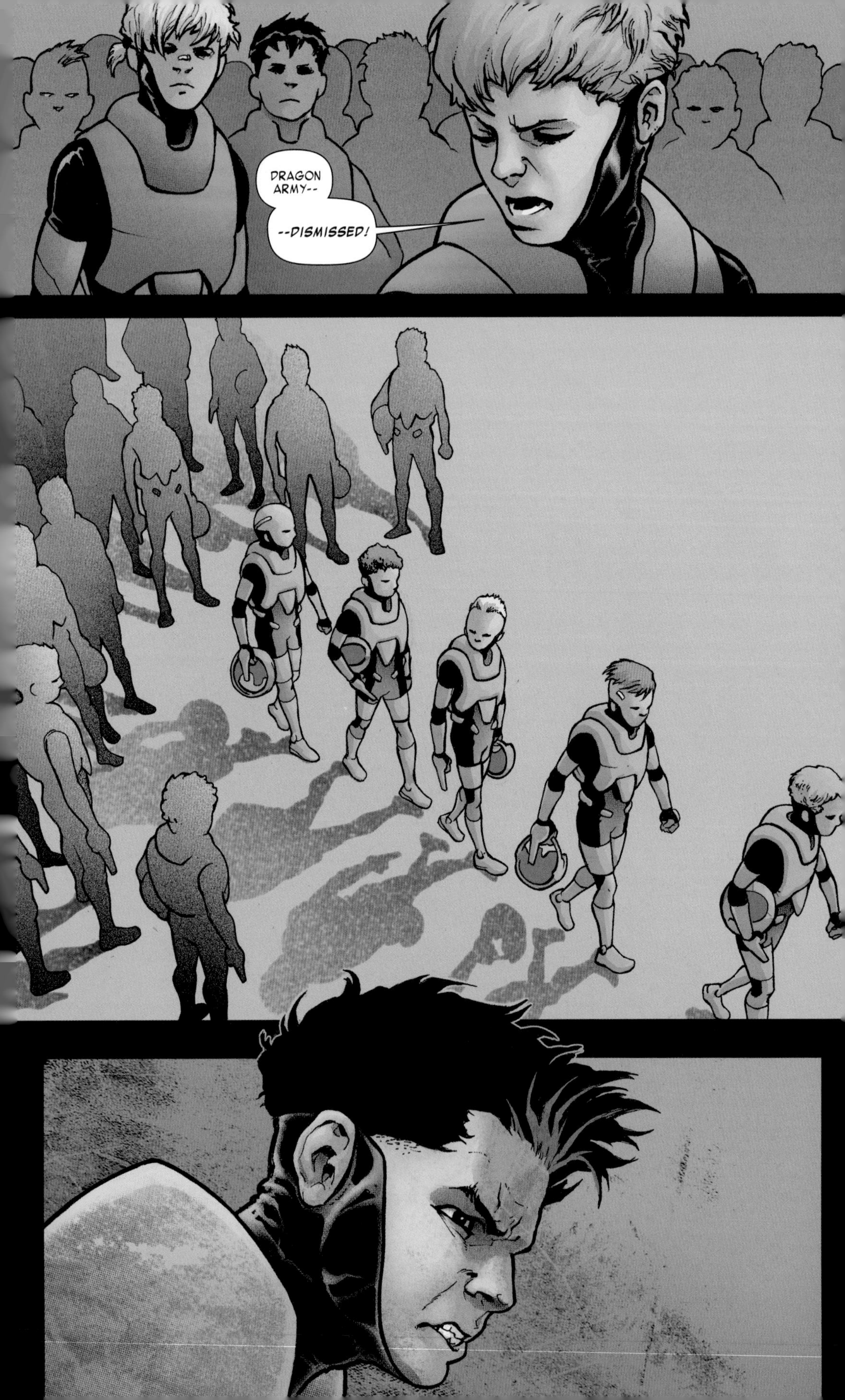
DRAGON ARMY--
--DISMISSED!

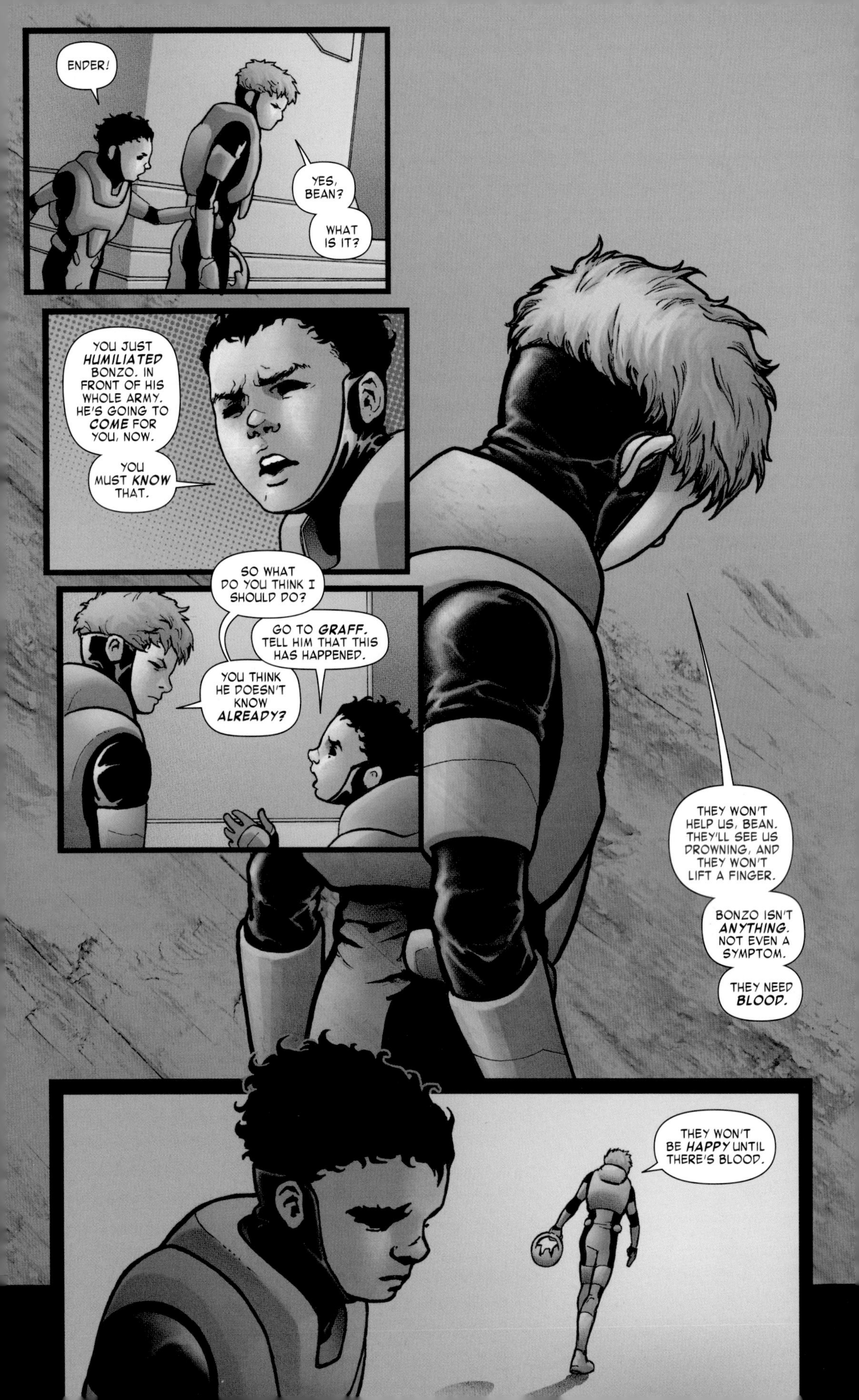
ENDER!
YES, BEAN?
WHAT IS IT?
YOU JUST *HUMILIATED* BONZO. IN FRONT OF HIS WHOLE ARMY. HE'S GOING TO *COME* FOR YOU, NOW.
YOU MUST *KNOW* THAT.
SO WHAT DO YOU THINK I SHOULD DO?
GO TO *GRAFF.* TELL HIM THAT THIS HAS HAPPENED.
YOU THINK HE DOESN'T KNOW *ALREADY?*
THEY WON'T HELP US, BEAN. THEY'LL SEE US DROWNING, AND THEY WON'T LIFT A FINGER.
BONZO ISN'T *ANYTHING.* NOT EVEN A SYMPTOM.
THEY NEED *BLOOD.*
THEY WON'T BE *HAPPY* UNTIL THERE'S BLOOD.

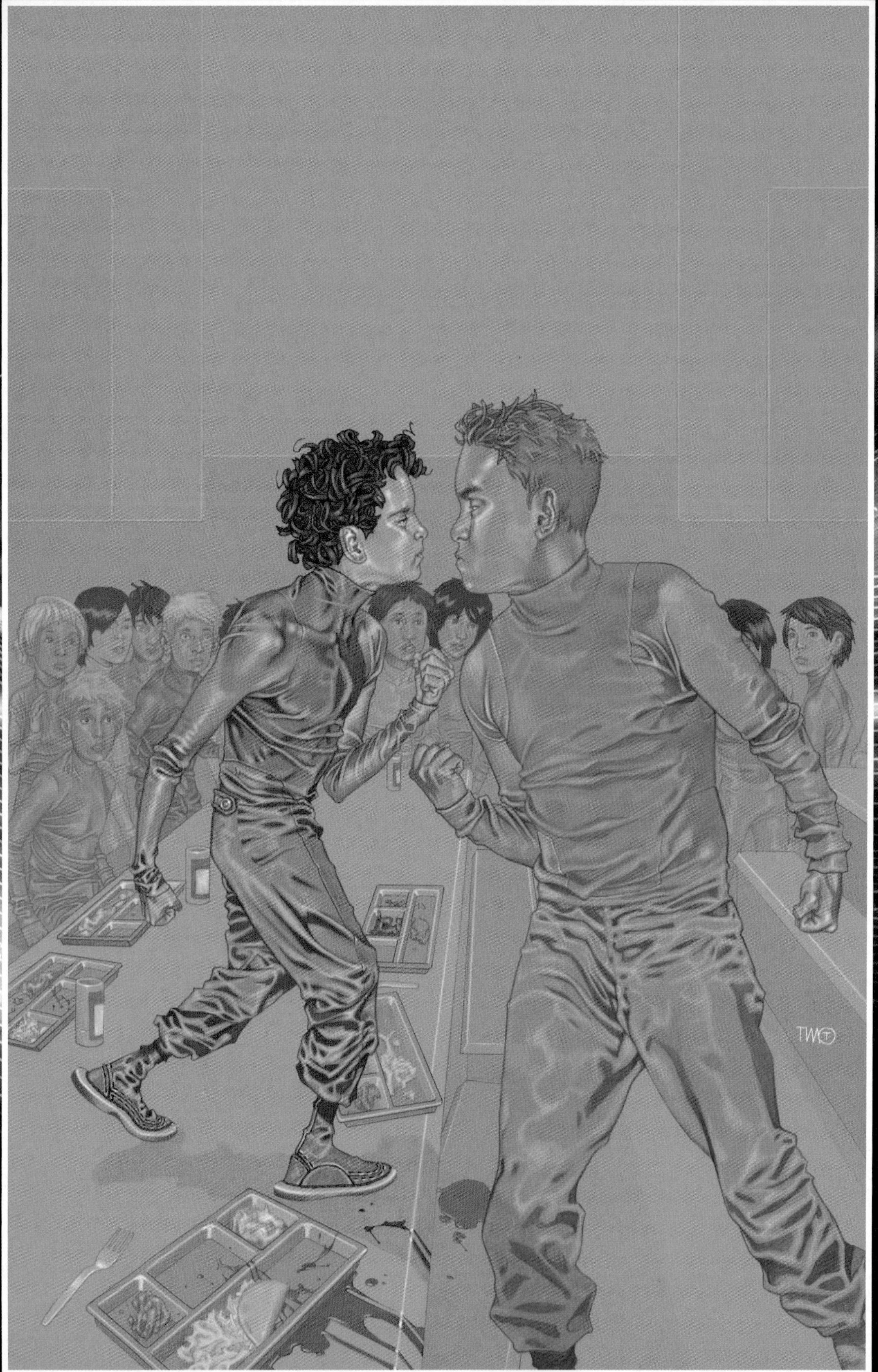

T H R E E

"Permission to speak freely, Colonel?"

"Denied."

"This situation is escalating beyond your ability to control it."

"I said denied, Captain. Perhaps you didn't hear me."

"Bonzo Madrid is berserk. Being defeated by Dragon army – and in such an extreme, humiliating way – has sent him over the edge. You can see that. Why won't you allow me to intervene?"

"You know my reasons. I'm not going to rehearse them again."

"Ender himself is close to breaking point. He sees you – us – as the enemy now. And Bean has identified with Ender far enough to share that view. Yet you continue to push the pair of them towards a psychological abyss whose far side you can't see."

"Nicely put. I never claimed to be a psychiatrist."

"No. What do you claim to be, Colonel Graff?"

"Well if we're talking in metaphors, then I suppose I'm a blacksmith. Hand me another nail, would you?"

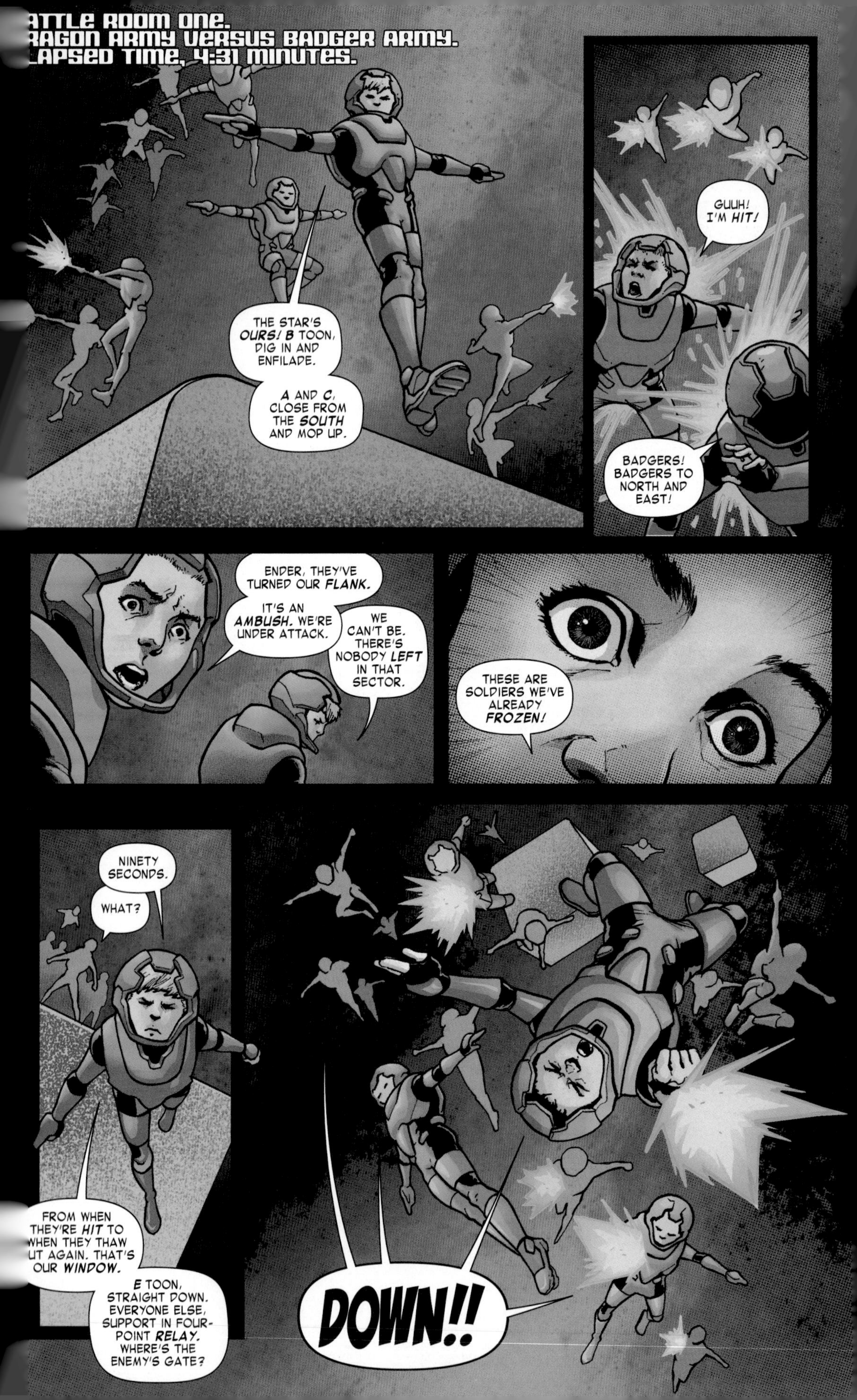
ATTLE ROOM ONE.
RAGON ARMY VERSUS BADGER ARMY.
LAPSED TIME, 4:31 MINUTES.
THE STAR'S OURS! B TOON, DIG IN AND ENFILADE.
A AND C, CLOSE FROM THE SOUTH AND MOP UP.
GUUH! I'M HIT!
BADGERS! BADGERS TO NORTH AND EAST!
ENDER, THEY'VE TURNED OUR FLANK.
IT'S AN AMBUSH. WE'RE UNDER ATTACK.
WE CAN'T BE. THERE'S NOBODY LEFT IN THAT SECTOR.
THESE ARE SOLDIERS WE'VE ALREADY FROZEN!
NINETY SECONDS.
WHAT?
FROM WHEN THEY'RE HIT TO WHEN THEY THAW UT AGAIN. THAT'S OUR WINDOW.
E TOON, STRAIGHT DOWN. EVERYONE ELSE, SUPPORT IN FOUR-POINT RELAY. WHERE'S THE ENEMY'S GATE?
DOWN!!

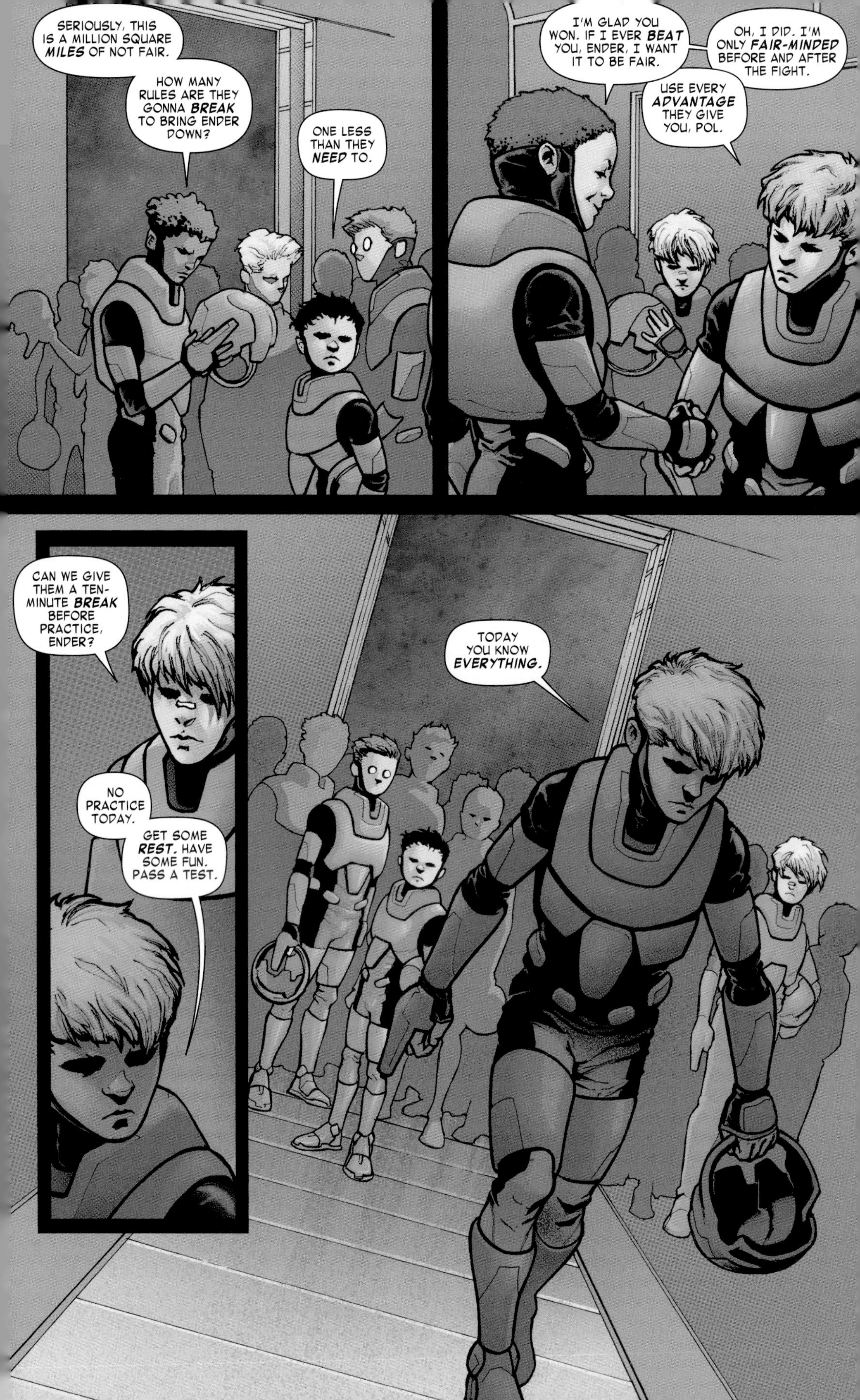

SERIOUSLY, THIS IS A MILLION SQUARE MILES OF NOT FAIR.
HOW MANY RULES ARE THEY GONNA BREAK TO BRING ENDER DOWN?
ONE LESS THAN THEY NEED TO.
I'M GLAD YOU WON. IF I EVER BEAT YOU, ENDER, I WANT IT TO BE FAIR.
OH, I DID. I'M ONLY FAIR-MINDED BEFORE AND AFTER THE FIGHT.
USE EVERY ADVANTAGE THEY GIVE YOU, POL.
CAN WE GIVE THEM A TEN-MINUTE BREAK BEFORE PRACTICE, ENDER?
NO PRACTICE TODAY.
GET SOME REST. HAVE SOME FUN. PASS A TEST.
TODAY YOU KNOW EVERYTHING.

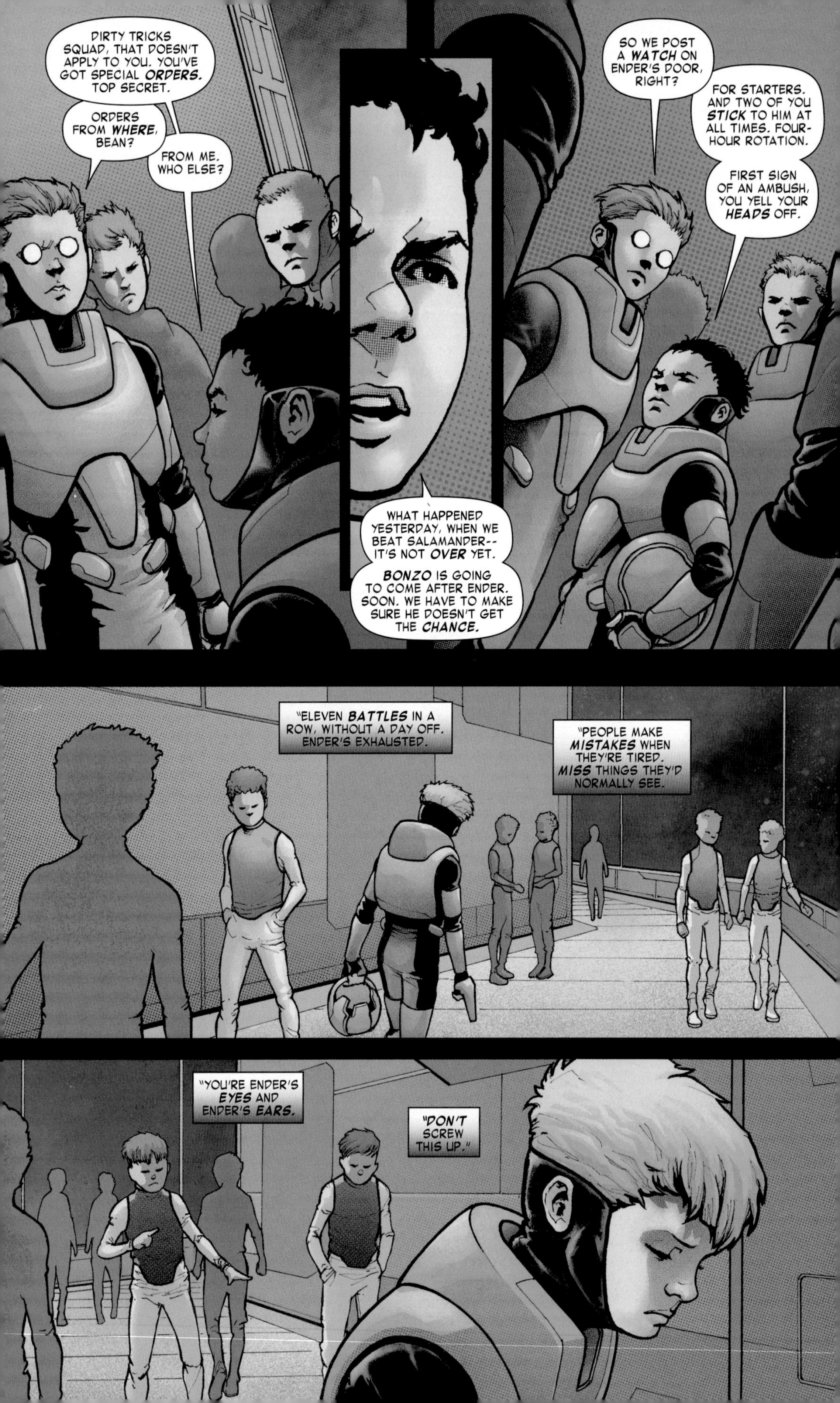
DIRTY TRICKS SQUAD, THAT DOESN'T APPLY TO YOU. YOU'VE GOT SPECIAL ORDERS. TOP SECRET.
ORDERS FROM WHERE, BEAN?
FROM ME. WHO ELSE?
WHAT HAPPENED YESTERDAY, WHEN WE BEAT SALAMANDER-- IT'S NOT OVER YET.
BONZO IS GOING TO COME AFTER ENDER. SOON. WE HAVE TO MAKE SURE HE DOESN'T GET THE CHANCE.
SO WE POST A WATCH ON ENDER'S DOOR, RIGHT?
FOR STARTERS. AND TWO OF YOU STICK TO HIM AT ALL TIMES. FOUR-HOUR ROTATION.
FIRST SIGN OF AN AMBUSH, YOU YELL YOUR HEADS OFF.
"ELEVEN BATTLES IN A ROW, WITHOUT A DAY OFF. ENDER'S EXHAUSTED.
"PEOPLE MAKE MISTAKES WHEN THEY'RE TIRED. MISS THINGS THEY'D NORMALLY SEE.
"YOU'RE ENDER'S EYES AND ENDER'S EARS.
"DON'T SCREW THIS UP."

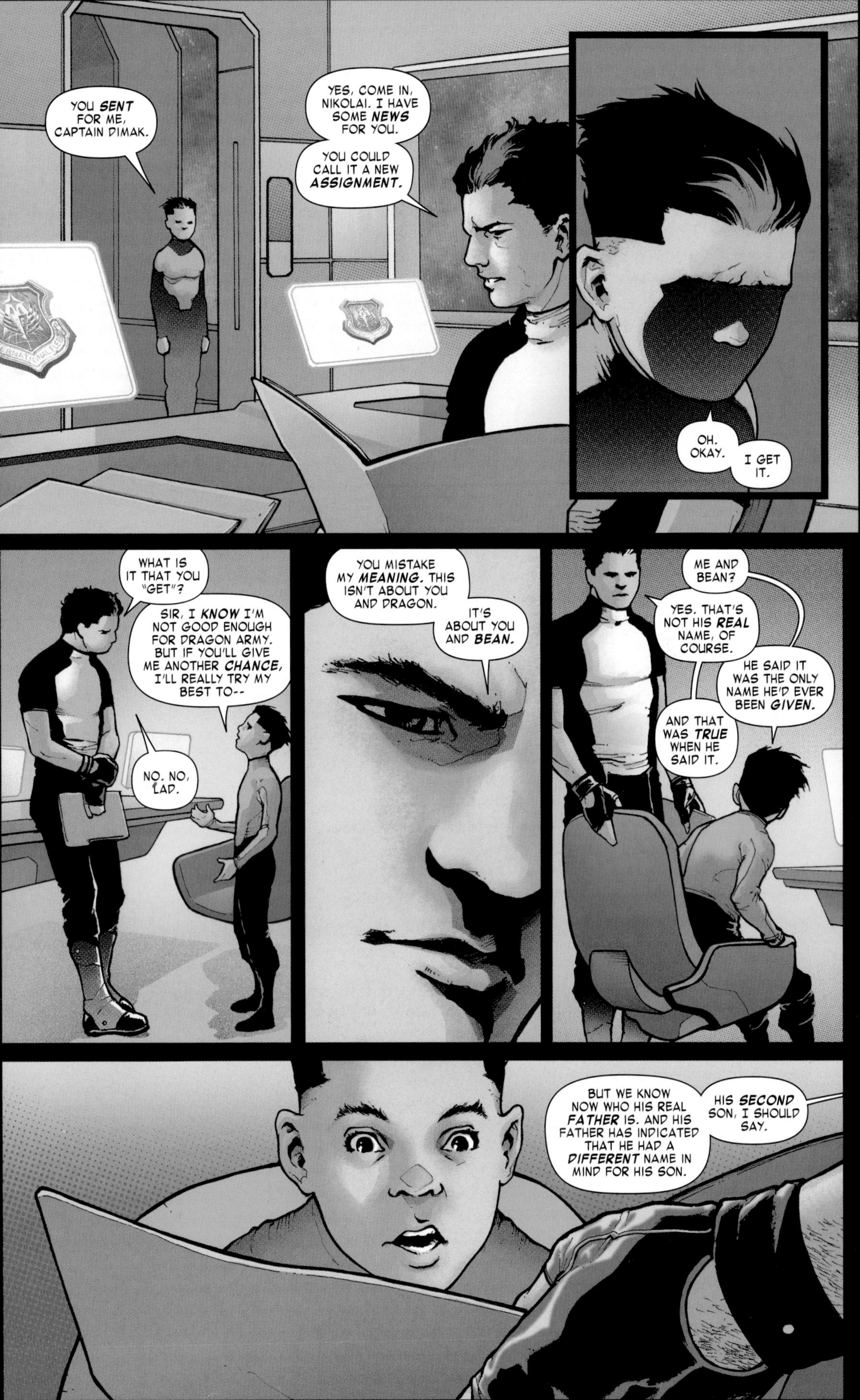
YOU SENT FOR ME, CAPTAIN DIMAK.
YES, COME IN, NIKOLAI. I HAVE SOME NEWS FOR YOU.
YOU COULD CALL IT A NEW ASSIGNMENT.
OH. OKAY.
I GET IT.
WHAT IS IT THAT YOU "GET"?
SIR, I KNOW I'M NOT GOOD ENOUGH FOR DRAGON ARMY. BUT IF YOU'LL GIVE ME ANOTHER CHANCE, I'LL REALLY TRY MY BEST TO--
NO. NO, LAD.
YOU MISTAKE MY MEANING. THIS ISN'T ABOUT YOU AND DRAGON.
IT'S ABOUT YOU AND BEAN.
ME AND BEAN?
YES. THAT'S NOT HIS REAL NAME, OF COURSE.
HE SAID IT WAS THE ONLY NAME HE'D EVER BEEN GIVEN.
AND THAT WAS TRUE WHEN HE SAID IT.
BUT WE KNOW NOW WHO HIS REAL FATHER IS. AND HIS FATHER HAS INDICATED THAT HE HAD A DIFFERENT NAME IN MIND FOR HIS SON.
HIS SECOND SON, I SHOULD SAY.

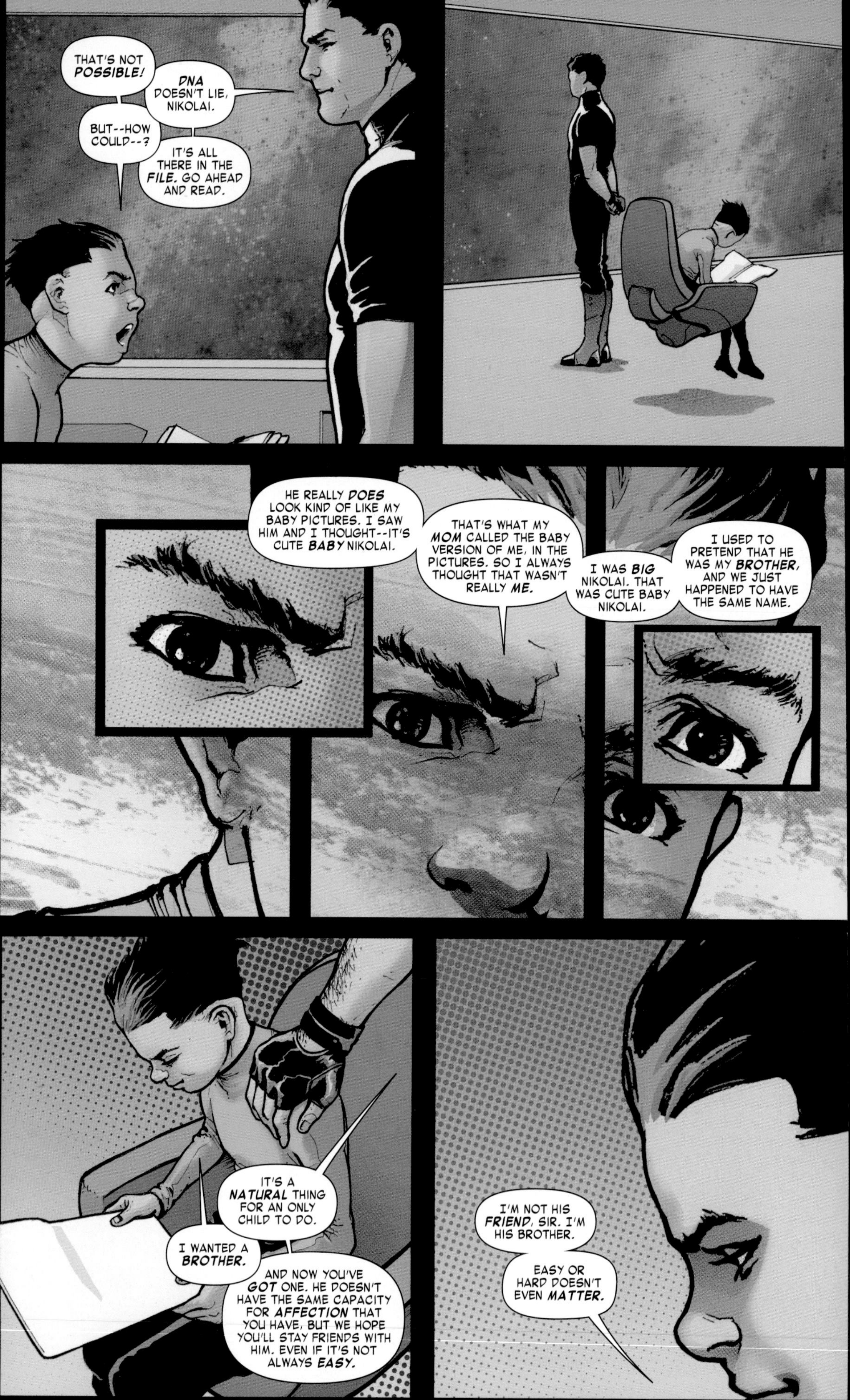
THAT'S NOT POSSIBLE!
DNA DOESN'T LIE, NIKOLAI.
BUT--HOW COULD--?
IT'S ALL THERE IN THE FILE. GO AHEAD AND READ.
HE REALLY DOES LOOK KIND OF LIKE MY BABY PICTURES. I SAW HIM AND I THOUGHT--IT'S CUTE BABY NIKOLAI.
THAT'S WHAT MY MOM CALLED THE BABY VERSION OF ME, IN THE PICTURES. SO I ALWAYS THOUGHT THAT WASN'T REALLY ME.
I WAS BIG NIKOLAI. THAT WAS CUTE BABY NIKOLAI.
I USED TO PRETEND THAT HE WAS MY BROTHER, AND WE JUST HAPPENED TO HAVE THE SAME NAME.
IT'S A NATURAL THING FOR AN ONLY CHILD TO DO.
I WANTED A BROTHER.
AND NOW YOU'VE GOT ONE. HE DOESN'T HAVE THE SAME CAPACITY FOR AFFECTION THAT YOU HAVE, BUT WE HOPE YOU'LL STAY FRIENDS WITH HIM. EVEN IF IT'S NOT ALWAYS EASY.
I'M NOT HIS FRIEND, SIR. I'M HIS BROTHER.
EASY OR HARD DOESN'T EVEN MATTER.

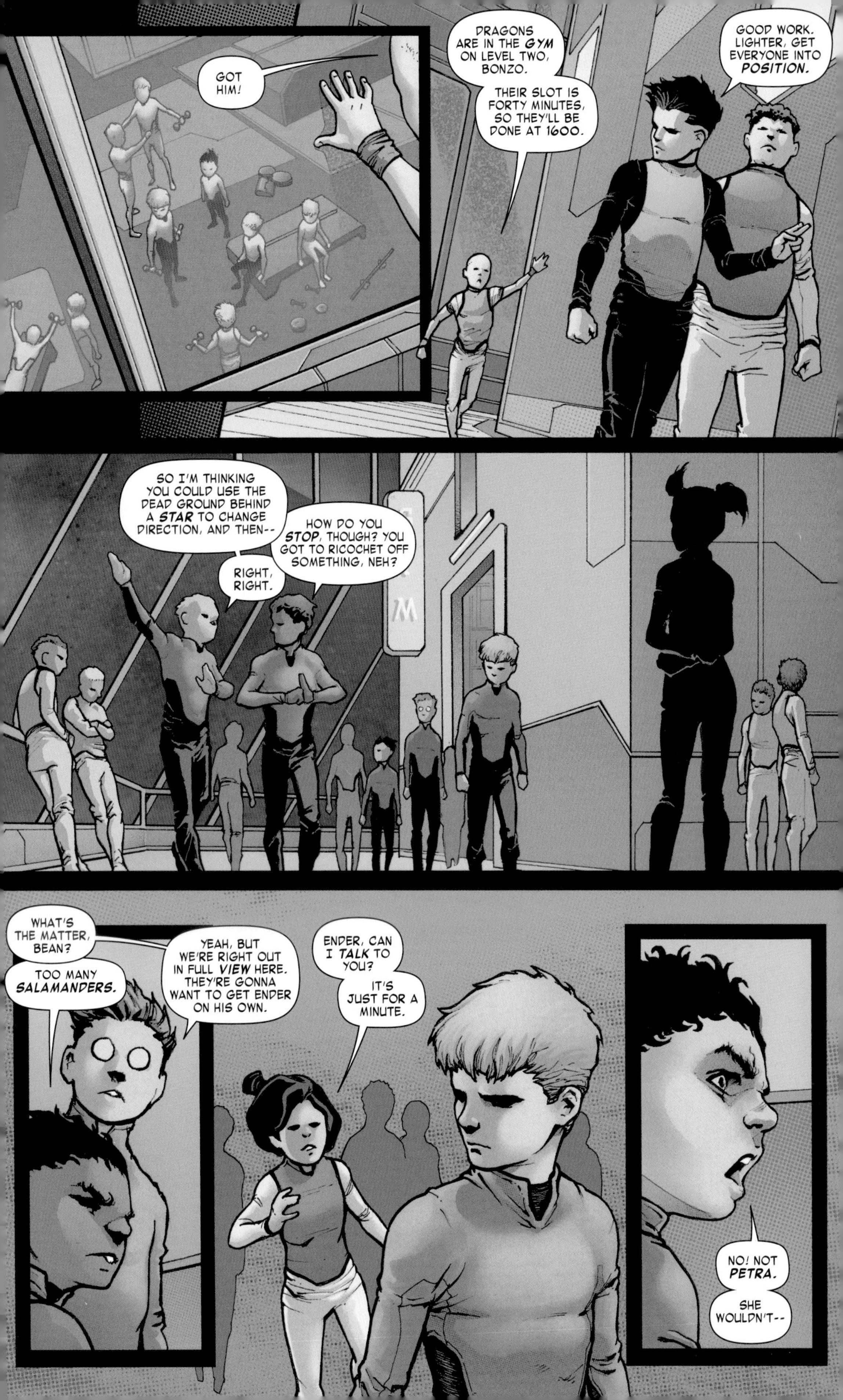
GOT HIM!
DRAGONS ARE IN THE GYM ON LEVEL TWO, BONZO.
THEIR SLOT IS FORTY MINUTES, SO THEY'LL BE DONE AT 1600.
GOOD WORK. LIGHTER, GET EVERYONE INTO POSITION.
SO I'M THINKING YOU COULD USE THE DEAD GROUND BEHIND A STAR TO CHANGE DIRECTION, AND THEN--
RIGHT, RIGHT.
HOW DO YOU STOP, THOUGH? YOU GOT TO RICOCHET OFF SOMETHING, NEH?
WHAT'S THE MATTER, BEAN?
TOO MANY SALAMANDERS.
YEAH, BUT WE'RE RIGHT OUT IN FULL VIEW HERE. THEY'RE GONNA WANT TO GET ENDER ON HIS OWN.
ENDER, CAN I TALK TO YOU?
IT'S JUST FOR A MINUTE.
NO! NOT PETRA.
SHE WOULDN'T--

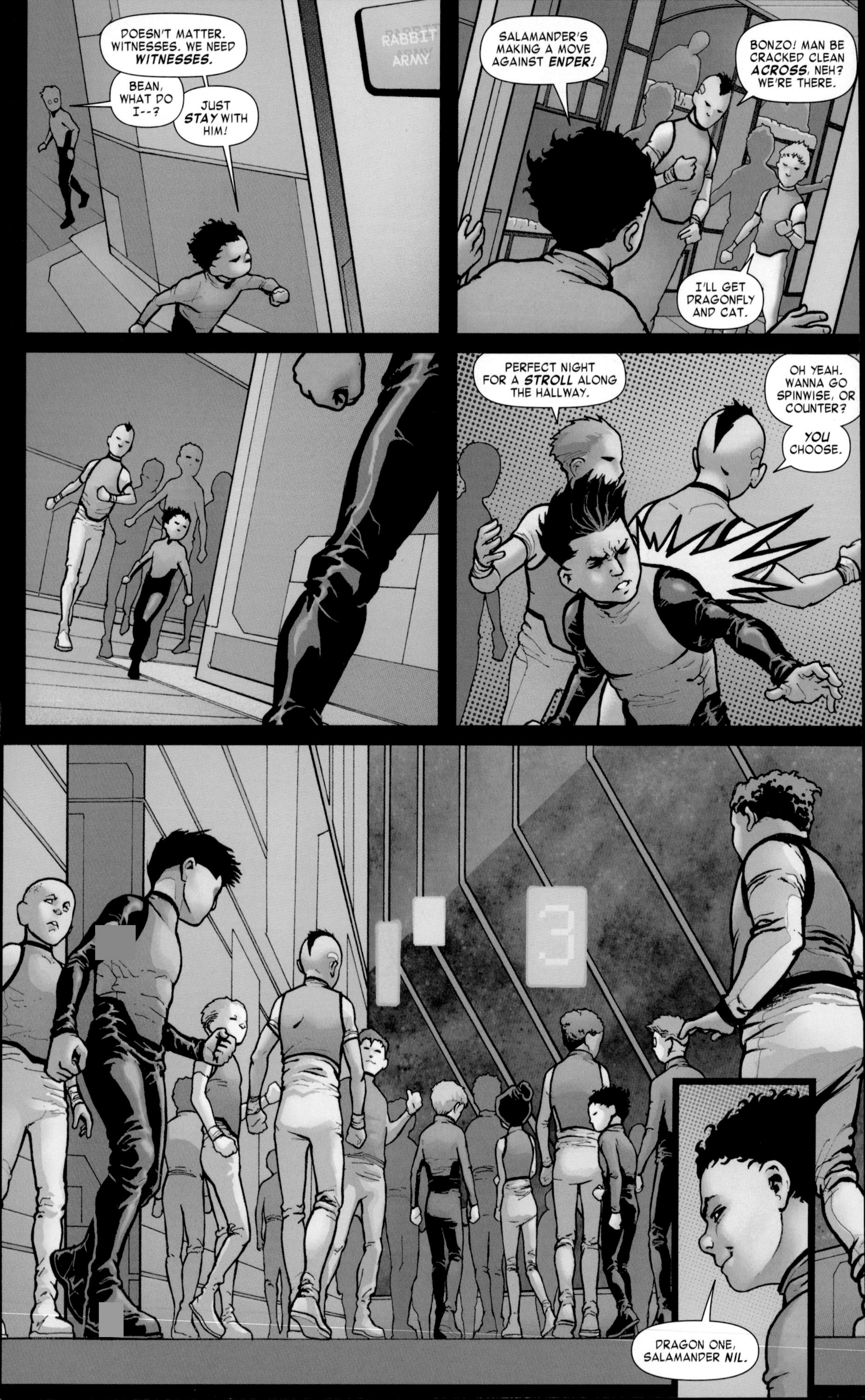
DOESN'T MATTER. WITNESSES. WE NEED WITNESSES.
RABBIT ARMY
BEAN, WHAT DO I--?
JUST STAY WITH HIM!
SALAMANDER'S MAKING A MOVE AGAINST ENDER!
BONZO! MAN BE CRACKED CLEAN ACROSS, NEH? WE'RE THERE.
I'LL GET DRAGONFLY AND CAT.
PERFECT NIGHT FOR A STROLL ALONG THE HALLWAY.
OH YEAH. WANNA GO SPINWISE, OR COUNTER? YOU CHOOSE.
DRAGON ONE, SALAMANDER NIL.

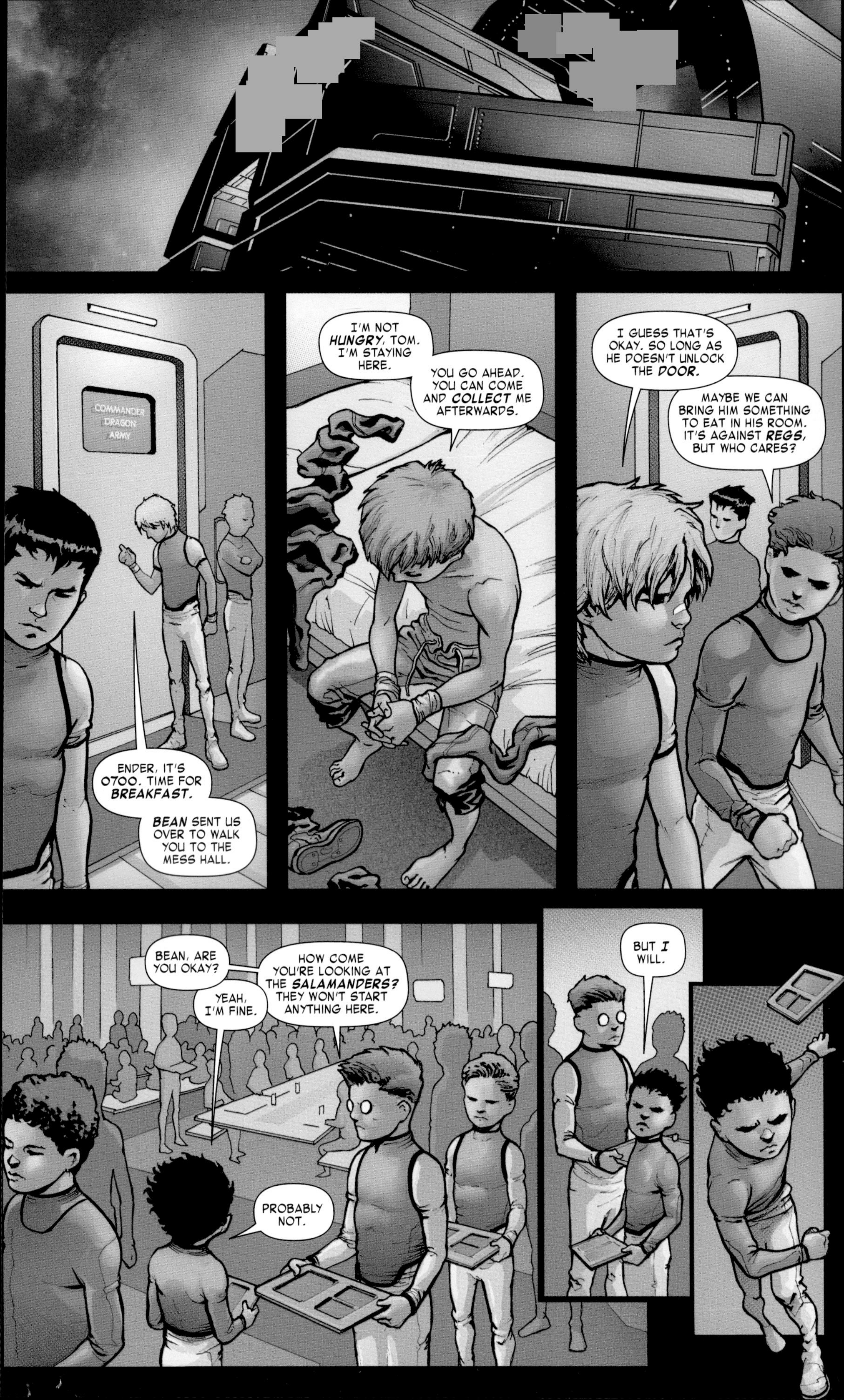
COMMANDER DRAGON ARMY
ENDER, IT'S 0700. TIME FOR BREAKFAST.
BEAN SENT US OVER TO WALK YOU TO THE MESS HALL.
I'M NOT HUNGRY, TOM. I'M STAYING HERE.
YOU GO AHEAD. YOU CAN COME AND COLLECT ME AFTERWARDS.
I GUESS THAT'S OKAY. SO LONG AS HE DOESN'T UNLOCK THE DOOR.
MAYBE WE CAN BRING HIM SOMETHING TO EAT IN HIS ROOM. IT'S AGAINST REGS, BUT WHO CARES?
BEAN, ARE YOU OKAY?
YEAH, I'M FINE.
HOW COME YOU'RE LOOKING AT THE SALAMANDERS? THEY WON'T START ANYTHING HERE.
PROBABLY NOT.
BUT I WILL.

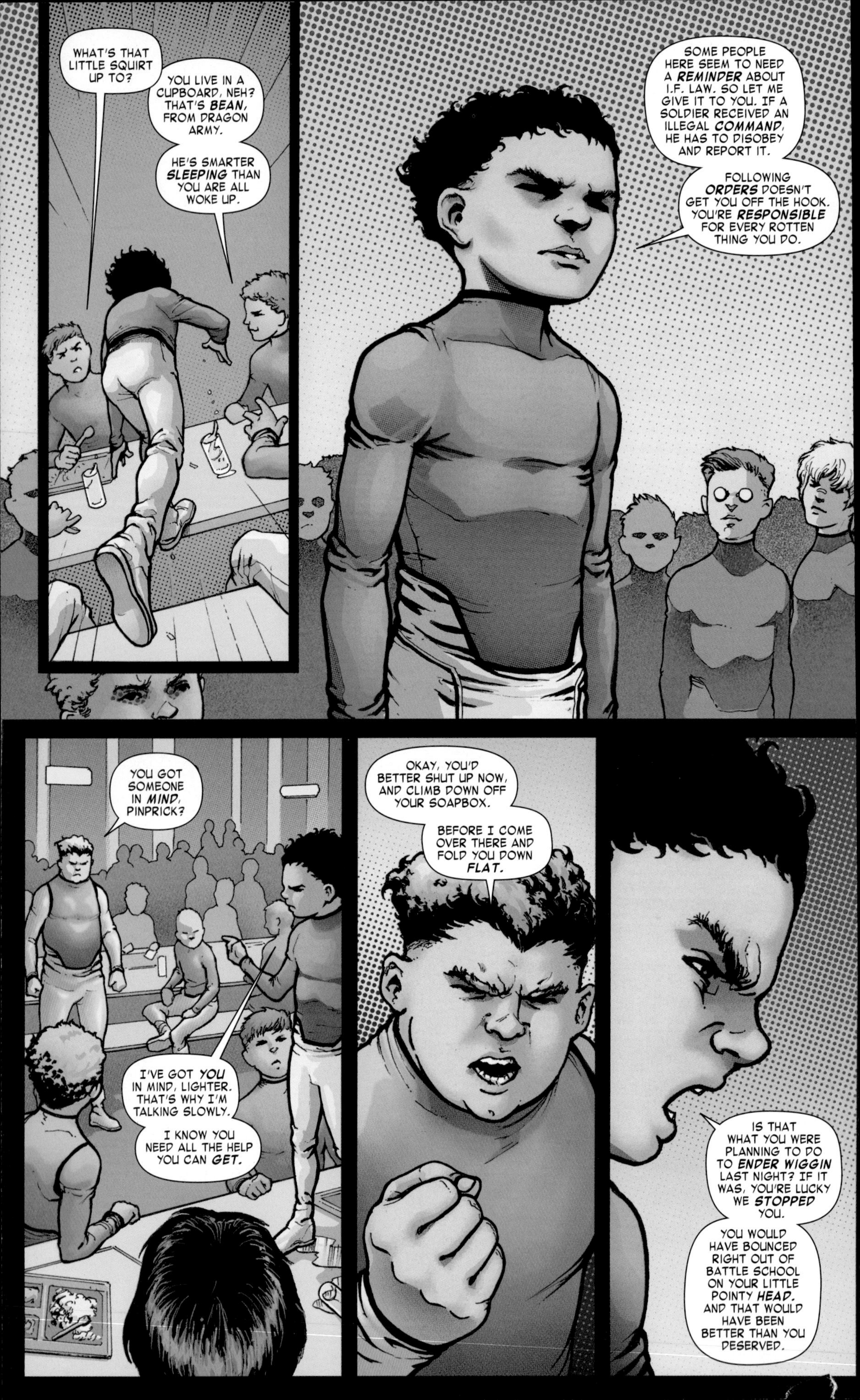

WHAT'S THAT LITTLE SQUIRT UP TO?
YOU LIVE IN A CUPBOARD, NEH? THAT'S BEAN, FROM DRAGON ARMY.
HE'S SMARTER SLEEPING THAN YOU ARE ALL WOKE UP.
SOME PEOPLE HERE SEEM TO NEED A REMINDER ABOUT I.F. LAW. SO LET ME GIVE IT TO YOU. IF A SOLDIER RECEIVED AN ILLEGAL COMMAND, HE HAS TO DISOBEY AND REPORT IT.
FOLLOWING ORDERS DOESN'T GET YOU OFF THE HOOK. YOU'RE RESPONSIBLE FOR EVERY ROTTEN THING YOU DO.
YOU GOT SOMEONE IN MIND, PINPRICK?
I'VE GOT YOU IN MIND, LIGHTER. THAT'S WHY I'M TALKING SLOWLY.
I KNOW YOU NEED ALL THE HELP YOU CAN GET.
OKAY, YOU'D BETTER SHUT UP NOW, AND CLIMB DOWN OFF YOUR SOAPBOX.
BEFORE I COME OVER THERE AND FOLD YOU DOWN FLAT.
IS THAT WHAT YOU WERE PLANNING TO DO TO ENDER WIGGIN LAST NIGHT? IF IT WAS, YOU'RE LUCKY WE STOPPED YOU.
YOU WOULD HAVE BOUNCED RIGHT OUT OF BATTLE SCHOOL ON YOUR LITTLE POINTY HEAD. AND THAT WOULD HAVE BEEN BETTER THAN YOU DESERVED.

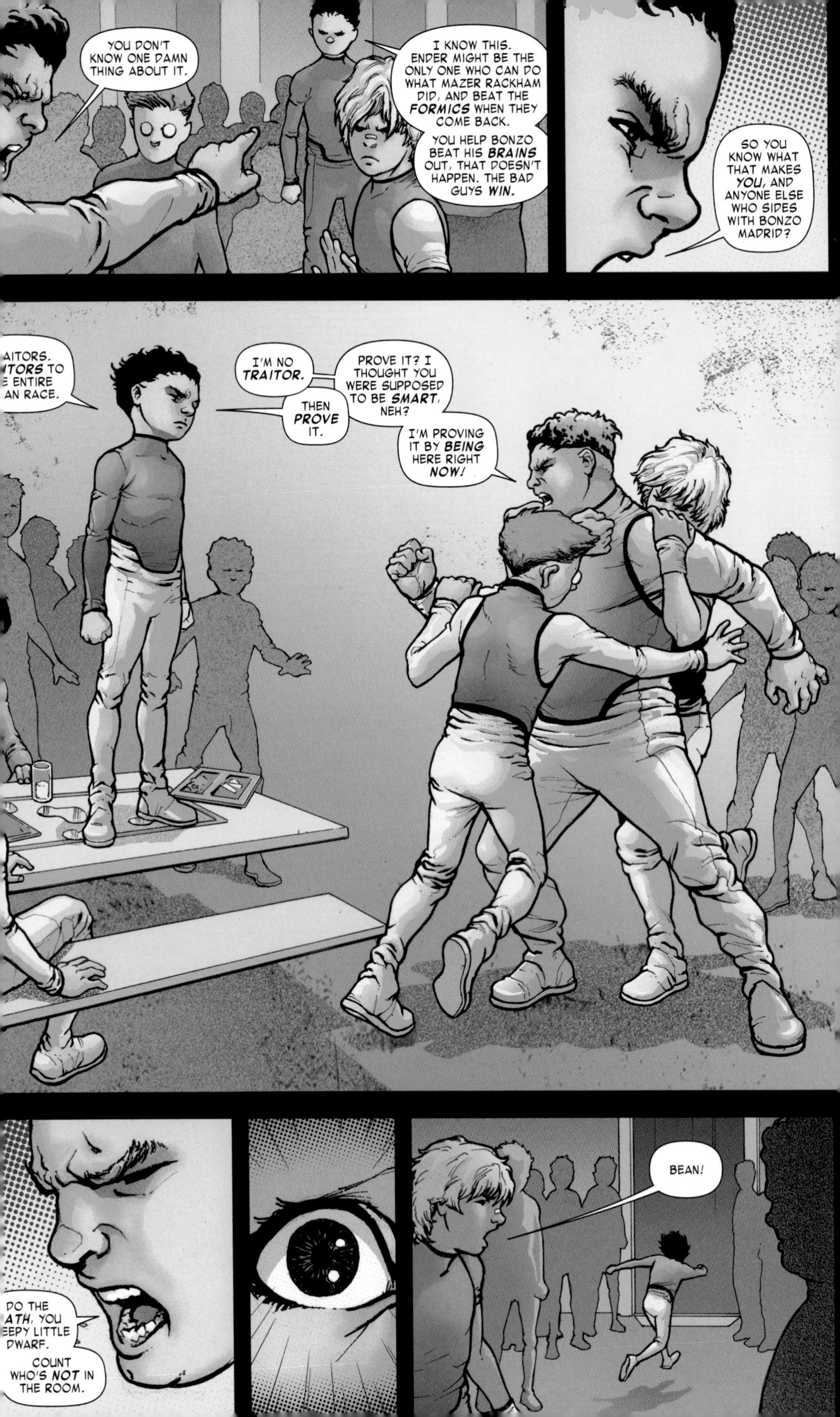

YOU DON'T KNOW ONE DAMN THING ABOUT IT.
I KNOW THIS. ENDER MIGHT BE THE ONLY ONE WHO CAN DO WHAT MAZER RACKHAM DID, AND BEAT THE FORMICS WHEN THEY COME BACK.
YOU HELP BONZO BEAT HIS BRAINS OUT, THAT DOESN'T HAPPEN. THE BAD GUYS WIN.
SO YOU KNOW WHAT THAT MAKES YOU, AND ANYONE ELSE WHO SIDES WITH BONZO MADRID?
AITORS. ITORS TO E ENTIRE AN RACE.
I'M NO TRAITOR.
THEN PROVE IT.
PROVE IT? I THOUGHT YOU WERE SUPPOSED TO BE SMART, NEH?
I'M PROVING IT BY BEING HERE RIGHT NOW!
DO THE ATH, YOU EEPY LITTLE DWARF.
COUNT WHO'S NOT IN THE ROOM.
BEAN!

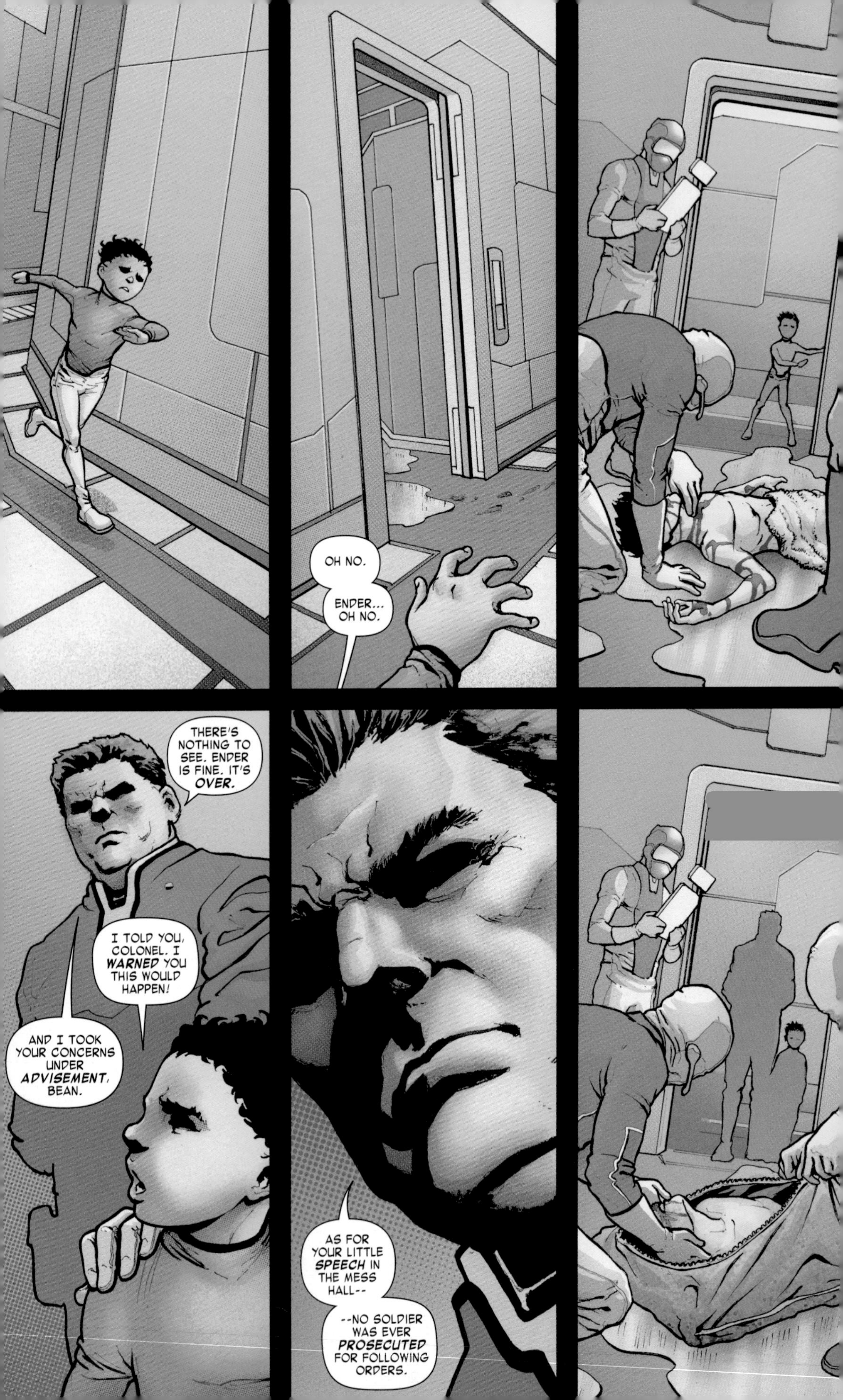
OH NO.
ENDER... OH NO.
THERE'S NOTHING TO SEE. ENDER IS FINE. IT'S OVER.
I TOLD YOU, COLONEL. I WARNED YOU THIS WOULD HAPPEN!
AND I TOOK YOUR CONCERNS UNDER ADVISEMENT, BEAN.
AS FOR YOUR LITTLE SPEECH IN THE MESS HALL--
--NO SOLDIER WAS EVER PROSECUTED FOR FOLLOWING ORDERS.

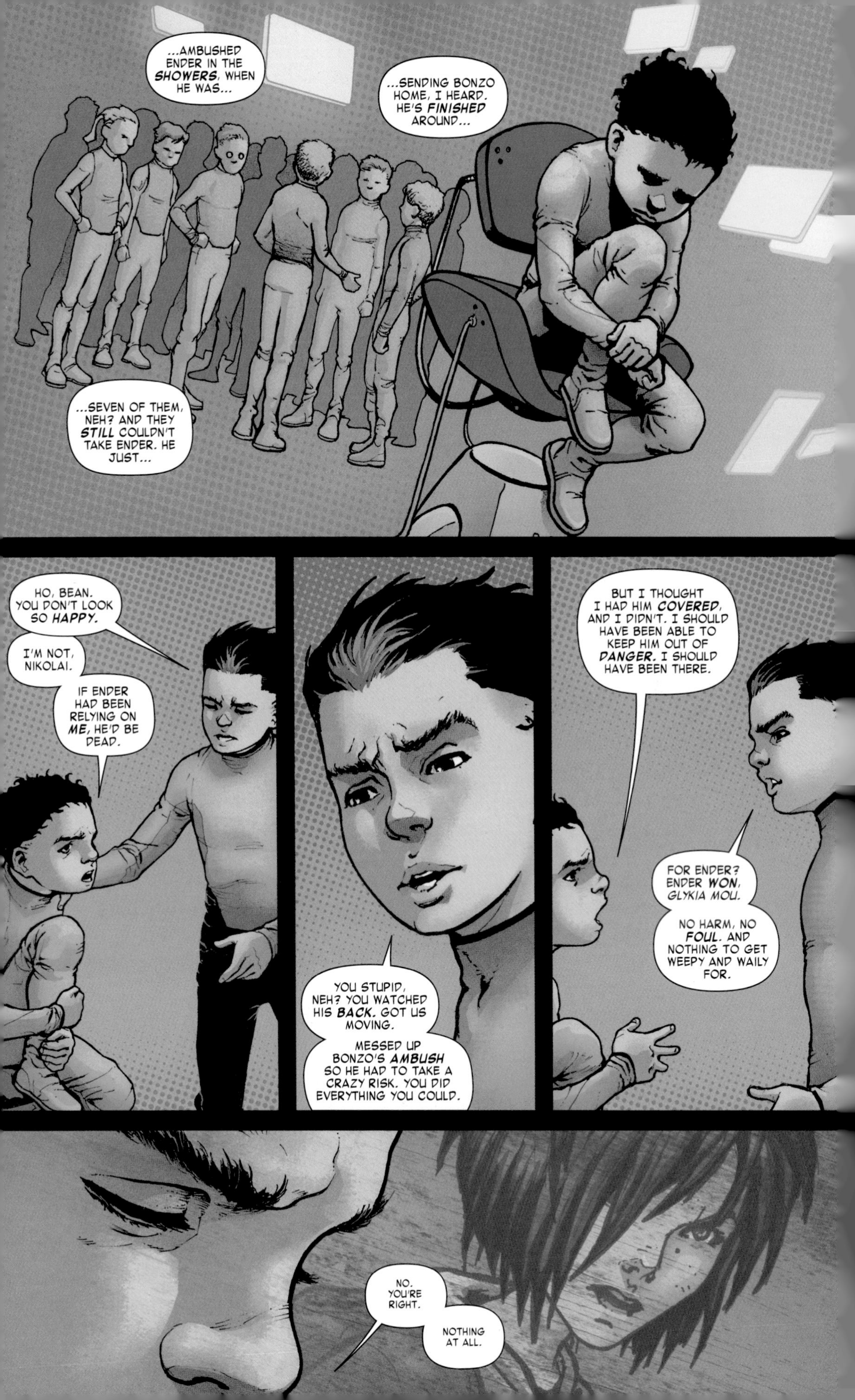
...AMBUSHED ENDER IN THE SHOWERS, WHEN HE WAS...
...SENDING BONZO HOME, I HEARD. HE'S FINISHED AROUND...
...SEVEN OF THEM, NEH? AND THEY STILL COULDN'T TAKE ENDER. HE JUST...
HO, BEAN. YOU DON'T LOOK SO HAPPY.
I'M NOT, NIKOLAI.
IF ENDER HAD BEEN RELYING ON ME, HE'D BE DEAD.
YOU STUPID, NEH? YOU WATCHED HIS BACK. GOT US MOVING.
MESSED UP BONZO'S AMBUSH SO HE HAD TO TAKE A CRAZY RISK. YOU DID EVERYTHING YOU COULD.
BUT I THOUGHT I HAD HIM COVERED, AND I DIDN'T. I SHOULD HAVE BEEN ABLE TO KEEP HIM OUT OF DANGER. I SHOULD HAVE BEEN THERE.
FOR ENDER? ENDER WON, GLYKIA MOU.
NO HARM, NO FOUL. AND NOTHING TO GET WEEPY AND WAILY FOR.
NO. YOU'RE RIGHT.
NOTHING AT ALL.

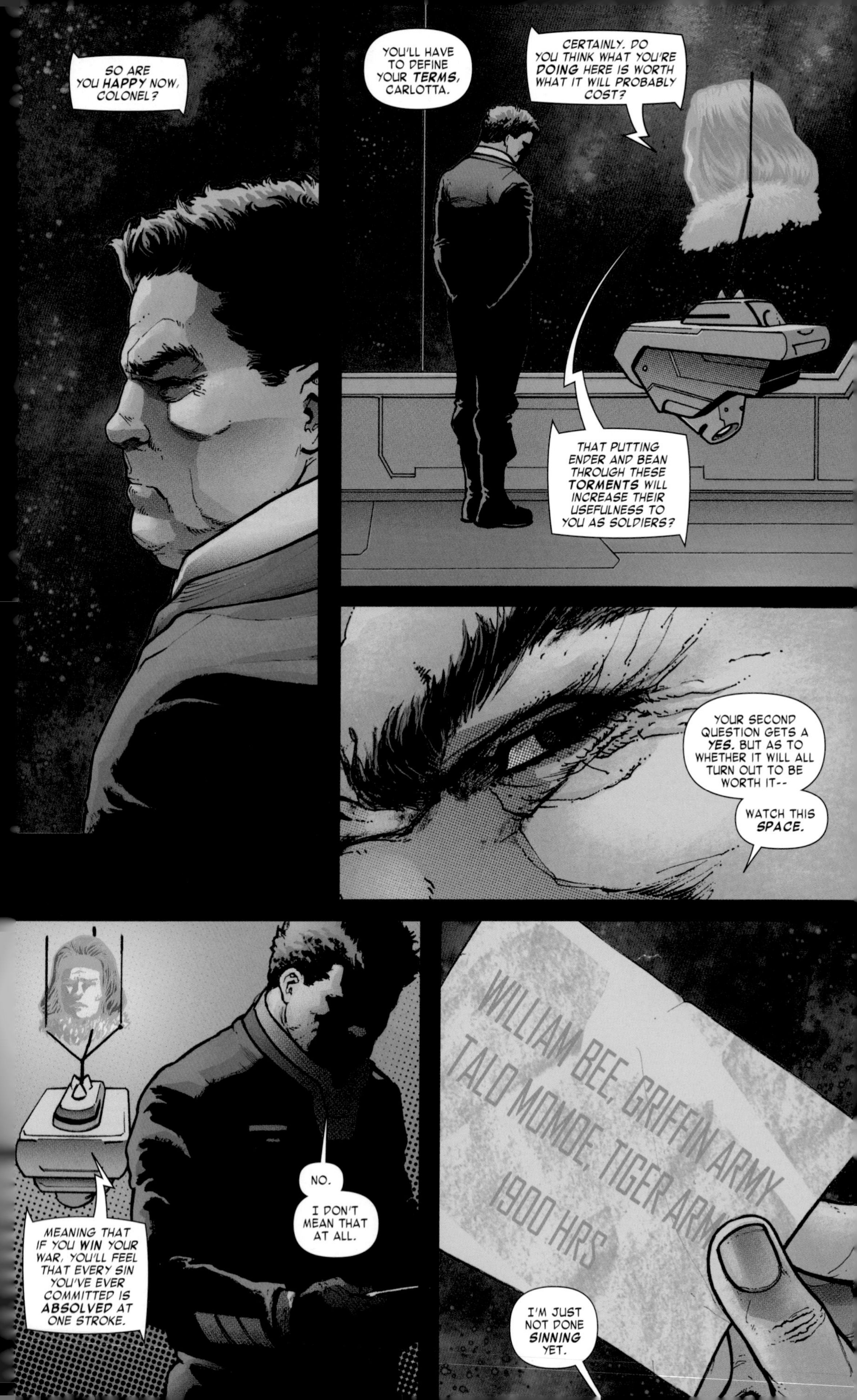
SO ARE YOU HAPPY NOW, COLONEL?
YOU'LL HAVE TO DEFINE YOUR TERMS, CARLOTTA.
CERTAINLY. DO YOU THINK WHAT YOU'RE DOING HERE IS WORTH WHAT IT WILL PROBABLY COST?
THAT PUTTING ENDER AND BEAN THROUGH THESE TORMENTS WILL INCREASE THEIR USEFULNESS TO YOU AS SOLDIERS?
YOUR SECOND QUESTION GETS A YES. BUT AS TO WHETHER IT WILL ALL TURN OUT TO BE WORTH IT--
WATCH THIS SPACE.
MEANING THAT IF YOU WIN YOUR WAR, YOU'LL FEEL THAT EVERY SIN YOU'VE EVER COMMITTED IS ABSOLVED AT ONE STROKE.
NO.
I DON'T MEAN THAT AT ALL.
WILLIAM BEE, GRIFFIN ARMY
TALO MOMOE, TIGER ARMY
1900 HRS
I'M JUST NOT DONE SINNING YET.

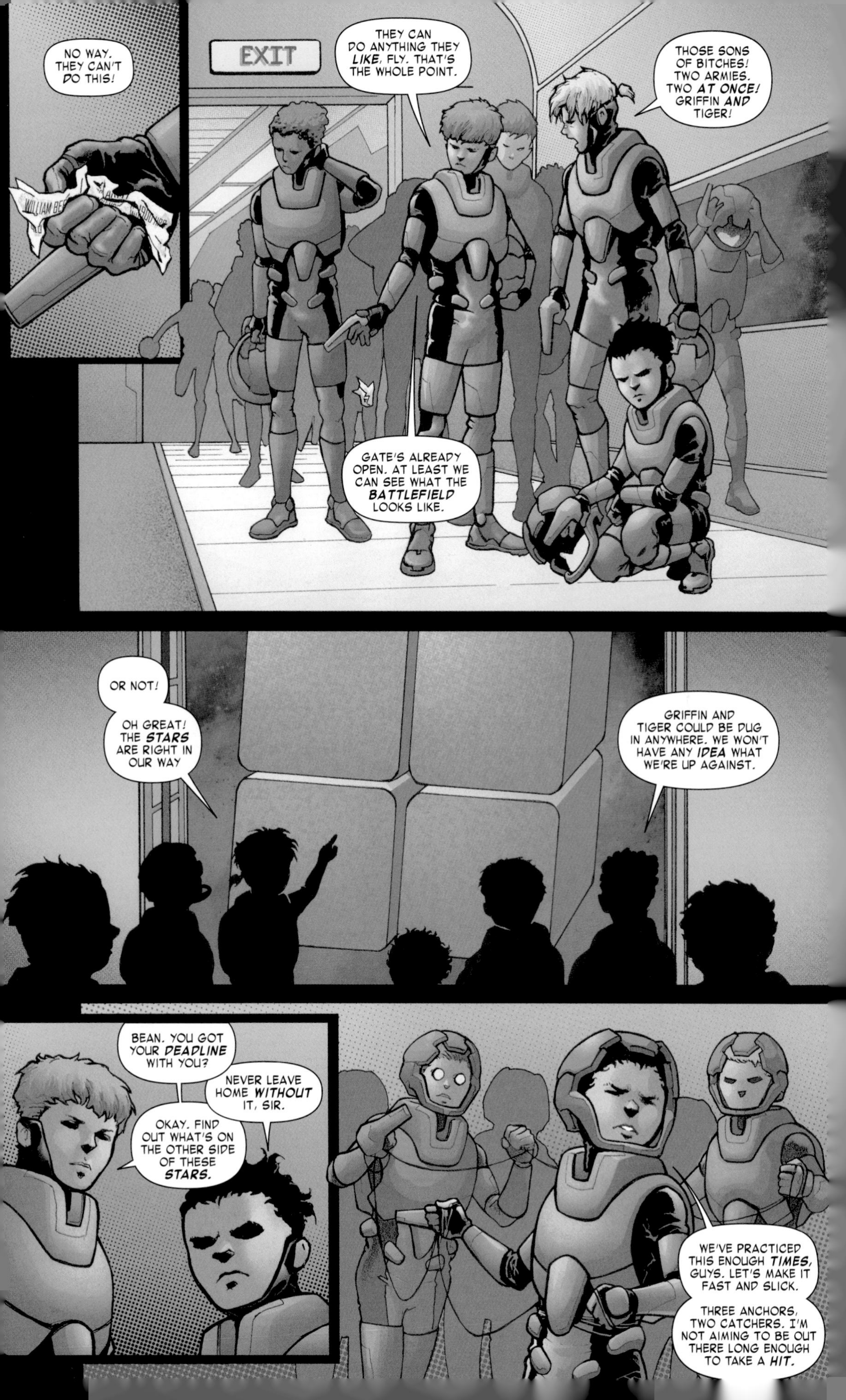

NO WAY. THEY CAN'T DO THIS!
WILLIAM BE
THEY CAN DO ANYTHING THEY LIKE, FLY. THAT'S THE WHOLE POINT.
THOSE SONS OF BITCHES! TWO ARMIES. TWO AT ONCE! GRIFFIN AND TIGER!
EXIT
GATE'S ALREADY OPEN. AT LEAST WE CAN SEE WHAT THE BATTLEFIELD LOOKS LIKE.
OR NOT!
OH GREAT! THE STARS ARE RIGHT IN OUR WAY
GRIFFIN AND TIGER COULD BE DUG IN ANYWHERE. WE WON'T HAVE ANY IDEA WHAT WE'RE UP AGAINST.
BEAN. YOU GOT YOUR DEADLINE WITH YOU?
NEVER LEAVE HOME WITHOUT IT, SIR.
OKAY. FIND OUT WHAT'S ON THE OTHER SIDE OF THESE STARS.
WE'VE PRACTICED THIS ENOUGH TIMES, GUYS. LET'S MAKE IT FAST AND SLICK.
THREE ANCHORS, TWO CATCHERS. I'M NOT AIMING TO BE OUT THERE LONG ENOUGH TO TAKE A HIT.

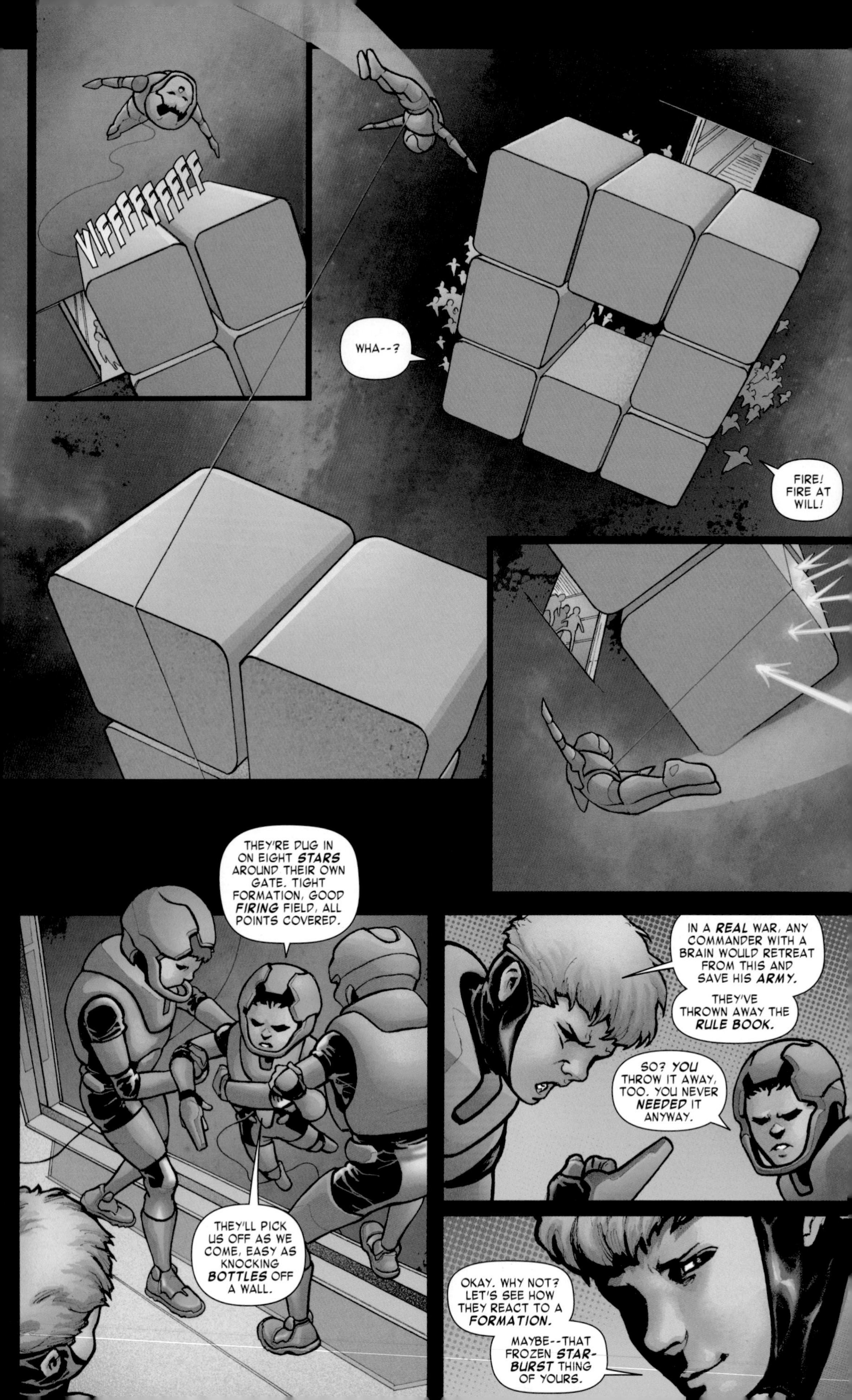
VIFFFFFFFF
WHA--?
FIRE! FIRE AT WILL!
THEY'RE DUG IN ON EIGHT STARS AROUND THEIR OWN GATE. TIGHT FORMATION, GOOD FIRING FIELD, ALL POINTS COVERED.
THEY'LL PICK US OFF AS WE COME, EASY AS KNOCKING BOTTLES OFF A WALL.
IN A REAL WAR, ANY COMMANDER WITH A BRAIN WOULD RETREAT FROM THIS AND SAVE HIS ARMY.
THEY'VE THROWN AWAY THE RULE BOOK.
SO? YOU THROW IT AWAY, TOO. YOU NEVER NEEDED IT ANYWAY.
OKAY. WHY NOT? LET'S SEE HOW THEY REACT TO A FORMATION.
MAYBE--THAT FROZEN STAR-BURST THING OF YOURS.

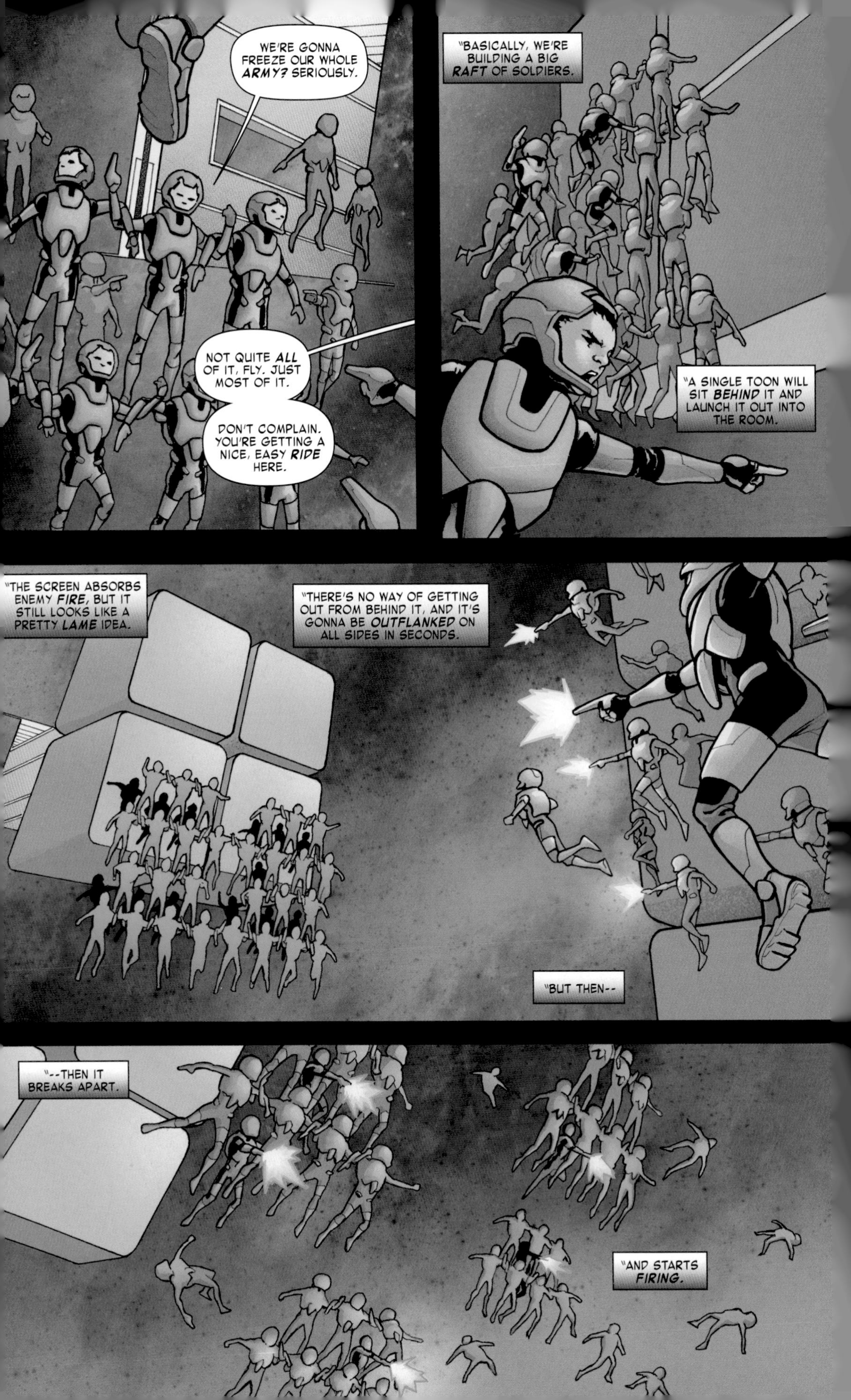
WE'RE GONNA FREEZE OUR WHOLE ARMY? SERIOUSLY.
NOT QUITE ALL OF IT, FLY. JUST MOST OF IT.
DON'T COMPLAIN. YOU'RE GETTING A NICE, EASY RIDE HERE.
"BASICALLY, WE'RE BUILDING A BIG RAFT OF SOLDIERS.
"A SINGLE TOON WILL SIT BEHIND IT AND LAUNCH IT OUT INTO THE ROOM.
"THE SCREEN ABSORBS ENEMY FIRE, BUT IT STILL LOOKS LIKE A PRETTY LAME IDEA.
"THERE'S NO WAY OF GETTING OUT FROM BEHIND IT, AND IT'S GONNA BE OUTFLANKED ON ALL SIDES IN SECONDS.
"BUT THEN--
"--THEN IT BREAKS APART.
"AND STARTS FIRING.

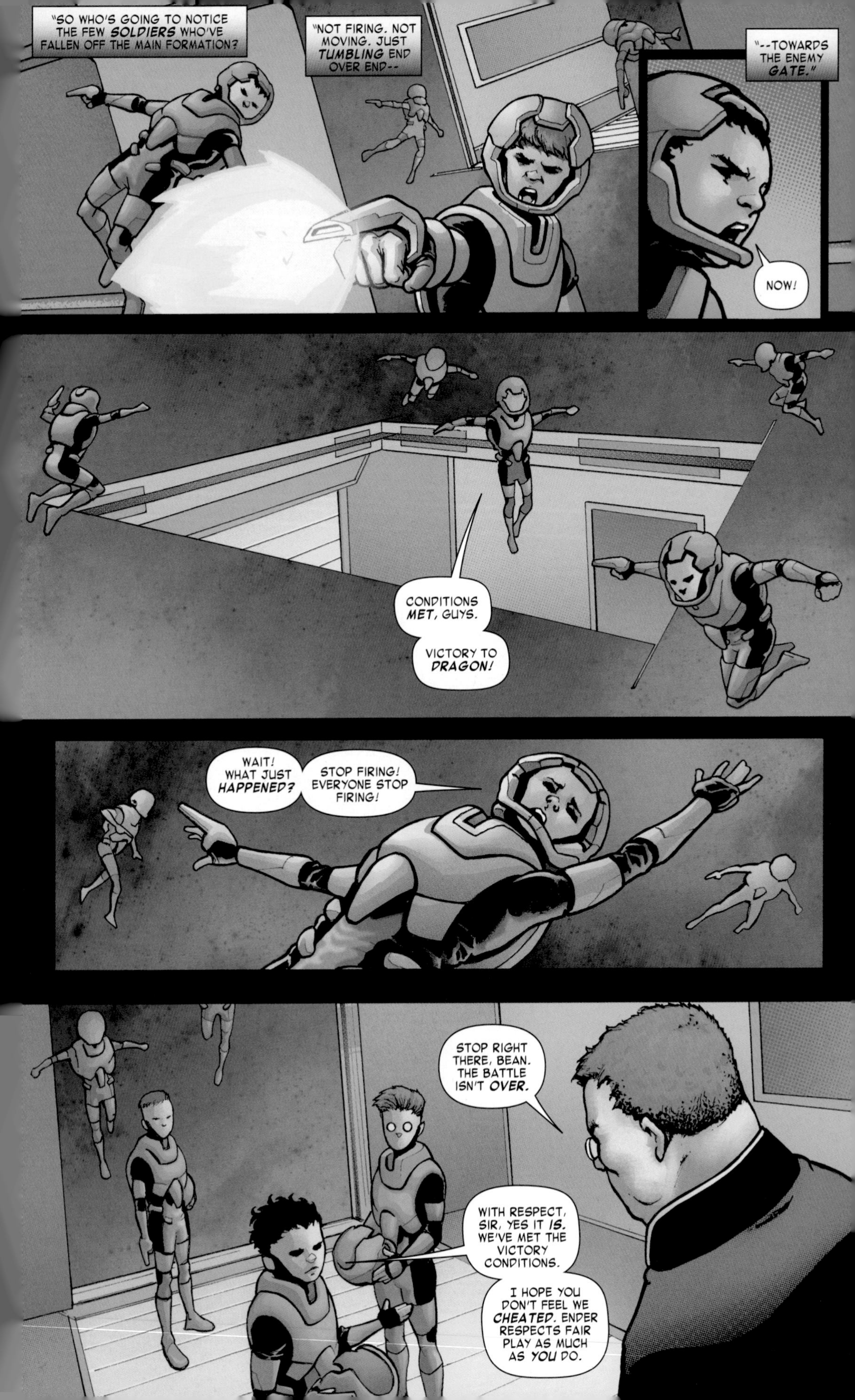
"SO WHO'S GOING TO NOTICE THE FEW SOLDIERS WHO'VE FALLEN OFF THE MAIN FORMATION?
"NOT FIRING. NOT MOVING. JUST TUMBLING END OVER END--
"--TOWARDS THE ENEMY GATE."
NOW!
CONDITIONS MET, GUYS.
VICTORY TO DRAGON!
WAIT! WHAT JUST HAPPENED?
STOP FIRING! EVERYONE STOP FIRING!
STOP RIGHT THERE, BEAN. THE BATTLE ISN'T OVER.
WITH RESPECT, SIR, YES IT IS. WE'VE MET THE VICTORY CONDITIONS.
I HOPE YOU DON'T FEEL WE CHEATED. ENDER RESPECTS FAIR PLAY AS MUCH AS YOU DO.

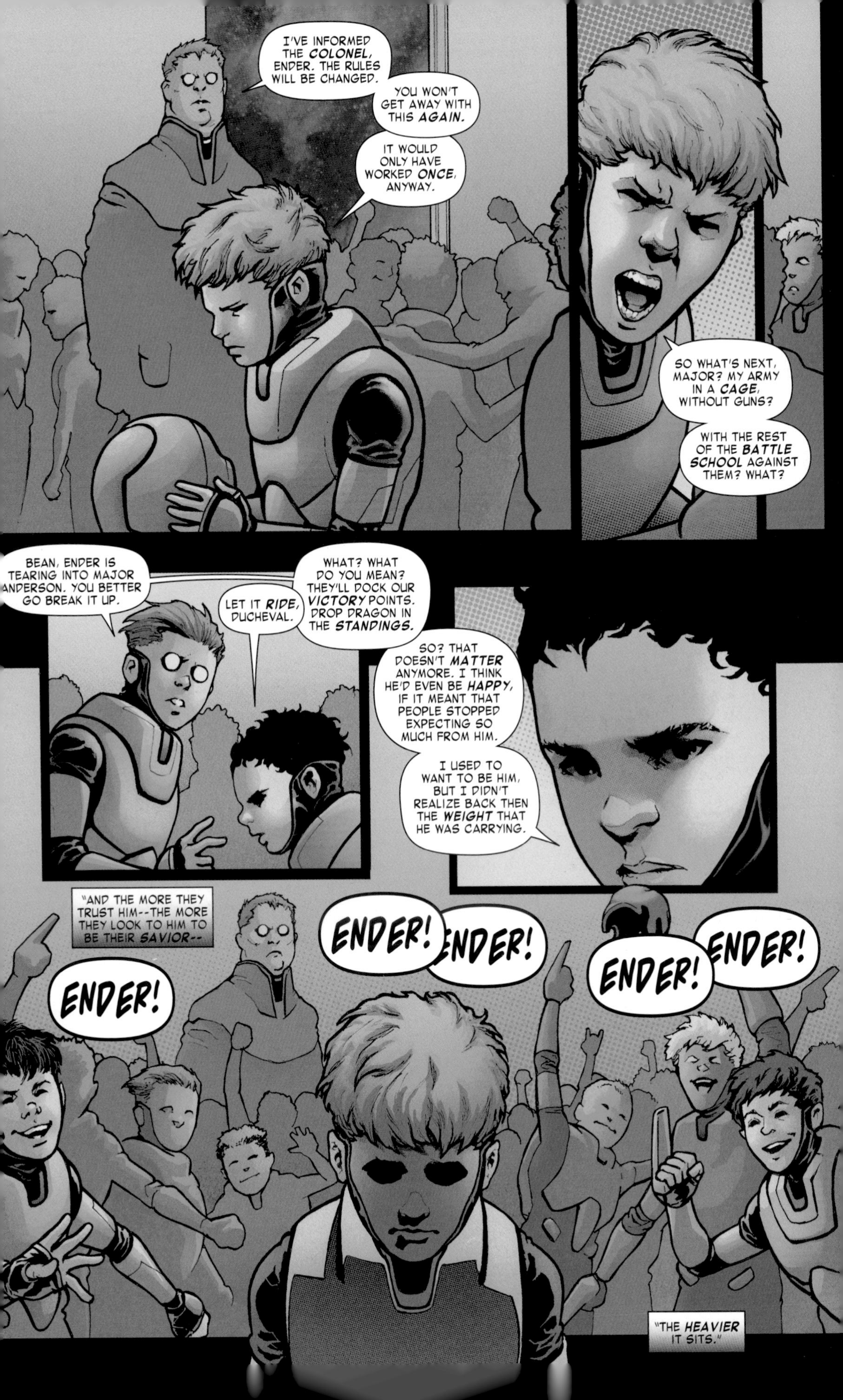
I'VE INFORMED THE COLONEL, ENDER. THE RULES WILL BE CHANGED.
YOU WON'T GET AWAY WITH THIS AGAIN.
IT WOULD ONLY HAVE WORKED ONCE, ANYWAY.
SO WHAT'S NEXT, MAJOR? MY ARMY IN A CAGE, WITHOUT GUNS?
WITH THE REST OF THE BATTLE SCHOOL AGAINST THEM? WHAT?
BEAN, ENDER IS TEARING INTO MAJOR ANDERSON. YOU BETTER GO BREAK IT UP.
LET IT RIDE, DUCHEVAL.
WHAT? WHAT DO YOU MEAN? THEY'LL DOCK OUR VICTORY POINTS. DROP DRAGON IN THE STANDINGS.
SO? THAT DOESN'T MATTER ANYMORE. I THINK HE'D EVEN BE HAPPY, IF IT MEANT THAT PEOPLE STOPPED EXPECTING SO MUCH FROM HIM.
I USED TO WANT TO BE HIM, BUT I DIDN'T REALIZE BACK THEN THE WEIGHT THAT HE WAS CARRYING.
"AND THE MORE THEY TRUST HIM--THE MORE THEY LOOK TO HIM TO BE THEIR SAVIOR--
ENDER!
ENDER!
ENDER!
ENDER!
ENDER!
"THE HEAVIER IT SITS."

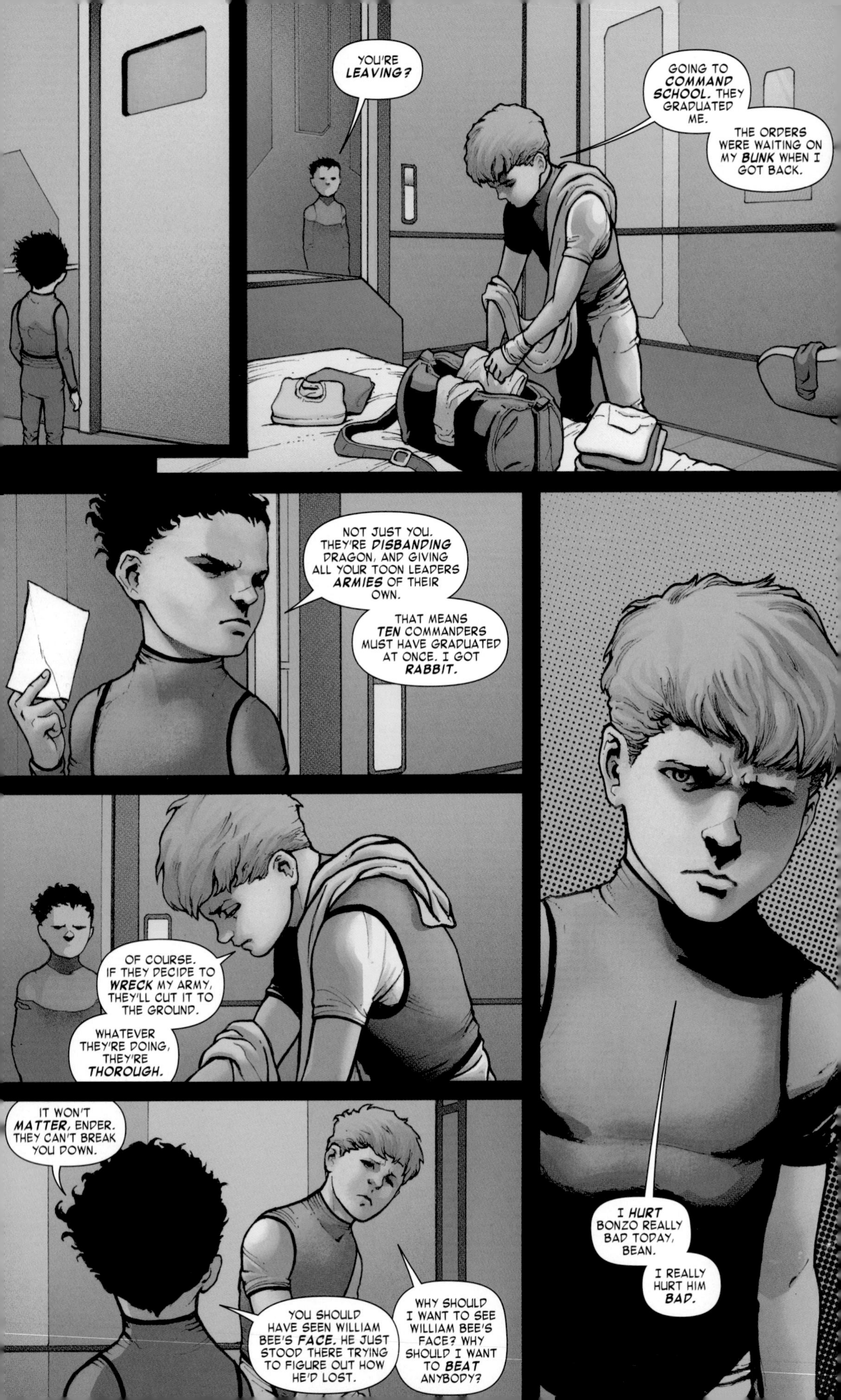

YOU'RE LEAVING?
GOING TO COMMAND SCHOOL. THEY GRADUATED ME.
THE ORDERS WERE WAITING ON MY BUNK WHEN I GOT BACK.
NOT JUST YOU. THEY'RE DISBANDING DRAGON, AND GIVING ALL YOUR TOON LEADERS ARMIES OF THEIR OWN.
THAT MEANS TEN COMMANDERS MUST HAVE GRADUATED AT ONCE. I GOT RABBIT.
OF COURSE. IF THEY DECIDE TO WRECK MY ARMY, THEY'LL CUT IT TO THE GROUND.
WHATEVER THEY'RE DOING, THEY'RE THOROUGH.
IT WON'T MATTER, ENDER. THEY CAN'T BREAK YOU DOWN.
YOU SHOULD HAVE SEEN WILLIAM BEE'S FACE. HE JUST STOOD THERE TRYING TO FIGURE OUT HOW HE'D LOST.
WHY SHOULD I WANT TO SEE WILLIAM BEE'S FACE? WHY SHOULD I WANT TO BEAT ANYBODY?
I HURT BONZO REALLY BAD TODAY, BEAN.
I REALLY HURT HIM BAD.

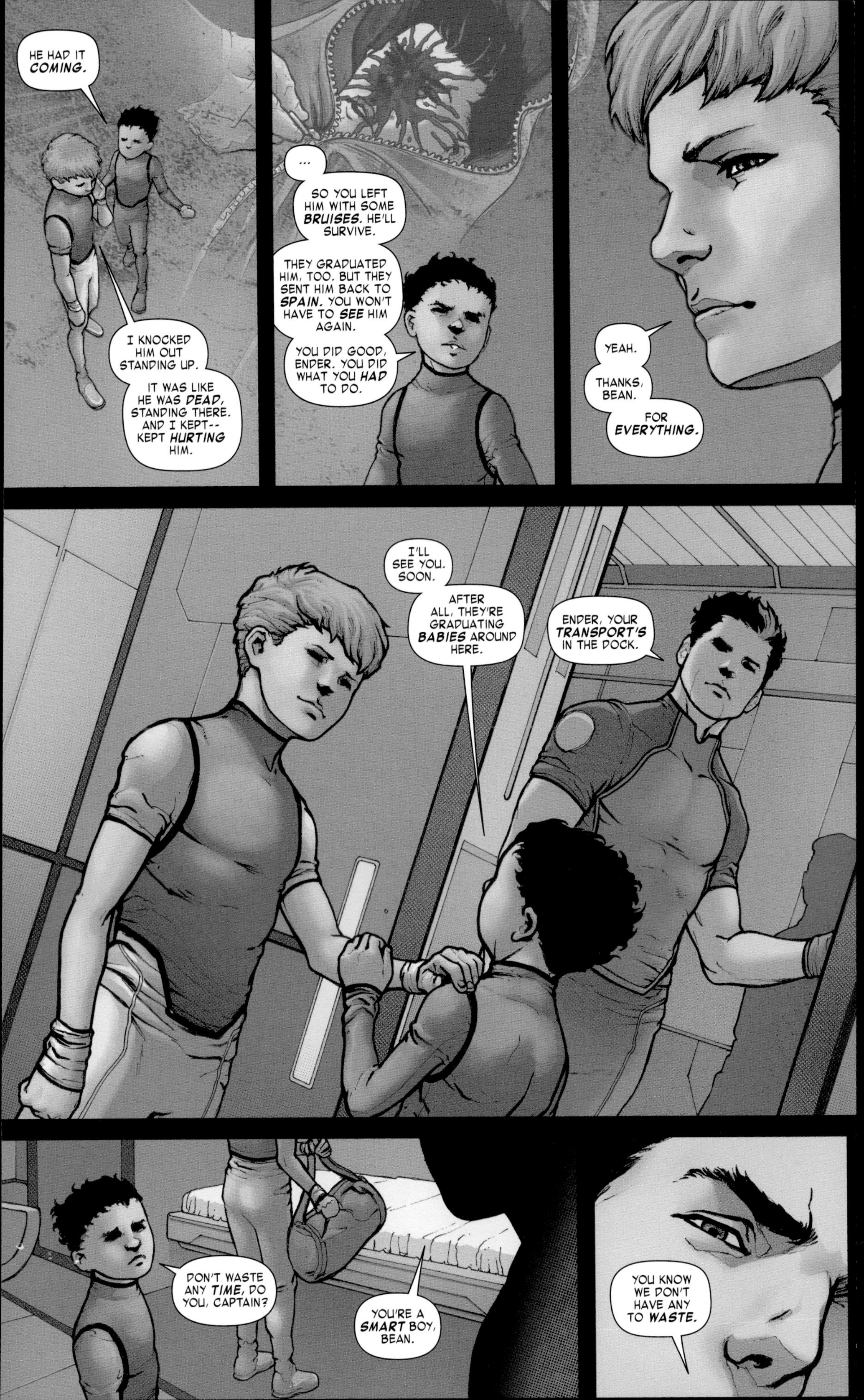
HE HAD IT COMING.
I KNOCKED HIM OUT STANDING UP.
IT WAS LIKE HE WAS DEAD, STANDING THERE. AND I KEPT-- KEPT HURTING HIM.
...
SO YOU LEFT HIM WITH SOME BRUISES. HE'LL SURVIVE.
THEY GRADUATED HIM, TOO. BUT THEY SENT HIM BACK TO SPAIN. YOU WON'T HAVE TO SEE HIM AGAIN.
YOU DID GOOD, ENDER. YOU DID WHAT YOU HAD TO DO.
YEAH.
THANKS, BEAN.
FOR EVERYTHING.
I'LL SEE YOU. SOON.
AFTER ALL, THEY'RE GRADUATING BABIES AROUND HERE.
ENDER, YOUR TRANSPORT'S IN THE DOCK.
DON'T WASTE ANY TIME, DO YOU, CAPTAIN?
YOU'RE A SMART BOY, BEAN.
YOU KNOW WE DON'T HAVE ANY TO WASTE.

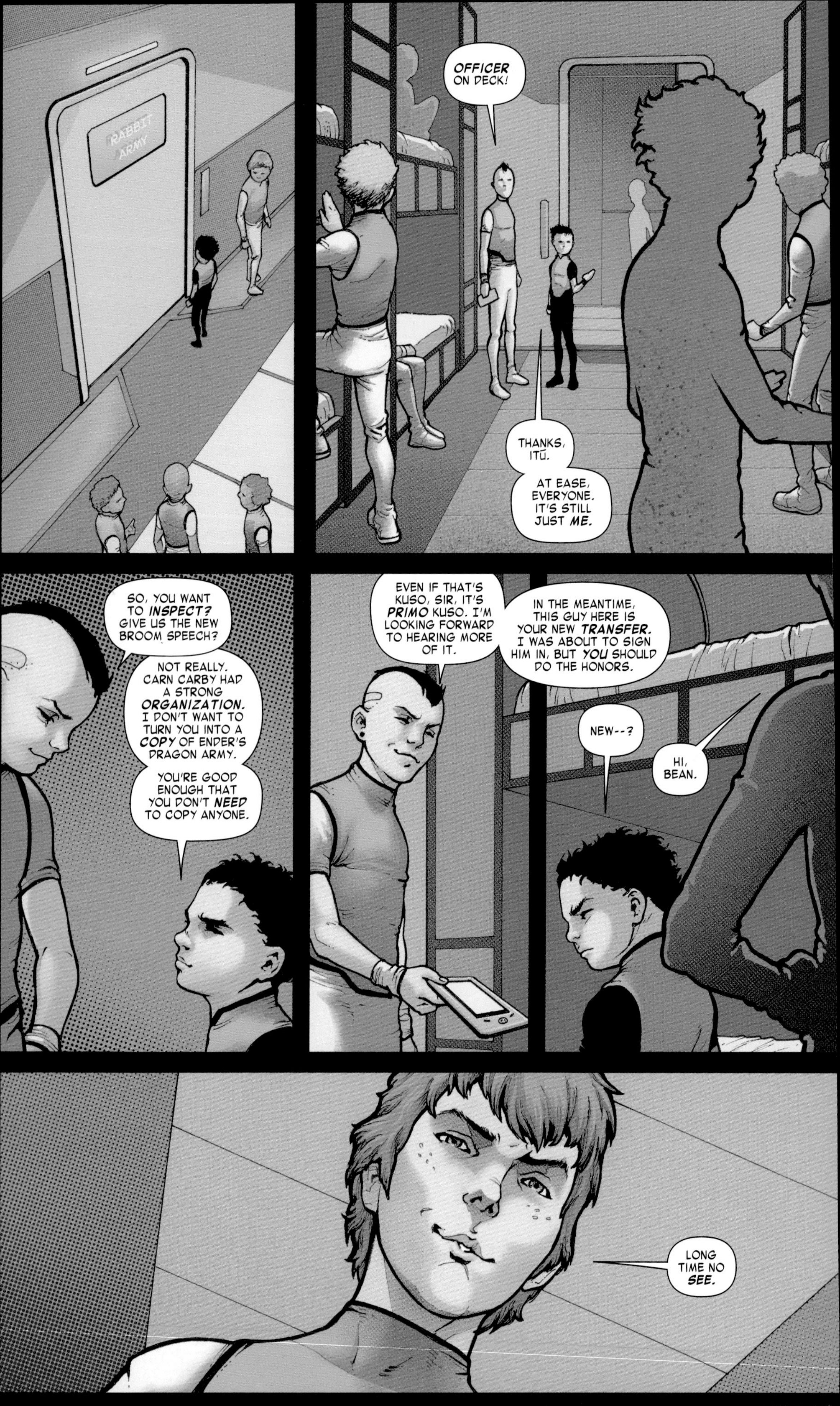
RABBIT ARMY
OFFICER ON DECK!
THANKS, ITŪ.
AT EASE, EVERYONE. IT'S STILL JUST ME.
SO, YOU WANT TO INSPECT? GIVE US THE NEW BROOM SPEECH?
NOT REALLY. CARN CARBY HAD A STRONG ORGANIZATION. I DON'T WANT TO TURN YOU INTO A COPY OF ENDER'S DRAGON ARMY.
YOU'RE GOOD ENOUGH THAT YOU DON'T NEED TO COPY ANYONE.
EVEN IF THAT'S KUSO, SIR, IT'S PRIMO KUSO. I'M LOOKING FORWARD TO HEARING MORE OF IT.
IN THE MEANTIME, THIS GUY HERE IS YOUR NEW TRANSFER. I WAS ABOUT TO SIGN HIM IN, BUT YOU SHOULD DO THE HONORS.
NEW--?
HI, BEAN.
LONG TIME NO SEE.

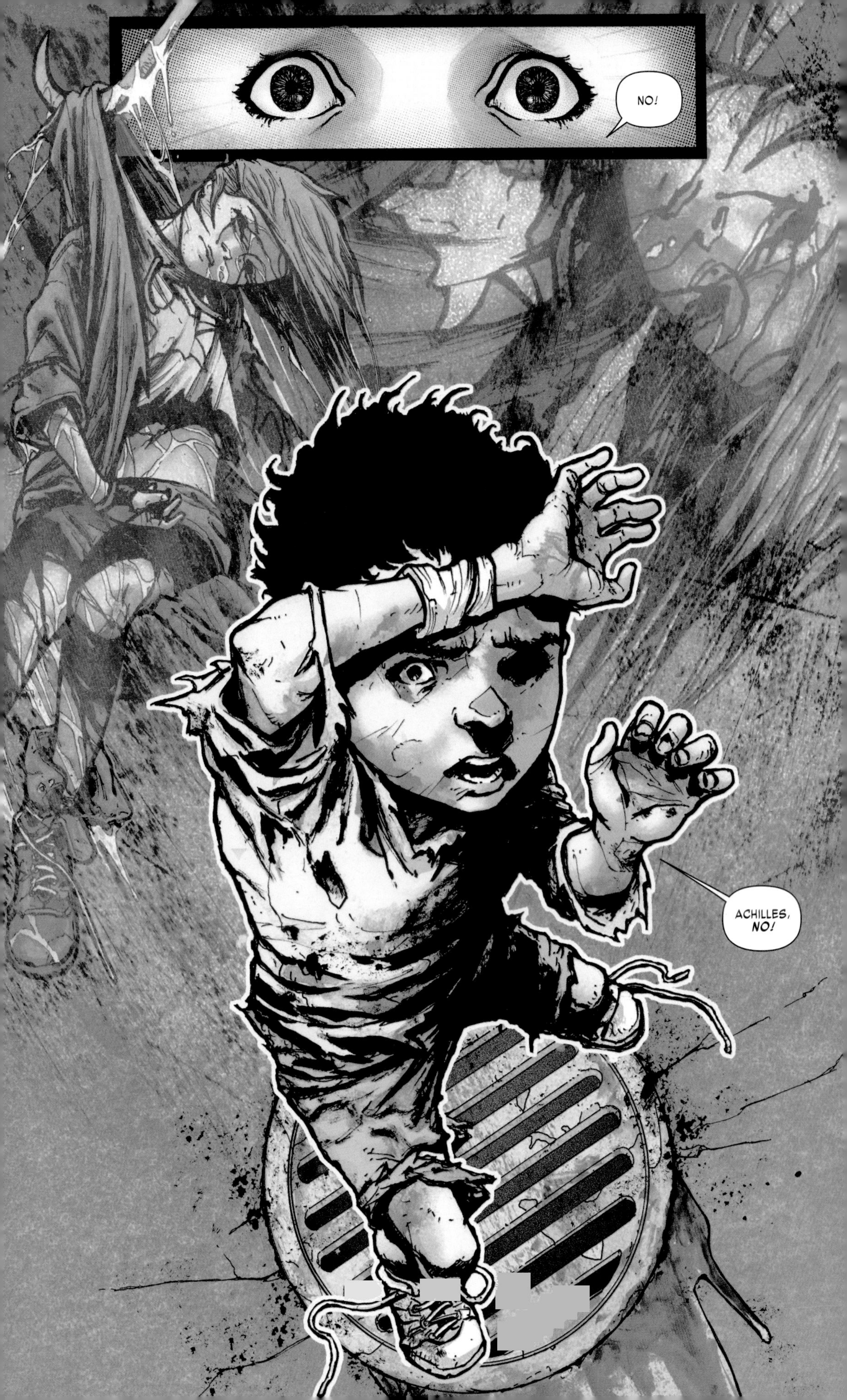
NO!
ACHILLES, NO!

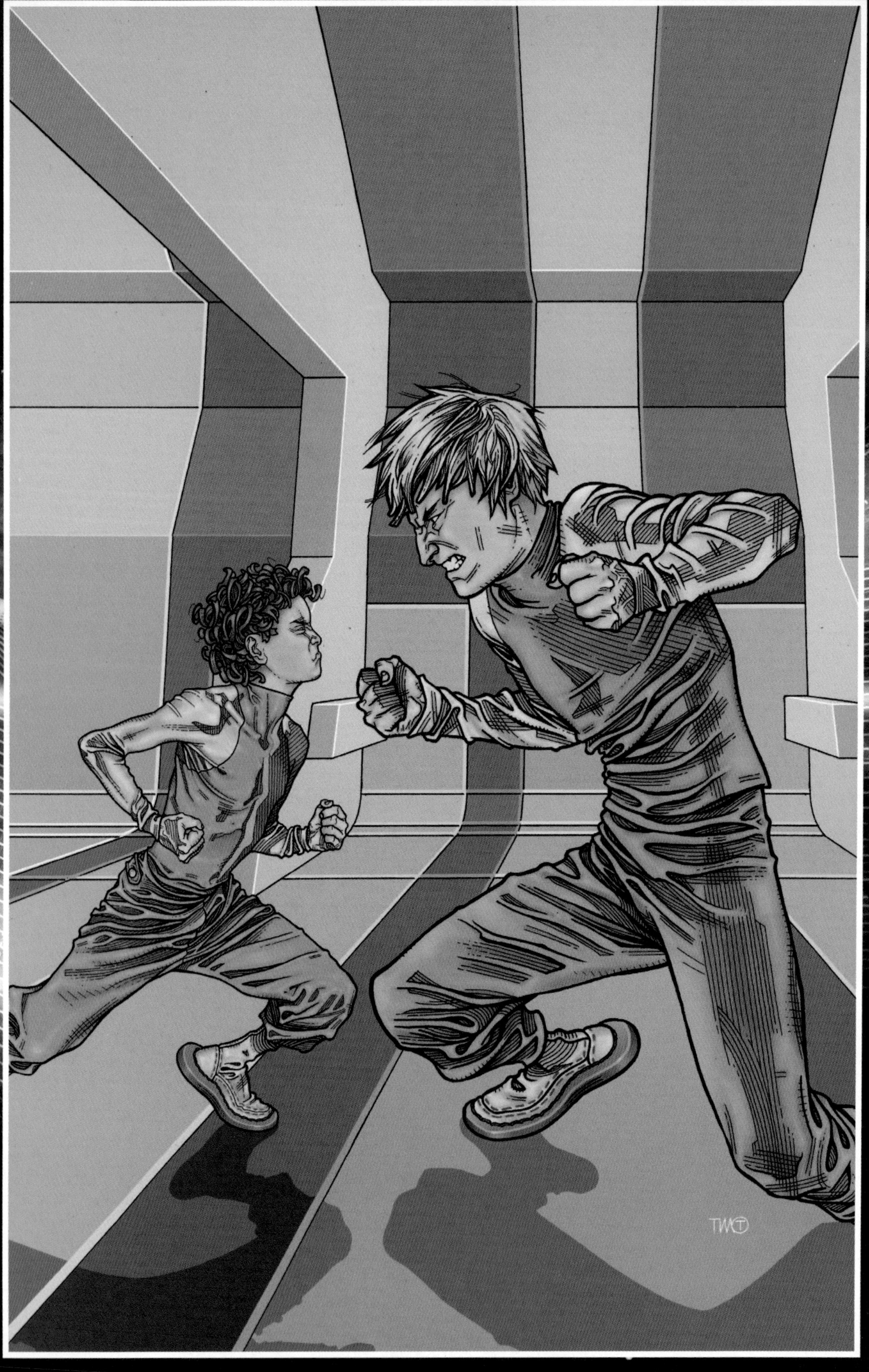
TMT

F O U R

"Putting in Achilles was Graff's last act, and we know that there were grave concerns. Why not play it safe and at least change Achilles to another army?"

"This is not necessarily a Bonzo Madrid situation for Bean."

"But we have no assurance that it's not, sir. Colonel Graff kept a lot of information to himself. A lot of conversations with Sister Carlotta, for instance, with no memo of what was said. Graff knows things about Bean, and about Achilles as well. I think he's laid a trap for us."

"Wrong, Captain Dimak. If Graff laid a trap, it wasn't for us. He doesn't play bureaucratic games. If he laid a trap, it's for Bean."

"Well, that's my point."

"I understand your point, but Achilles stays."

"Why?"

"Because we still know so little about Bean. About his motivations, his drives. This will give us invaluable information."

"It's a risk."

"A calculated one. Achilles' tests show him to be of a remarkably even temperament. But still, every precaution will be taken. I am not playing Russian roulette the way Graff was."

"Yes you are, sir. The only difference is that he knew he had an empty chamber because he loaded the gun."

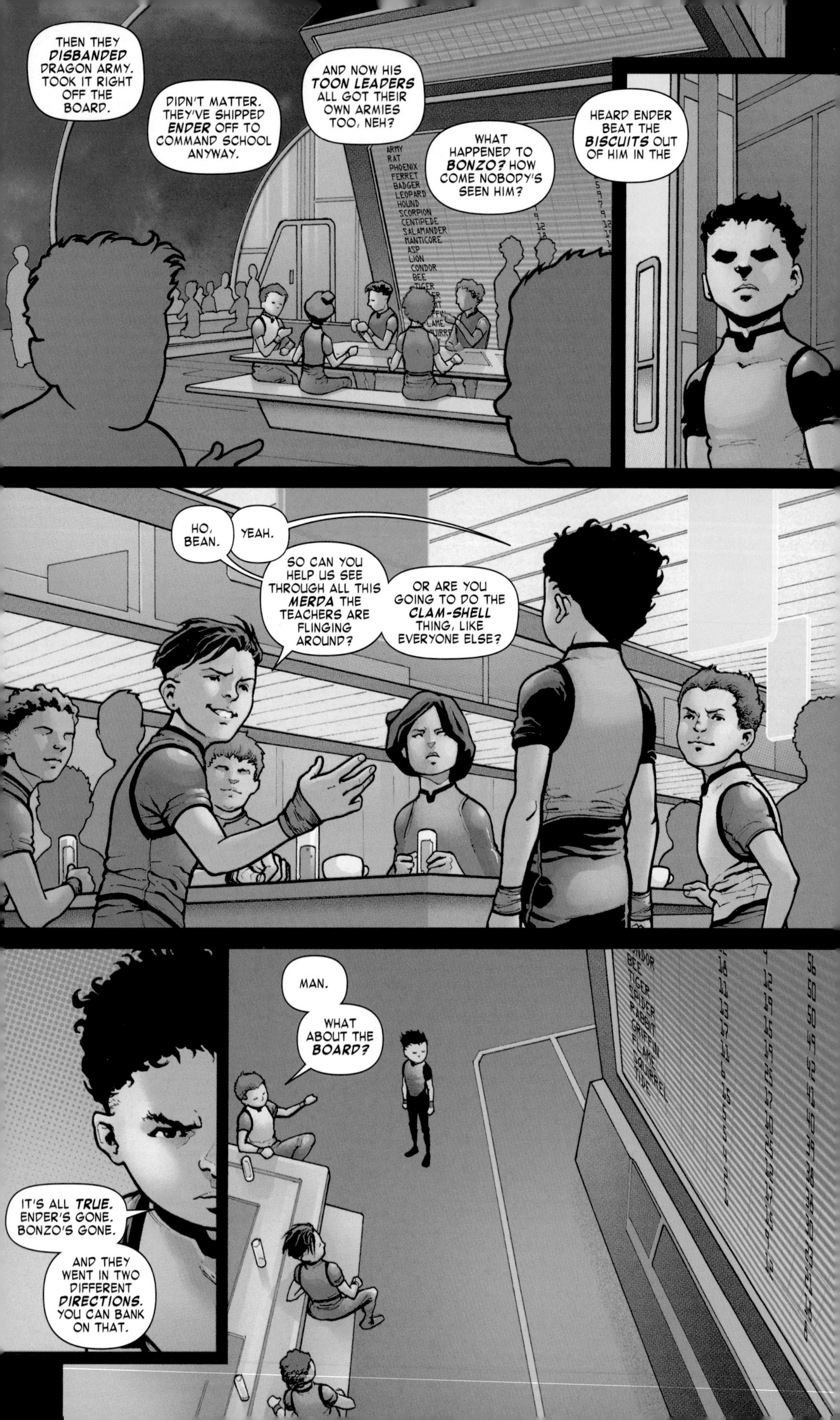
THEN THEY DISBANDED DRAGON ARMY. TOOK IT RIGHT OFF THE BOARD.
DIDN'T MATTER. THEY'VE SHIPPED ENDER OFF TO COMMAND SCHOOL ANYWAY.
AND NOW HIS TOON LEADERS ALL GOT THEIR OWN ARMIES TOO, NEH?
WHAT HAPPENED TO BONZO? HOW COME NOBODY'S SEEN HIM?
HEARD ENDER BEAT THE BISCUITS OUT OF HIM IN THE
ARMY
RAT
PHOENIX
FERRET
BADGER
LEOPARD
HOUND
SCORPION
CENTIPEDE
SALAMANDER
MANTICORE
ASP
LION
CONDOR
BEE
HO, BEAN.
YEAH.
SO CAN YOU HELP US SEE THROUGH ALL THIS MERDA THE TEACHERS ARE FLINGING AROUND?
OR ARE YOU GOING TO DO THE CLAM-SHELL THING, LIKE EVERYONE ELSE?
MAN.
WHAT ABOUT THE BOARD?
BEE
TIGER
SPIDER
RABBIT
GRIFFIN
FLAME
SQUIRREL
TIDE
IT'S ALL TRUE. ENDER'S GONE. BONZO'S GONE.
AND THEY WENT IN TWO DIFFERENT DIRECTIONS. YOU CAN BANK ON THAT.

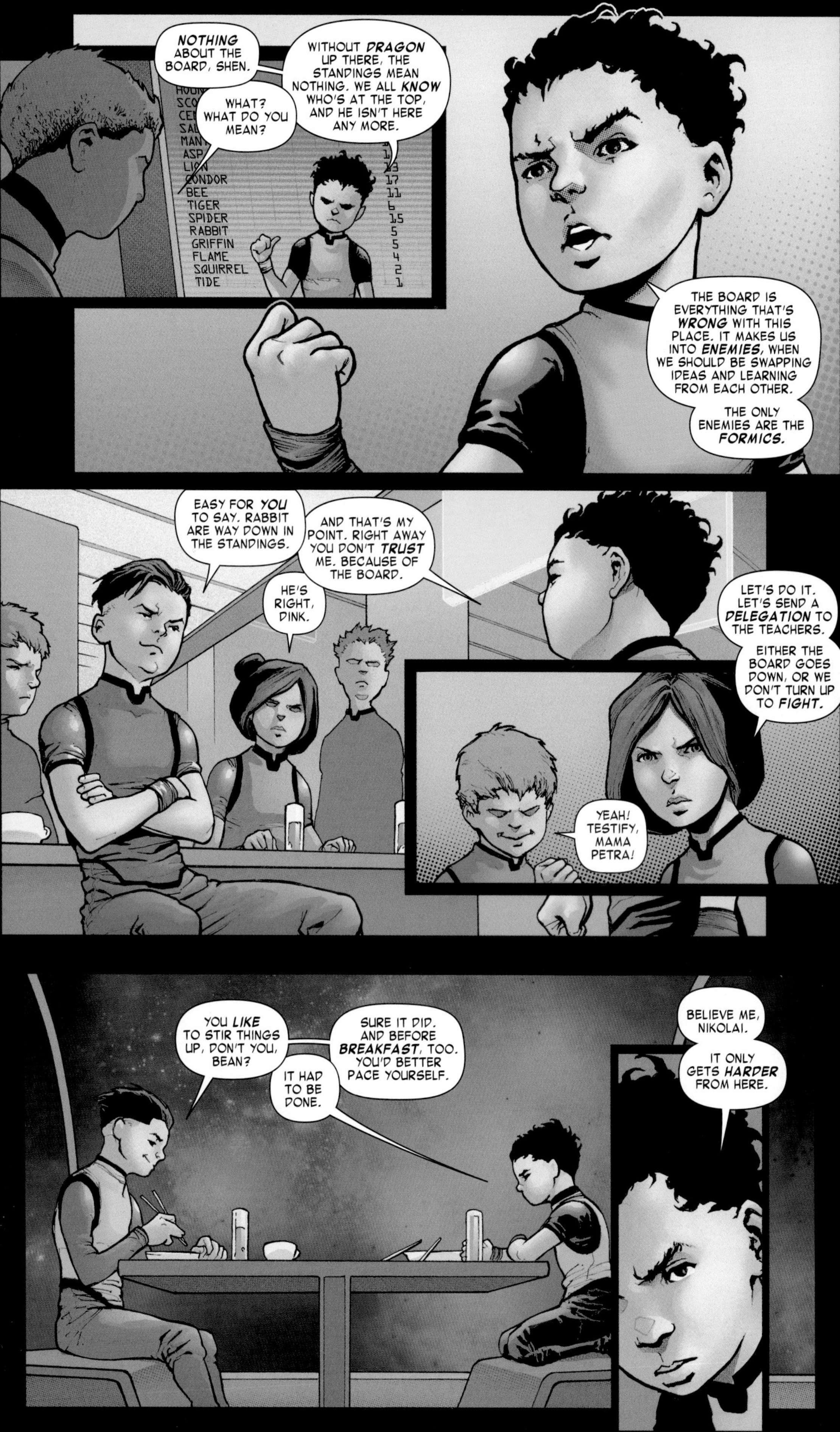
NOTHING ABOUT THE BOARD, SHEN.
WHAT? WHAT DO YOU MEAN?
WITHOUT DRAGON UP THERE, THE STANDINGS MEAN NOTHING. WE ALL KNOW WHO'S AT THE TOP, AND HE ISN'T HERE ANY MORE.
CONDOR
BEE
TIGER
SPIDER
RABBIT
GRIFFIN
FLAME
SQUIRREL
TIDE
THE BOARD IS EVERYTHING THAT'S WRONG WITH THIS PLACE. IT MAKES US INTO ENEMIES, WHEN WE SHOULD BE SWAPPING IDEAS AND LEARNING FROM EACH OTHER.
THE ONLY ENEMIES ARE THE FORMICS.
EASY FOR YOU TO SAY. RABBIT ARE WAY DOWN IN THE STANDINGS.
AND THAT'S MY POINT. RIGHT AWAY YOU DON'T TRUST ME. BECAUSE OF THE BOARD.
HE'S RIGHT, DINK.
LET'S DO IT. LET'S SEND A DELEGATION TO THE TEACHERS.
EITHER THE BOARD GOES DOWN, OR WE DON'T TURN UP TO FIGHT.
YEAH! TESTIFY, MAMA PETRA!
YOU LIKE TO STIR THINGS UP, DON'T YOU, BEAN?
IT HAD TO BE DONE.
SURE IT DID. AND BEFORE BREAKFAST, TOO. YOU'D BETTER PACE YOURSELF.
BELIEVE ME, NIKOLAI.
IT ONLY GETS HARDER FROM HERE.

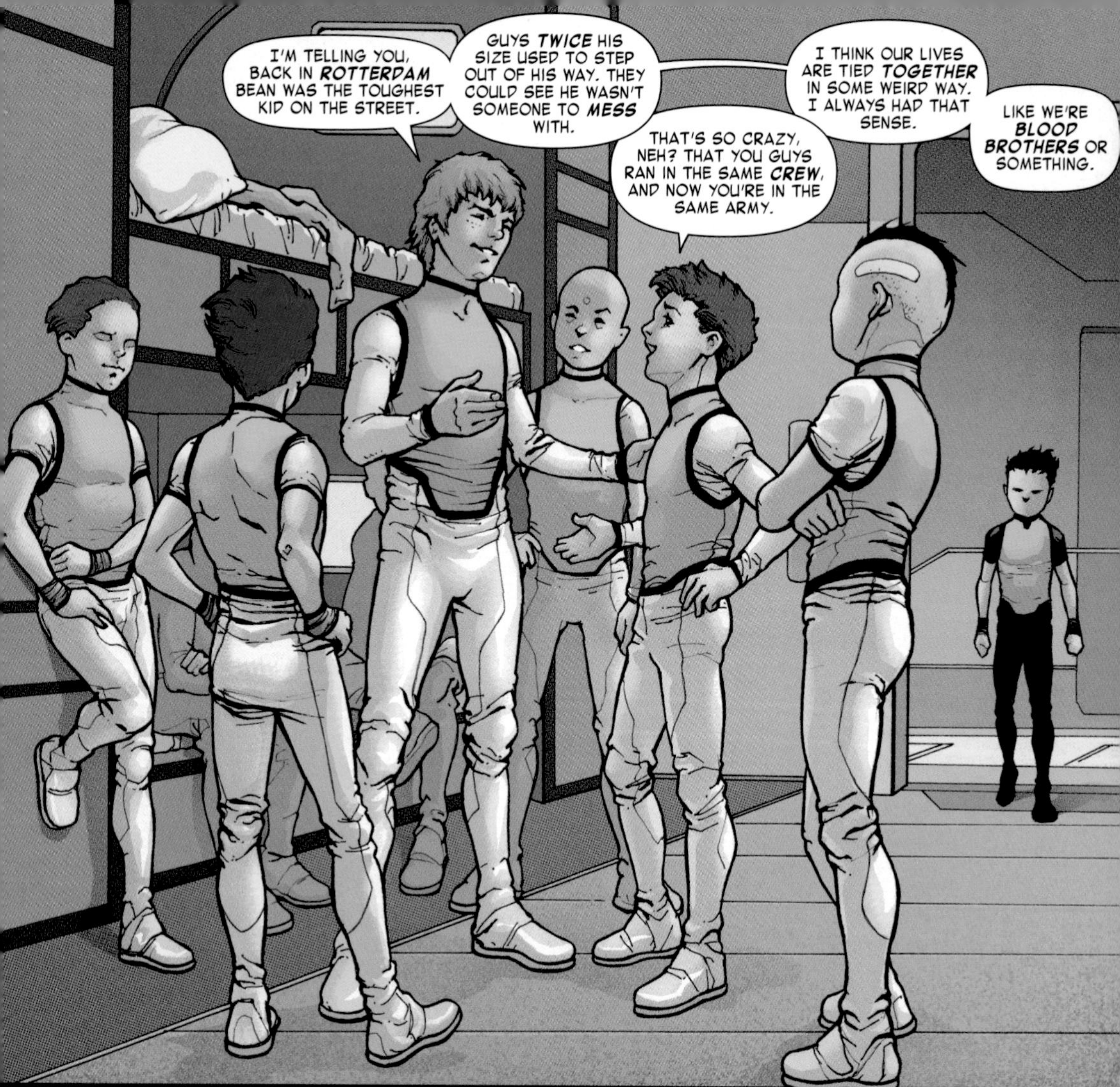
I'M TELLING YOU, BACK IN ROTTERDAM BEAN WAS THE TOUGHEST KID ON THE STREET.
GUYS TWICE HIS SIZE USED TO STEP OUT OF HIS WAY. THEY COULD SEE HE WASN'T SOMEONE TO MESS WITH.
THAT'S SO CRAZY, NEH? THAT YOU GUYS RAN IN THE SAME CREW, AND NOW YOU'RE IN THE SAME ARMY.
I THINK OUR LIVES ARE TIED TOGETHER IN SOME WEIRD WAY. I ALWAYS HAD THAT SENSE.
LIKE WE'RE BLOOD BROTHERS OR SOMETHING.

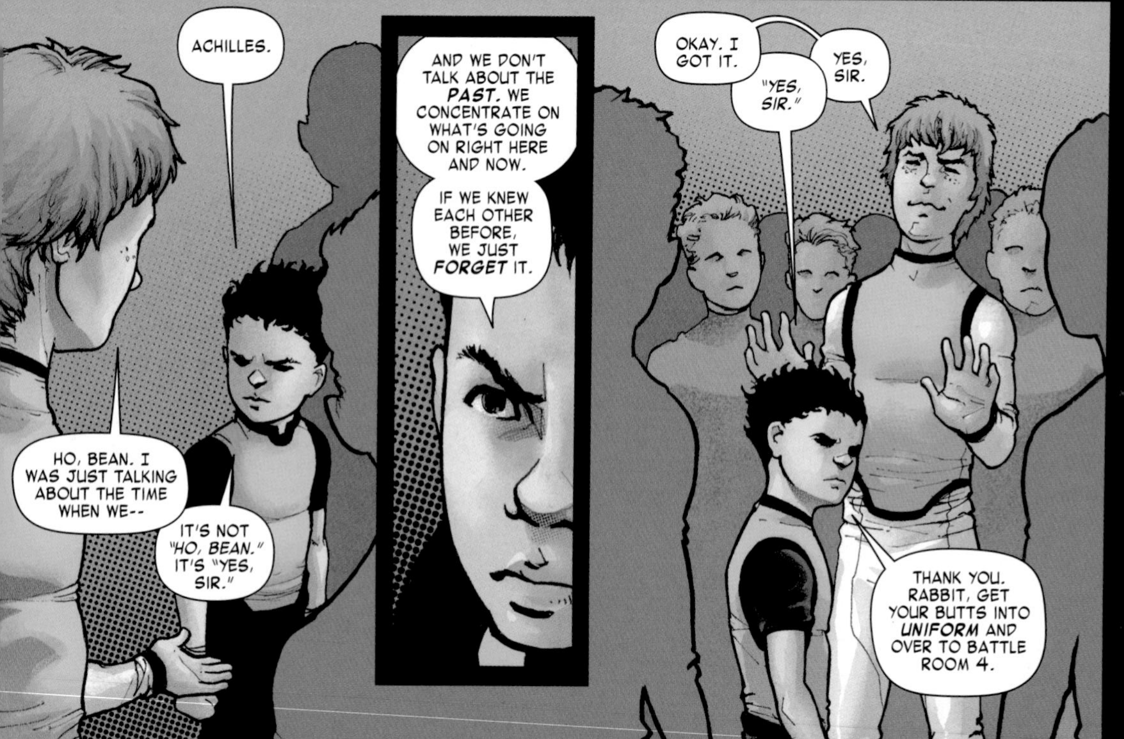
ACHILLES.
HO, BEAN. I WAS JUST TALKING ABOUT THE TIME WHEN WE--
IT'S NOT "HO, BEAN." IT'S "YES, SIR."
AND WE DON'T TALK ABOUT THE PAST. WE CONCENTRATE ON WHAT'S GOING ON RIGHT HERE AND NOW.
IF WE KNEW EACH OTHER BEFORE, WE JUST FORGET IT.
OKAY. I GOT IT.
"YES, SIR."
YES, SIR.
THANK YOU. RABBIT, GET YOUR BUTTS INTO UNIFORM AND OVER TO BATTLE ROOM 4.

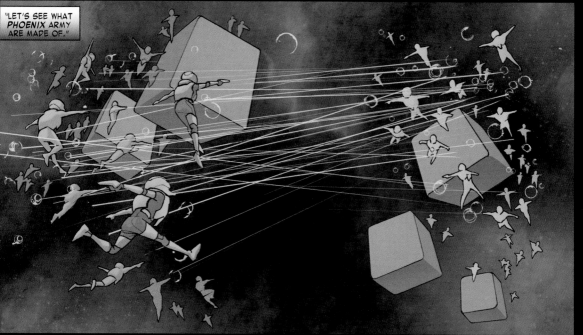

"LET'S SEE WHAT PHOENIX ARMY ARE MADE OF."

AMBUL, MAKE FOR THE OTHER STAR. WE'LL DROP AND *COVER* YOU FROM BELOW.

WE'LL BE IN *CROSSFIRE!*

NOT IF YOU MOVE *QUICK* ENOUGH. GO!

PHOENIX COMING IN FROM THE *WEST!*

ITŪ WILL HEAD THEM OFF.

ITŪ'S GOT *TROUBLES* OF HIS OWN!

SORRY, BABY BOYS!

THIS ROCK BELONGS TO *MAMA PETRA!*

UFFF!

MARCUS, FAILSAFE, DO THE HONORS.

PHOENIX *RISES!*

WELL THAT WAS KIND OF *HUMILIATING.*

EDUCATIONAL, THOUGH.

I WON'T TRY THAT AIR-TO-GROUND *ENFILADE* THING AGAIN IN A HURRY.

YOU *LOST* BECAUSE EVERY *TOON* WAS MAKING ITS OWN *TACTICS* ON THE FLY.

IF SOMEONE HAD TAKEN OVERALL *CONTROL*, RABBIT WOULD HAVE WON.

NO, ACHILLES. *I* WOULD HAVE WON, AND NOBODY ELSE WOULD HAVE GOT MUCH OUT OF IT.

THIS IS LEARNING BY *DOING.*

BUT WHAT SOLDIERS NEED TO LEARN, FIRST AND FOREMOST, IS *OBEDIENCE* TO THEIR COMMANDER.

HAVE YOU *STUDIED* THE SECOND FORMIC WAR? WE CAN'T MATCH THEM FOR *SPEED* AND SYNCHRONIZATION OF RESPONSE.

EVEN WITH THE BEST *GENERAL* IN THE WORLD, WE NEED FLEXIBILITY AS MUCH AS WE NEED GREAT *TACTICS.*

YOU SEE FLEXIBILITY. I SEE *CHAOS.*

THEN I'LL HAVE TO TEACH YOU THE *DIFFERENCE,* SOLDIER.

REPORT TO ME IN THE *GYM* ON LEVEL FIVE AT 22:00 HOURS, AFTER EVENING PRACTICE.

WELL *FOUGH* RABBIT

I'M PR OF *39* YOU

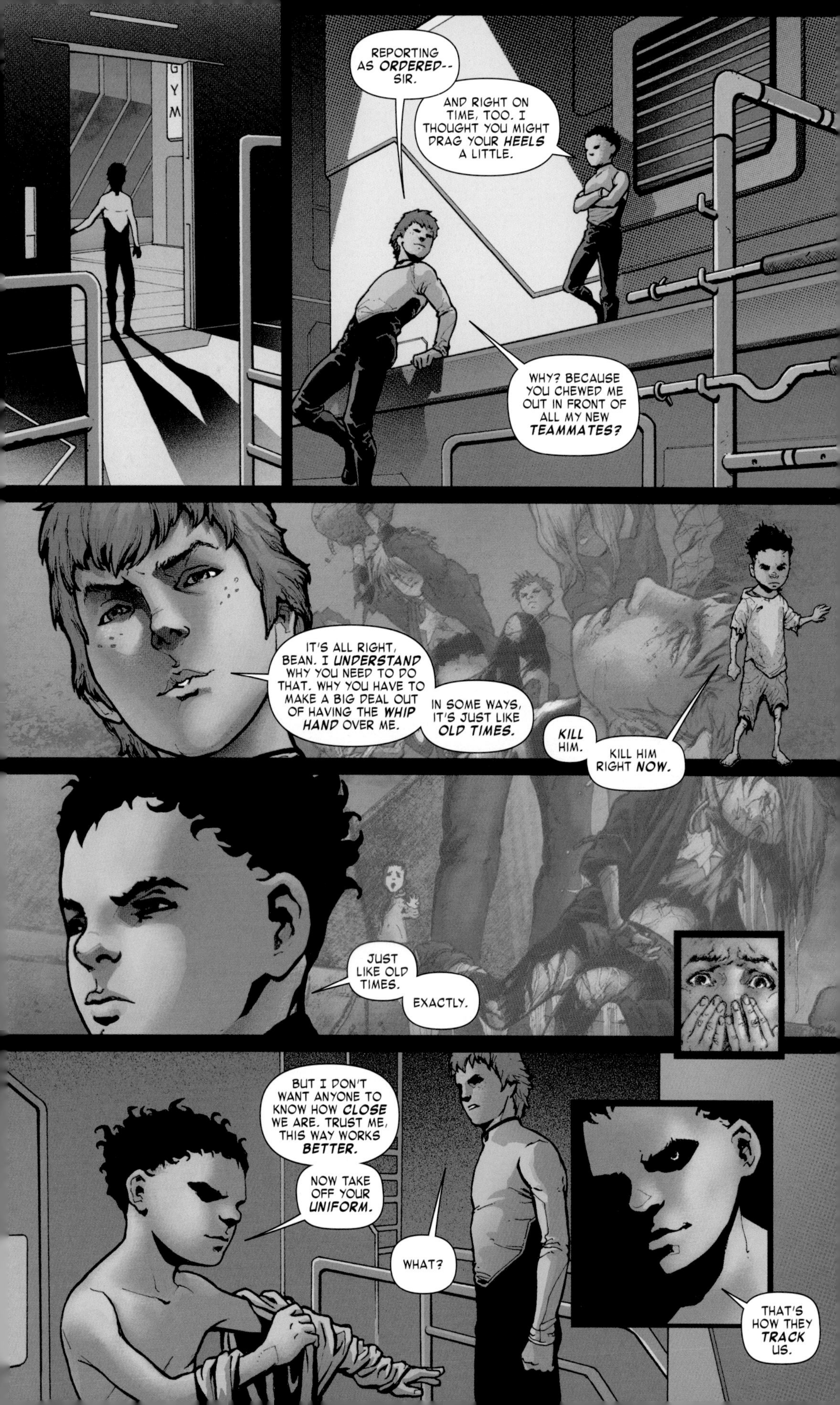

GYM
REPORTING AS ORDERED-- SIR.
AND RIGHT ON TIME, TOO. I THOUGHT YOU MIGHT DRAG YOUR HEELS A LITTLE.
WHY? BECAUSE YOU CHEWED ME OUT IN FRONT OF ALL MY NEW TEAMMATES?
IT'S ALL RIGHT, BEAN. I UNDERSTAND WHY YOU NEED TO DO THAT. WHY YOU HAVE TO MAKE A BIG DEAL OUT OF HAVING THE WHIP HAND OVER ME.
IN SOME WAYS, IT'S JUST LIKE OLD TIMES.
KILL HIM.
KILL HIM RIGHT NOW.
JUST LIKE OLD TIMES.
EXACTLY.
BUT I DON'T WANT ANYONE TO KNOW HOW CLOSE WE ARE. TRUST ME, THIS WAY WORKS BETTER.
NOW TAKE OFF YOUR UNIFORM.
WHAT?
THAT'S HOW THEY TRACK US.

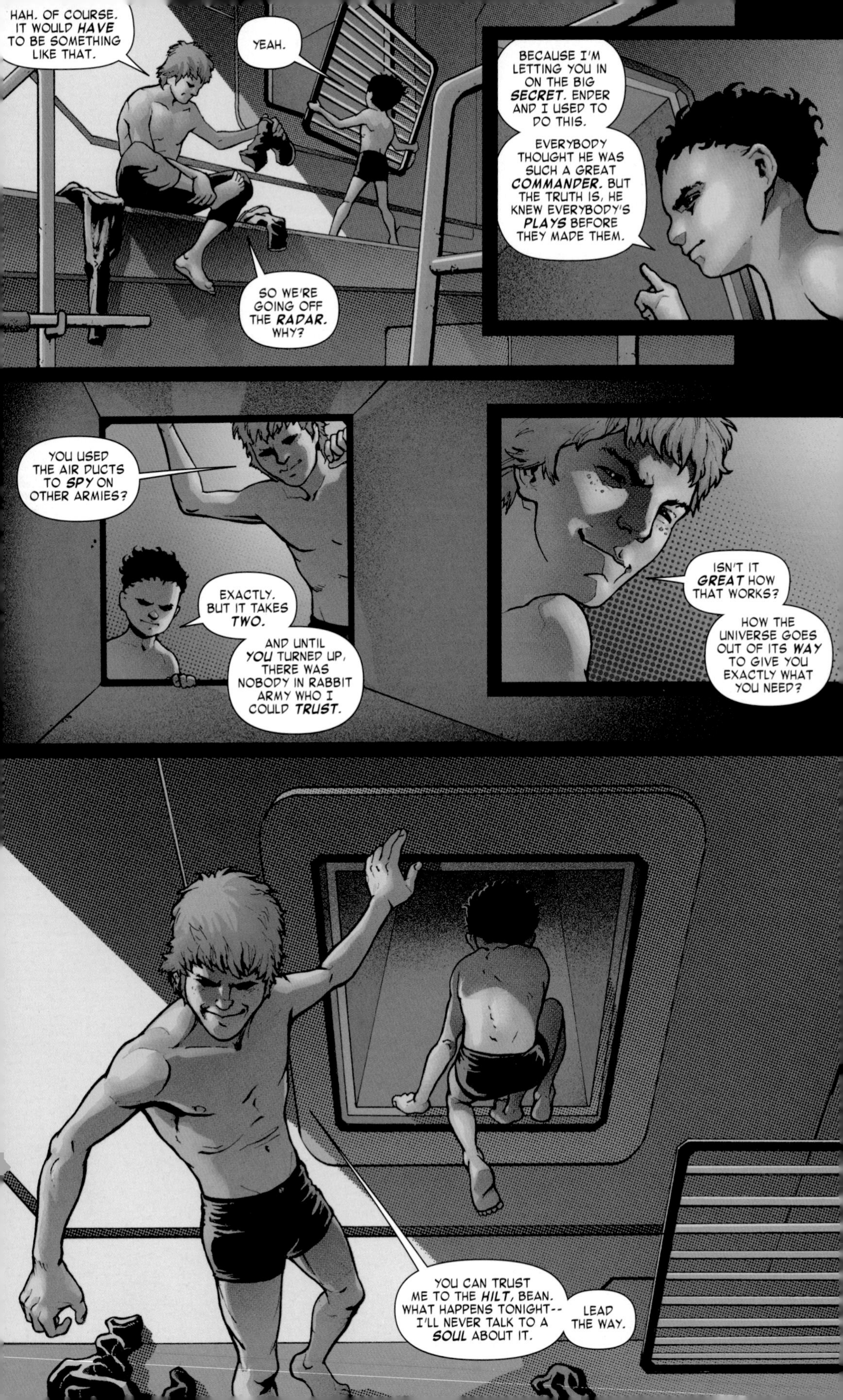
HAH. OF COURSE. IT WOULD HAVE TO BE SOMETHING LIKE THAT.
YEAH.
SO WE'RE GOING OFF THE RADAR. WHY?
BECAUSE I'M LETTING YOU IN ON THE BIG SECRET. ENDER AND I USED TO DO THIS.
EVERYBODY THOUGHT HE WAS SUCH A GREAT COMMANDER. BUT THE TRUTH IS, HE KNEW EVERYBODY'S PLAYS BEFORE THEY MADE THEM.
YOU USED THE AIR DUCTS TO SPY ON OTHER ARMIES?
EXACTLY. BUT IT TAKES TWO.
AND UNTIL YOU TURNED UP, THERE WAS NOBODY IN RABBIT ARMY WHO I COULD TRUST.
ISN'T IT GREAT HOW THAT WORKS?
HOW THE UNIVERSE GOES OUT OF ITS WAY TO GIVE YOU EXACTLY WHAT YOU NEED?
YOU CAN TRUST ME TO THE HILT, BEAN. WHAT HAPPENS TONIGHT-- I'LL NEVER TALK TO A SOUL ABOUT IT.
LEAD THE WAY.

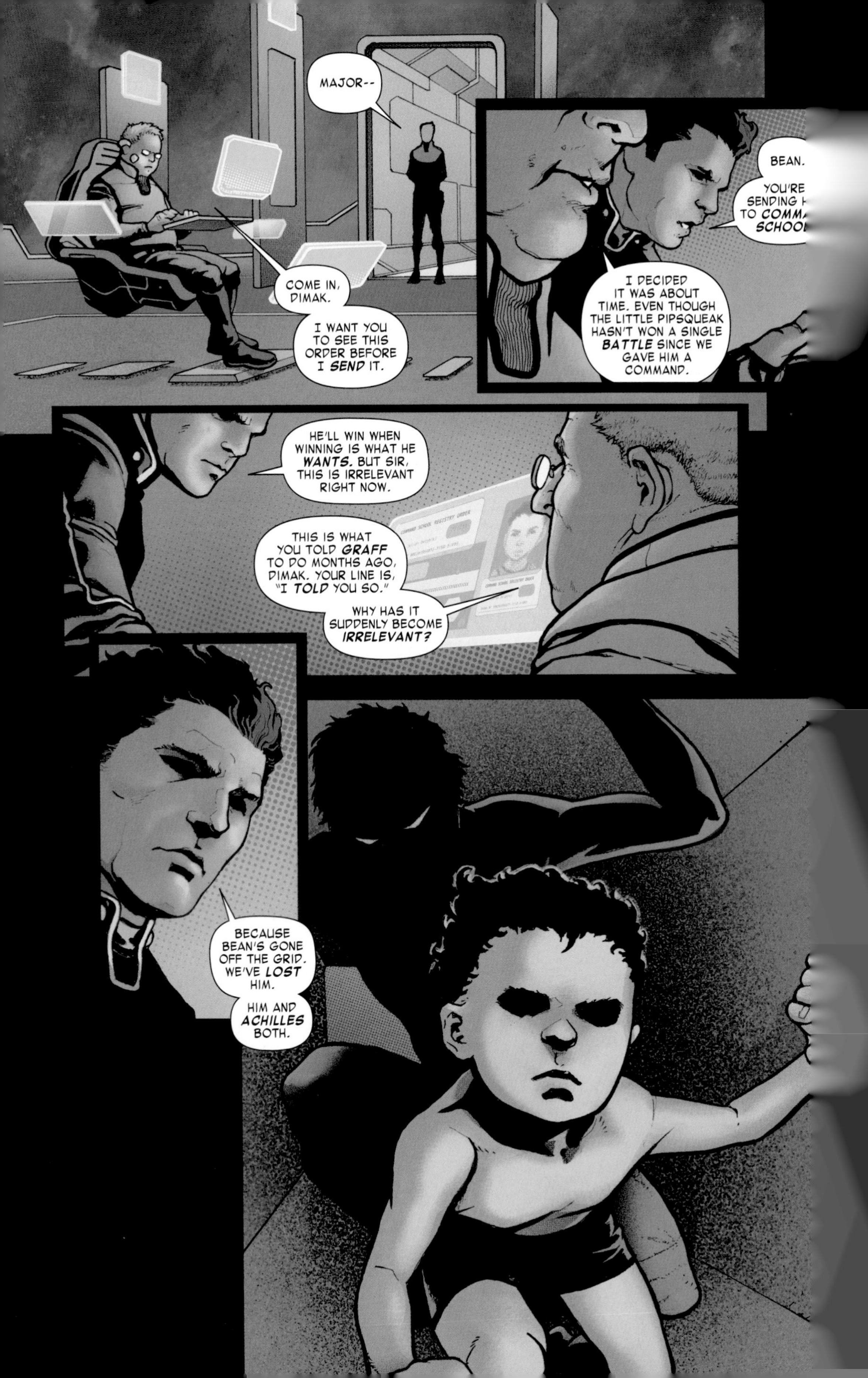
MAJOR--
COME IN, DIMAK.
I WANT YOU TO SEE THIS ORDER BEFORE I SEND IT.
BEAN.
YOU'RE SENDING
TO
I DECIDED IT WAS ABOUT TIME. EVEN THOUGH THE LITTLE PIPSQUEAK HASN'T WON A SINGLE BATTLE SINCE WE GAVE HIM A COMMAND.
HE'LL WIN WHEN WINNING IS WHAT HE WANTS. BUT SIR, THIS IS IRRELEVANT RIGHT NOW.
THIS IS WHAT YOU TOLD GRAFF TO DO MONTHS AGO, DIMAK. YOUR LINE IS, "I TOLD YOU SO."
WHY HAS IT SUDDENLY BECOME IRRELEVANT?
BECAUSE BEAN'S GONE OFF THE GRID. WE'VE LOST HIM.
HIM AND ACHILLES BOTH.

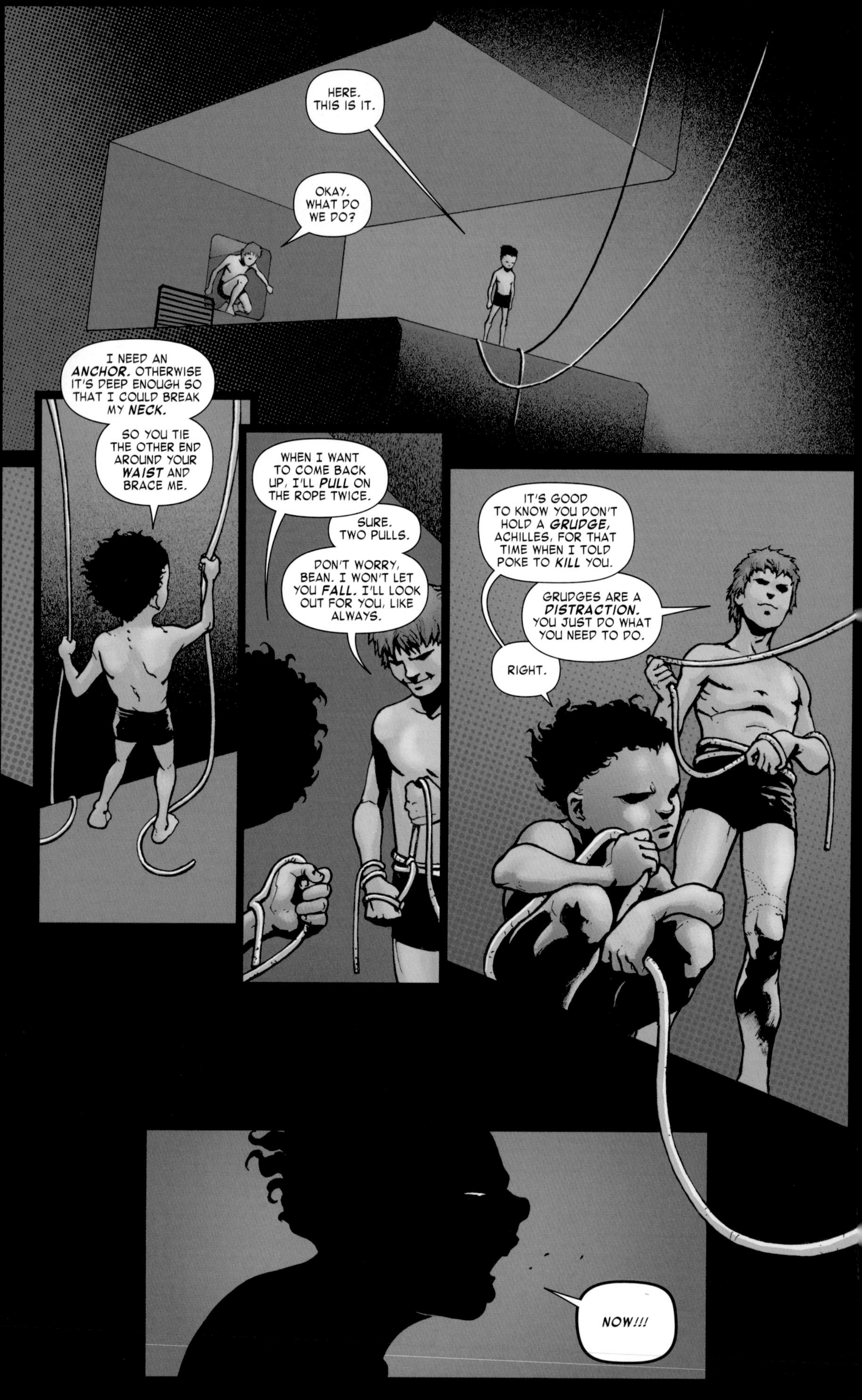
HERE. THIS IS IT.
OKAY. WHAT DO WE DO?
I NEED AN ANCHOR. OTHERWISE IT'S DEEP ENOUGH SO THAT I COULD BREAK MY NECK.
SO YOU TIE THE OTHER END AROUND YOUR WAIST AND BRACE ME.
WHEN I WANT TO COME BACK UP, I'LL PULL ON THE ROPE TWICE.
SURE. TWO PULLS.
DON'T WORRY, BEAN. I WON'T LET YOU FALL. I'LL LOOK OUT FOR YOU, LIKE ALWAYS.
IT'S GOOD TO KNOW YOU DON'T HOLD A GRUDGE, ACHILLES, FOR THAT TIME WHEN I TOLD POKE TO KILL YOU.
GRUDGES ARE A DISTRACTION. YOU JUST DO WHAT YOU NEED TO DO.
RIGHT.
NOW!!!

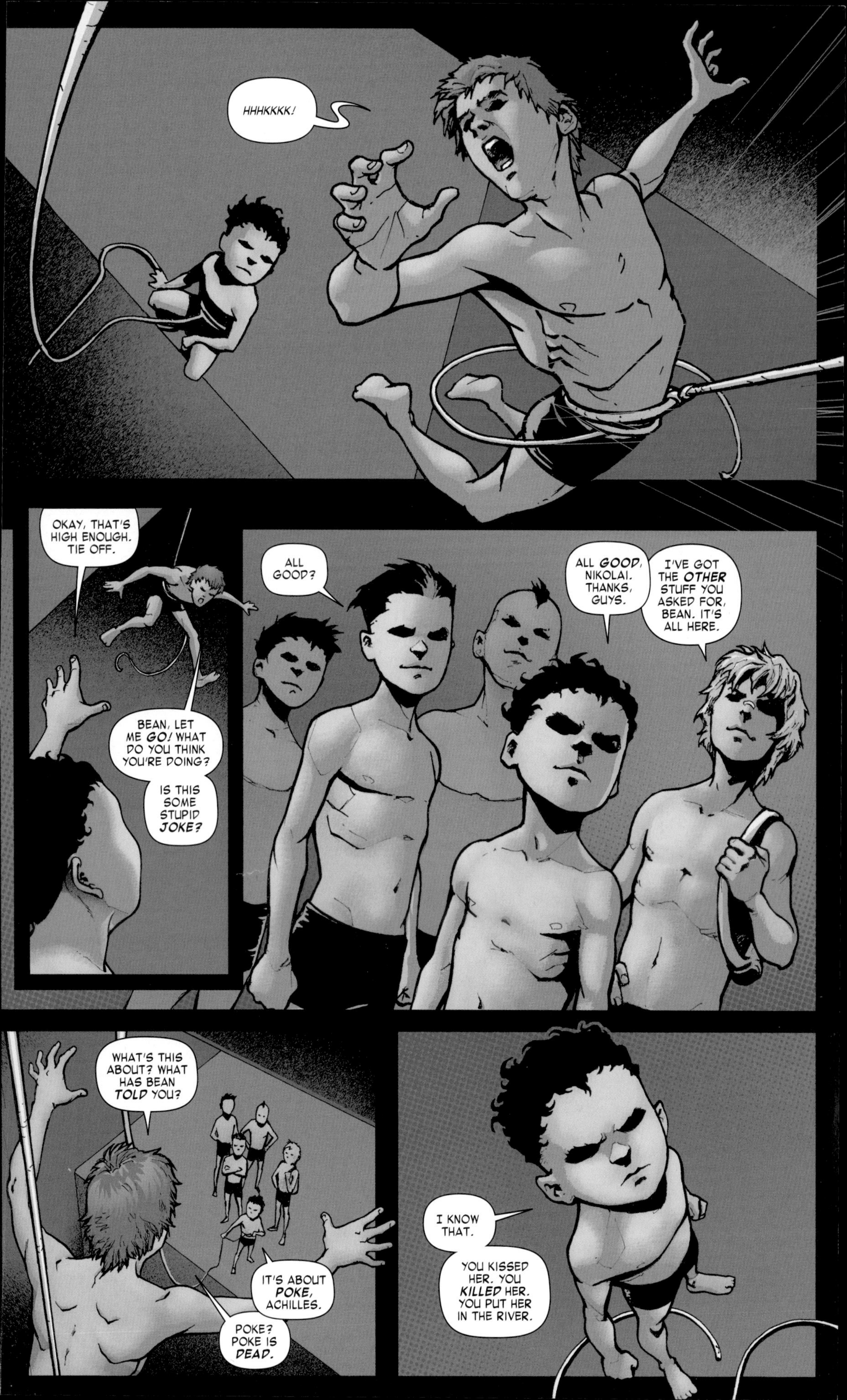
HHHKKKK!
OKAY, THAT'S HIGH ENOUGH. TIE OFF.
BEAN, LET ME GO! WHAT DO YOU THINK YOU'RE DOING?
IS THIS SOME STUPID JOKE?
ALL GOOD?
ALL GOOD, NIKOLAI. THANKS, GUYS.
I'VE GOT THE OTHER STUFF YOU ASKED FOR, BEAN. IT'S ALL HERE.
WHAT'S THIS ABOUT? WHAT HAS BEAN TOLD YOU?
IT'S ABOUT POKE, ACHILLES.
POKE? POKE IS DEAD.
I KNOW THAT.
YOU KISSED HER. YOU KILLED HER. YOU PUT HER IN THE RIVER.

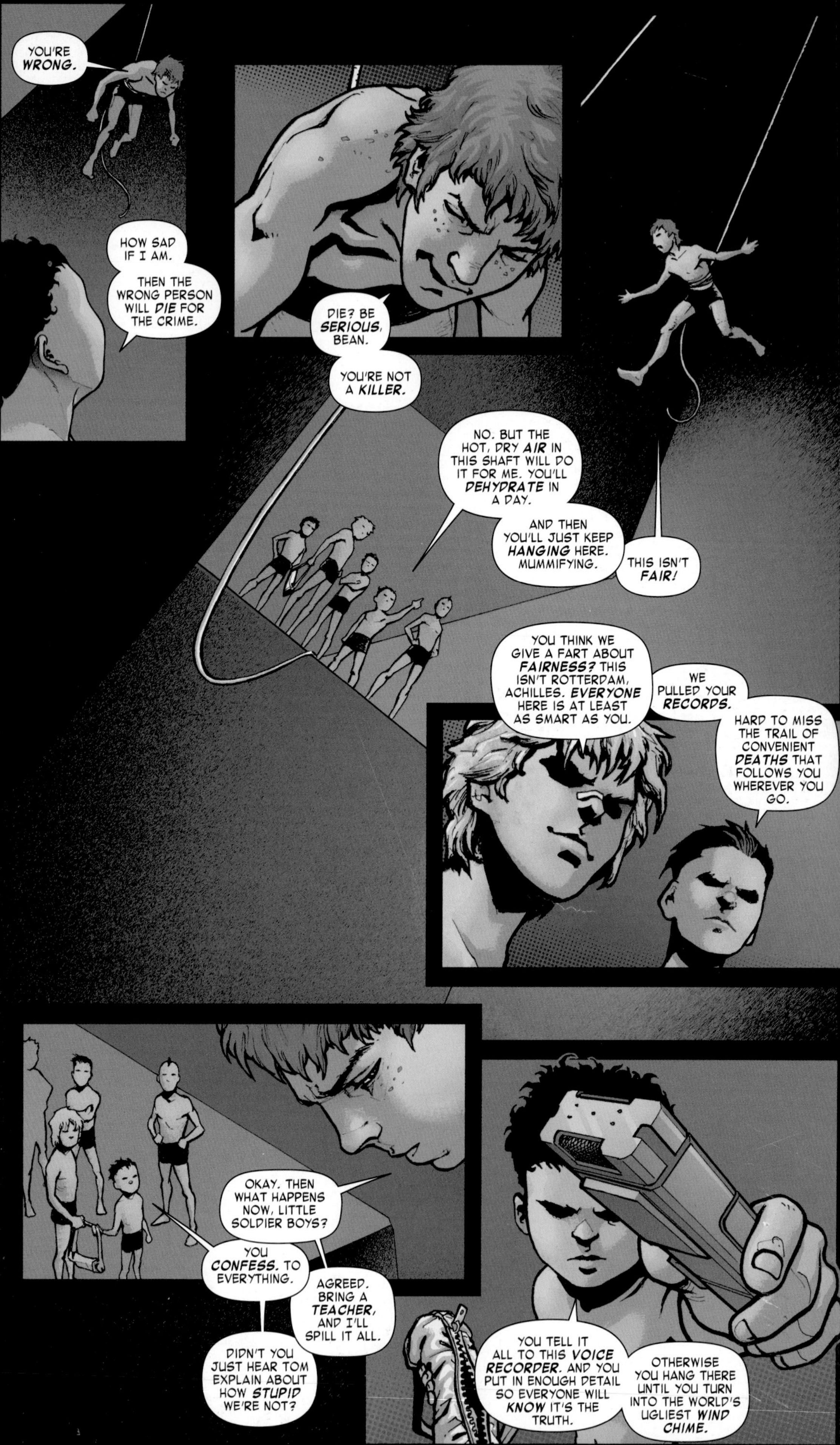
YOU'RE WRONG.
HOW SAD IF I AM.
THEN THE WRONG PERSON WILL DIE FOR THE CRIME.
DIE? BE SERIOUS, BEAN.
YOU'RE NOT A KILLER.
NO. BUT THE HOT, DRY AIR IN THIS SHAFT WILL DO IT FOR ME. YOU'LL DEHYDRATE IN A DAY.
AND THEN YOU'LL JUST KEEP HANGING HERE. MUMMIFYING.
THIS ISN'T FAIR!
YOU THINK WE GIVE A FART ABOUT FAIRNESS? THIS ISN'T ROTTERDAM, ACHILLES. EVERYONE HERE IS AT LEAST AS SMART AS YOU.
WE PULLED YOUR RECORDS.
HARD TO MISS THE TRAIL OF CONVENIENT DEATHS THAT FOLLOWS YOU WHEREVER YOU GO.
OKAY. THEN WHAT HAPPENS NOW, LITTLE SOLDIER BOYS?
YOU CONFESS. TO EVERYTHING.
AGREED. BRING A TEACHER, AND I'LL SPILL IT ALL.
DIDN'T YOU JUST HEAR TOM EXPLAIN ABOUT HOW STUPID WE'RE NOT?
YOU TELL IT ALL TO THIS VOICE RECORDER. AND YOU PUT IN ENOUGH DETAIL SO EVERYONE WILL KNOW IT'S THE TRUTH.
OTHERWISE YOU HANG THERE UNTIL YOU TURN INTO THE WORLD'S UGLIEST WIND CHIME.

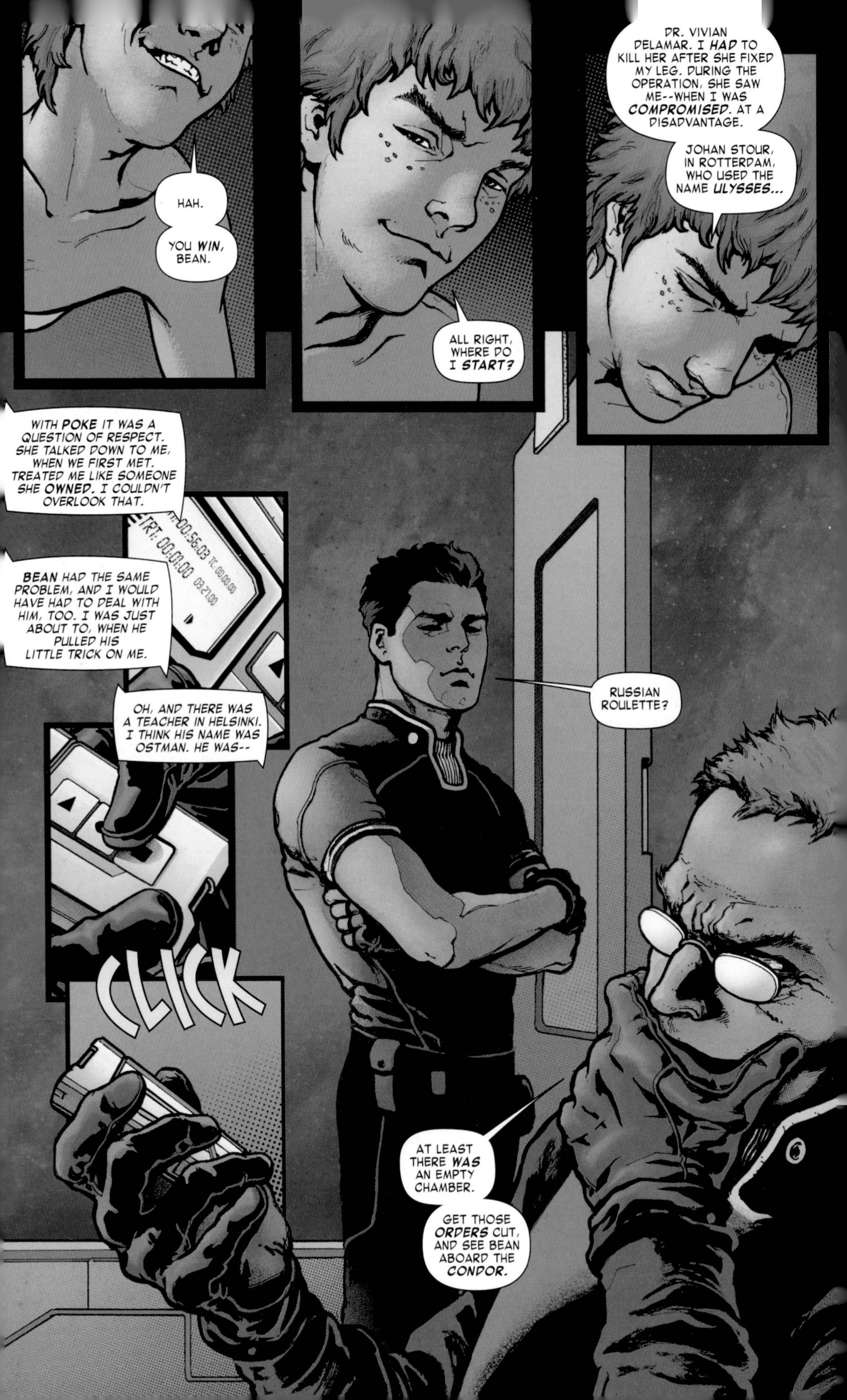
HAH.
YOU WIN, BEAN.
ALL RIGHT, WHERE DO I START?
DR. VIVIAN DELAMAR. I HAD TO KILL HER AFTER SHE FIXED MY LEG. DURING THE OPERATION, SHE SAW ME--WHEN I WAS COMPROMISED. AT A DISADVANTAGE.
JOHAN STOUR, IN ROTTERDAM, WHO USED THE NAME ULYSSES...
WITH POKE IT WAS A QUESTION OF RESPECT. SHE TALKED DOWN TO ME, WHEN WE FIRST MET. TREATED ME LIKE SOMEONE SHE OWNED. I COULDN'T OVERLOOK THAT.
TRT: 00:00:00
BEAN HAD THE SAME PROBLEM, AND I WOULD HAVE HAD TO DEAL WITH HIM, TOO. I WAS JUST ABOUT TO, WHEN HE PULLED HIS LITTLE TRICK ON ME.
OH, AND THERE WAS A TEACHER IN HELSINKI. I THINK HIS NAME WAS OSTMAN. HE WAS--
CLICK
RUSSIAN ROULETTE?
AT LEAST THERE WAS AN EMPTY CHAMBER.
GET THOSE ORDERS CUT, AND SEE BEAN ABOARD THE CONDOR.

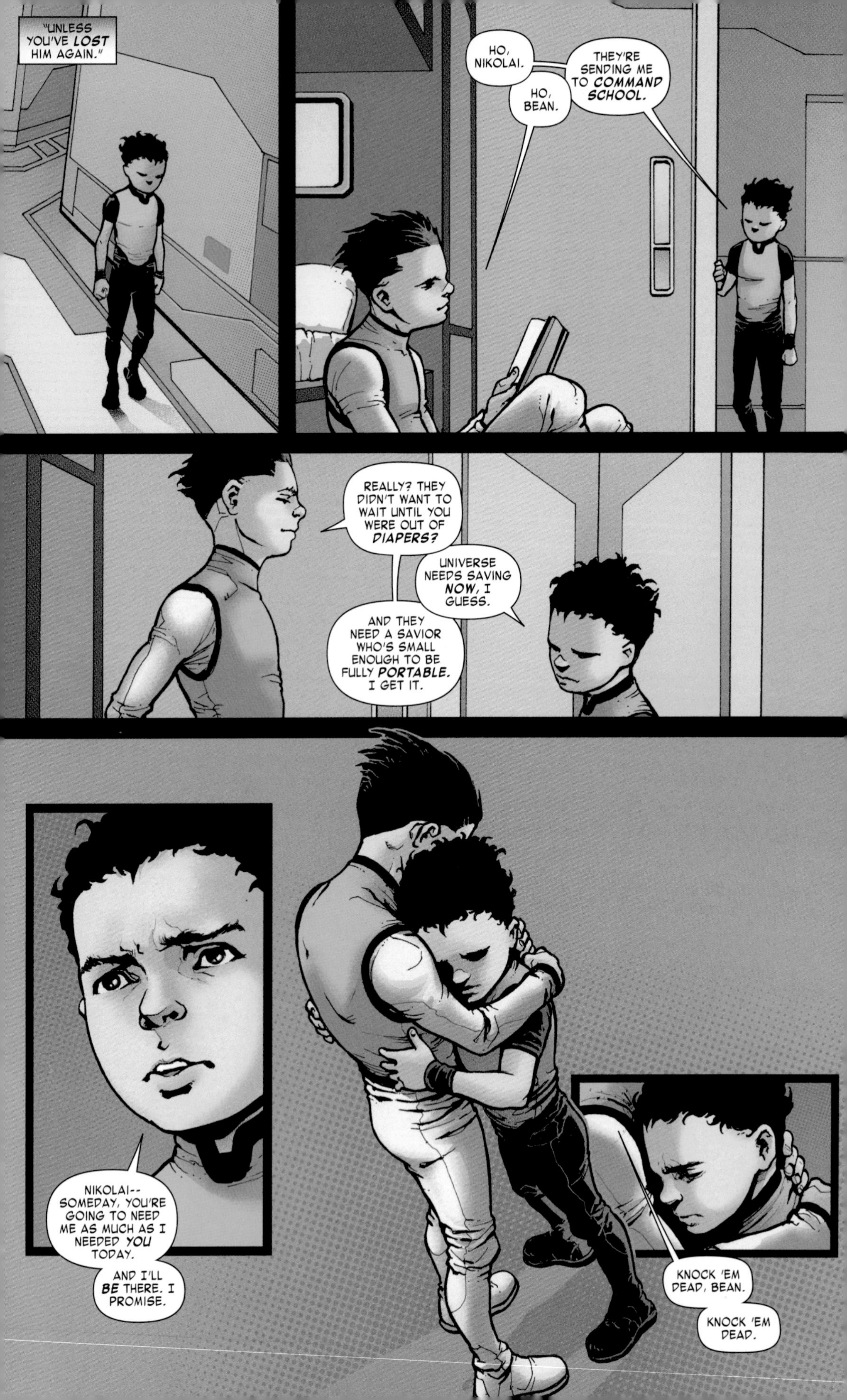
"UNLESS YOU'VE LOST HIM AGAIN."
HO, NIKOLAI.
HO, BEAN.
THEY'RE SENDING ME TO COMMAND SCHOOL.
REALLY? THEY DIDN'T WANT TO WAIT UNTIL YOU WERE OUT OF DIAPERS?
UNIVERSE NEEDS SAVING NOW, I GUESS.
AND THEY NEED A SAVIOR WHO'S SMALL ENOUGH TO BE FULLY PORTABLE. I GET IT.
NIKOLAI-- SOMEDAY, YOU'RE GOING TO NEED ME AS MUCH AS I NEEDED YOU TODAY.
AND I'LL BE THERE. I PROMISE.
KNOCK 'EM DEAD, BEAN.
KNOCK 'EM DEAD.

I.F. TRANSPORT CONDOR.
EROS RUN.

DISTANCE FROM EARTH 20.2 MILLION MILES.
ASTRAL POSITION 220 17 33.10 DEGREES SOUTH OF ECLIPTIC.

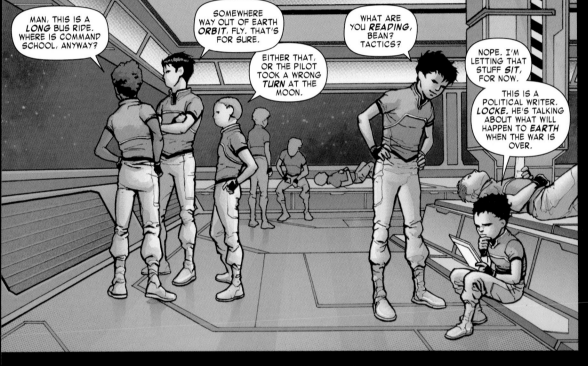

MAN, THIS IS A *LONG* BUS RIDE. WHERE IS COMMAND SCHOOL, ANYWAY?

SOMEWHERE WAY OUT OF EARTH *ORBIT*, FLY. THAT'S FOR SURE.

EITHER THAT, OR THE PILOT TOOK A WRONG *TURN* AT THE MOON.

WHAT ARE YOU *READING*, BEAN? TACTICS?

NOPE. I'M LETTING THAT STUFF *SIT*, FOR NOW.

THIS IS A POLITICAL WRITER. *LOCKE.* HE'S TALKING ABOUT WHAT WILL HAPPEN TO *EARTH* WHEN THE WAR IS OVER.

MAN, I ADMIRE HIS OPTIMISM.

HE'S ASSUMING THERE'LL STILL *BE* AN EARTH WHEN THE WAR IS OVER.

HERE. YOU SHOULD *READ* IT. HE'S MOSTLY INTERESTED IN WHAT WILL HAPPEN TO THE I.F.'S *ASSETS.* WHO GETS TO KEEP THEM AND *DEPLOY* THEM IF THEY STILL EXIST.

THE SHIPS WILL PROBABLY BE *MOTHBALLED*, WON'T THEY? THEY CAN'T BE USED IN *GROUND-BASED* CONFLICTS.

HE'S NOT THINKING ABOUT THE *SHIPS.*

HE MEANS *US.*

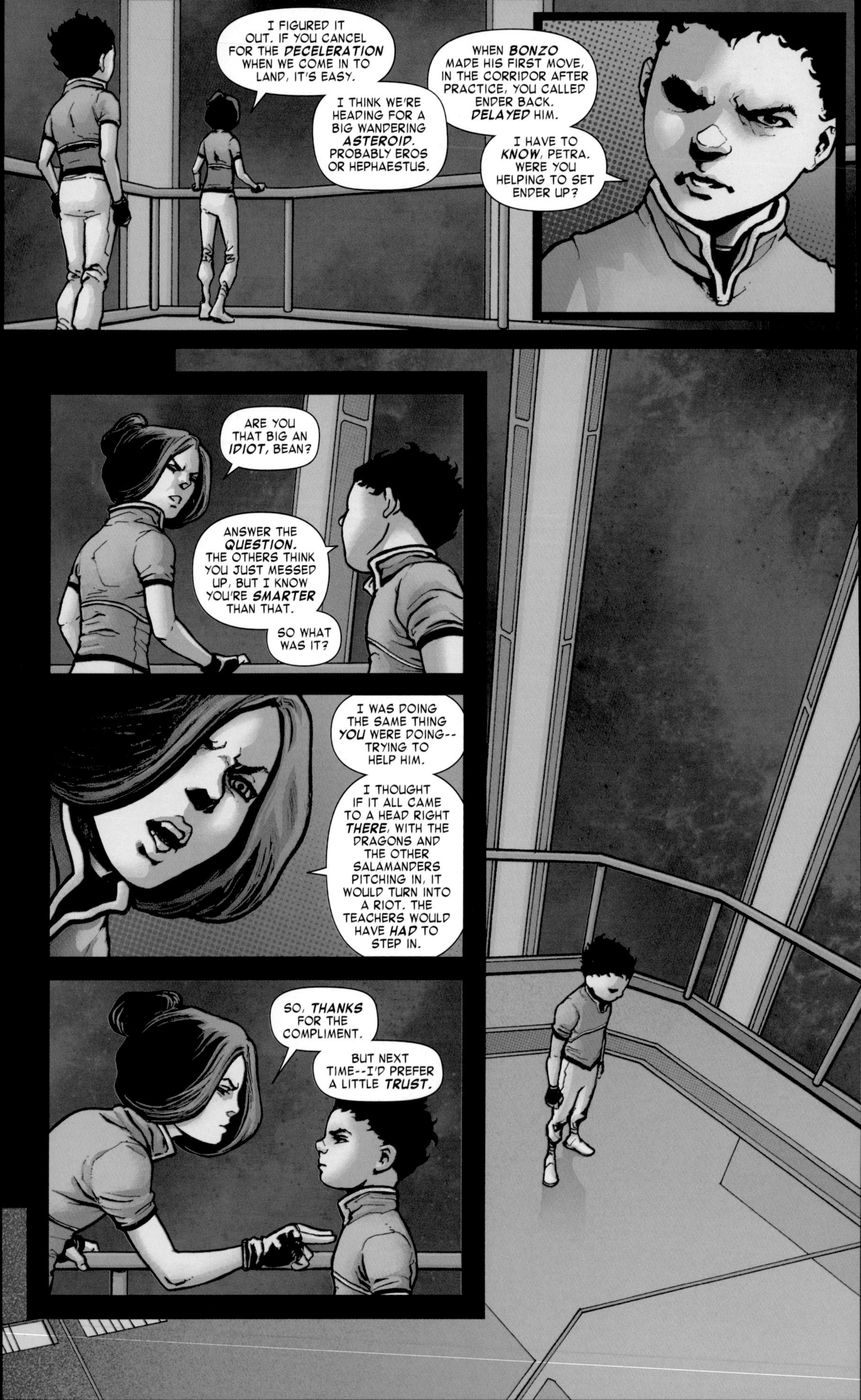
I FIGURED IT OUT. IF YOU CANCEL FOR THE DECELERATION WHEN WE COME IN TO LAND, IT'S EASY.
I THINK WE'RE HEADING FOR A BIG WANDERING ASTEROID. PROBABLY EROS OR HEPHAESTUS.
WHEN BONZO MADE HIS FIRST MOVE, IN THE CORRIDOR AFTER PRACTICE, YOU CALLED ENDER BACK. DELAYED HIM.
I HAVE TO KNOW, PETRA. WERE YOU HELPING TO SET ENDER UP?
ARE YOU THAT BIG AN IDIOT, BEAN?
ANSWER THE QUESTION. THE OTHERS THINK YOU JUST MESSED UP, BUT I KNOW YOU'RE SMARTER THAN THAT.
SO WHAT WAS IT?
I WAS DOING THE SAME THING YOU WERE DOING-- TRYING TO HELP HIM.
I THOUGHT IF IT ALL CAME TO A HEAD RIGHT THERE, WITH THE DRAGONS AND THE OTHER SALAMANDERS PITCHING IN, IT WOULD TURN INTO A RIOT. THE TEACHERS WOULD HAVE HAD TO STEP IN.
SO, THANKS FOR THE COMPLIMENT.
BUT NEXT TIME--I'D PREFER A LITTLE TRUST.

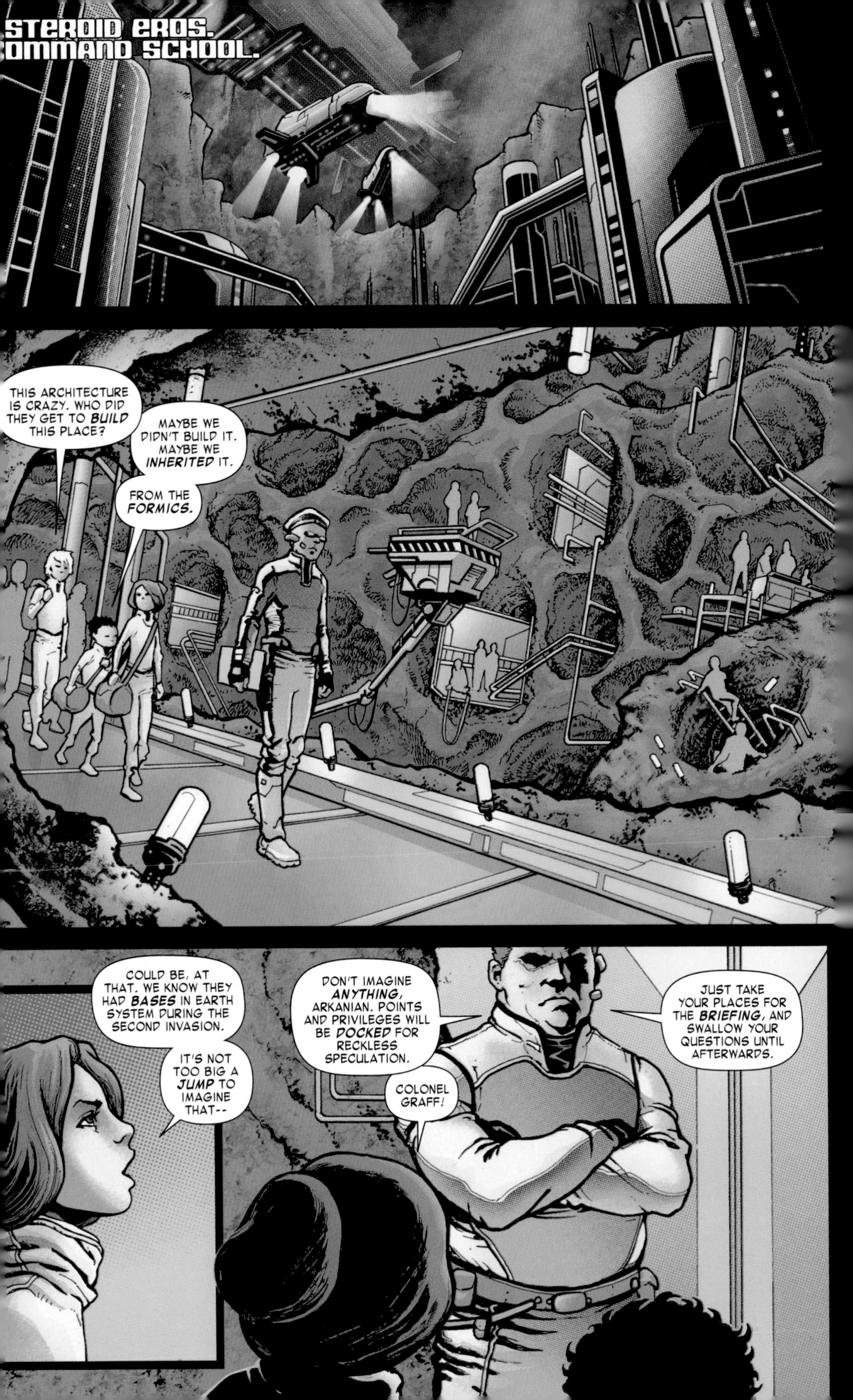
STEROID EROS.
OMMAND SCHOOL.
THIS ARCHITECTURE IS CRAZY. WHO DID THEY GET TO BUILD THIS PLACE?
MAYBE WE DIDN'T BUILD IT. MAYBE WE INHERITED IT.
FROM THE FORMICS.
COULD BE, AT THAT. WE KNOW THEY HAD BASES IN EARTH SYSTEM DURING THE SECOND INVASION.
IT'S NOT TOO BIG A JUMP TO IMAGINE THAT--
DON'T IMAGINE ANYTHING, ARKANIAN. POINTS AND PRIVILEGES WILL BE DOCKED FOR RECKLESS SPECULATION.
COLONEL GRAFF!
JUST TAKE YOUR PLACES FOR THE BRIEFING, AND SWALLOW YOUR QUESTIONS UNTIL AFTERWARDS.

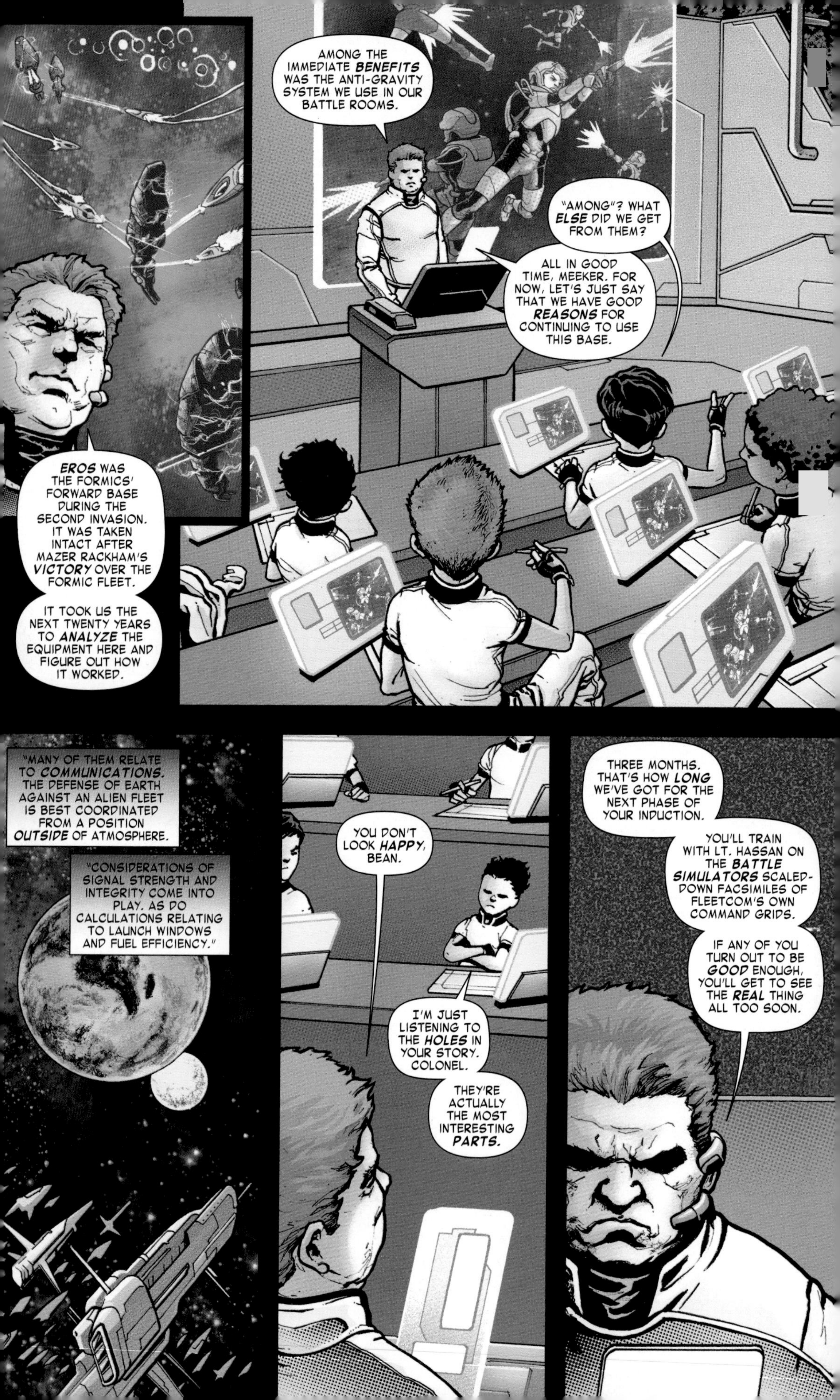
AMONG THE IMMEDIATE BENEFITS WAS THE ANTI-GRAVITY SYSTEM WE USE IN OUR BATTLE ROOMS.
EROS WAS THE FORMICS' FORWARD BASE DURING THE SECOND INVASION. IT WAS TAKEN INTACT AFTER MAZER RACKHAM'S VICTORY OVER THE FORMIC FLEET.
IT TOOK US THE NEXT TWENTY YEARS TO ANALYZE THE EQUIPMENT HERE AND FIGURE OUT HOW IT WORKED.
"AMONG"? WHAT ELSE DID WE GET FROM THEM?
ALL IN GOOD TIME, MEEKER. FOR NOW, LET'S JUST SAY THAT WE HAVE GOOD REASONS FOR CONTINUING TO USE THIS BASE.
"MANY OF THEM RELATE TO COMMUNICATIONS. THE DEFENSE OF EARTH AGAINST AN ALIEN FLEET IS BEST COORDINATED FROM A POSITION OUTSIDE OF ATMOSPHERE.
"CONSIDERATIONS OF SIGNAL STRENGTH AND INTEGRITY COME INTO PLAY. AS DO CALCULATIONS RELATING TO LAUNCH WINDOWS AND FUEL EFFICIENCY."
YOU DON'T LOOK HAPPY, BEAN.
I'M JUST LISTENING TO THE HOLES IN YOUR STORY. COLONEL.
THEY'RE ACTUALLY THE MOST INTERESTING PARTS.
THREE MONTHS. THAT'S HOW LONG WE'VE GOT FOR THE NEXT PHASE OF YOUR INDUCTION.
YOU'LL TRAIN WITH LT. HASSAN ON THE BATTLE SIMULATORS SCALED-DOWN FACSIMILES OF FLEETCOM'S OWN COMMAND GRIDS.
IF ANY OF YOU TURN OUT TO BE GOOD ENOUGH, YOU'LL GET TO SEE THE REAL THING ALL TOO SOON.

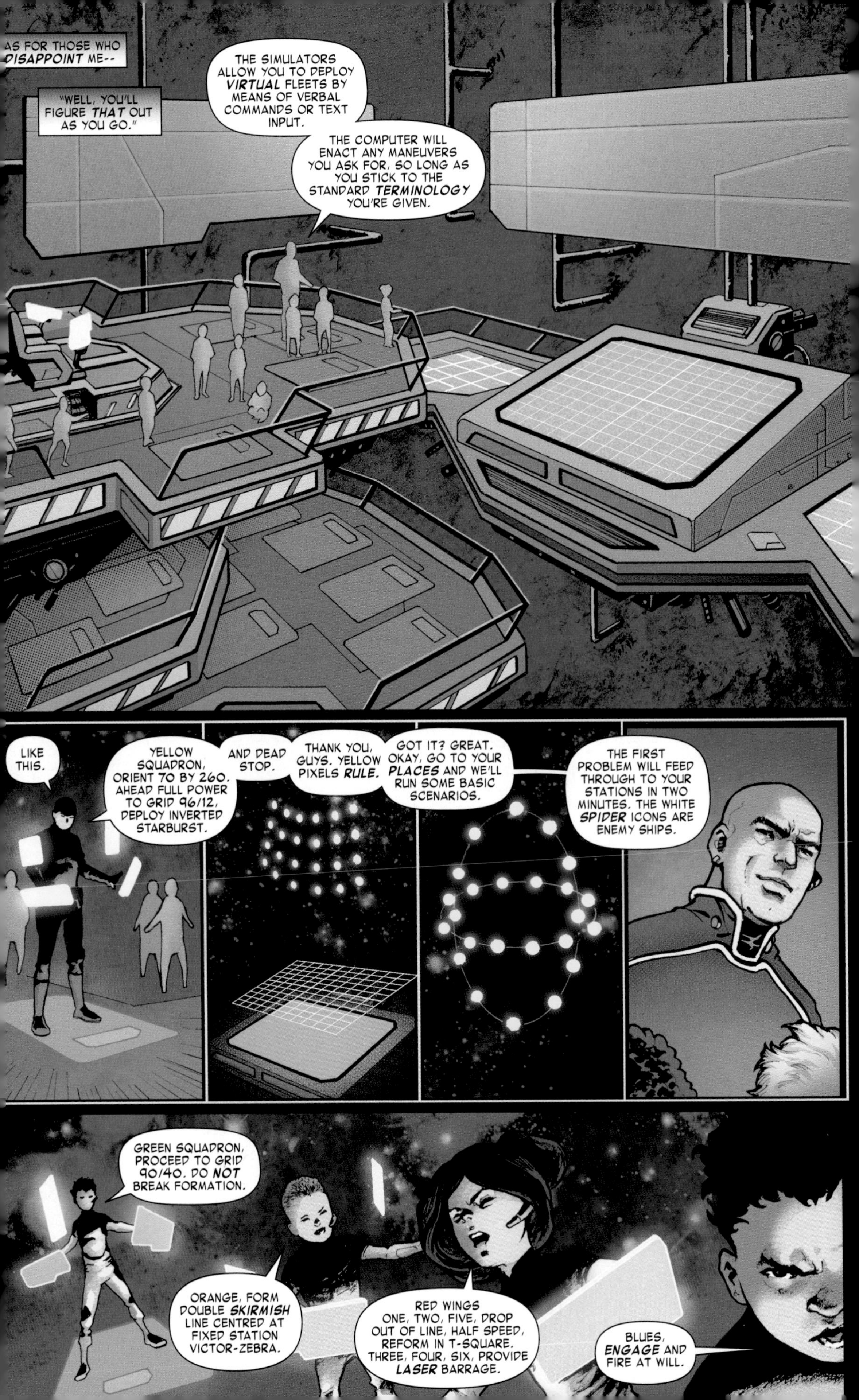
AS FOR THOSE WHO DISAPPOINT ME--
"WELL, YOU'LL FIGURE THAT OUT AS YOU GO."
THE SIMULATORS ALLOW YOU TO DEPLOY VIRTUAL FLEETS BY MEANS OF VERBAL COMMANDS OR TEXT INPUT.
THE COMPUTER WILL ENACT ANY MANEUVERS YOU ASK FOR, SO LONG AS YOU STICK TO THE STANDARD TERMINOLOGY YOU'RE GIVEN.
LIKE THIS.
YELLOW SQUADRON, ORIENT 70 BY 260. AHEAD FULL POWER TO GRID 96/12, DEPLOY INVERTED STARBURST.
AND DEAD STOP.
THANK YOU, GUYS. YELLOW PIXELS RULE.
GOT IT? GREAT. OKAY, GO TO YOUR PLACES AND WE'LL RUN SOME BASIC SCENARIOS.
THE FIRST PROBLEM WILL FEED THROUGH TO YOUR STATIONS IN TWO MINUTES. THE WHITE SPIDER ICONS ARE ENEMY SHIPS.
GREEN SQUADRON, PROCEED TO GRID 90/40. DO NOT BREAK FORMATION.
ORANGE, FORM DOUBLE SKIRMISH LINE CENTRED AT FIXED STATION VICTOR-ZEBRA.
RED WINGS ONE, TWO, FIVE, DROP OUT OF LINE, HALF SPEED, REFORM IN T-SQUARE. THREE, FOUR, SIX, PROVIDE LASER BARRAGE.
BLUES, ENGAGE AND FIRE AT WILL.

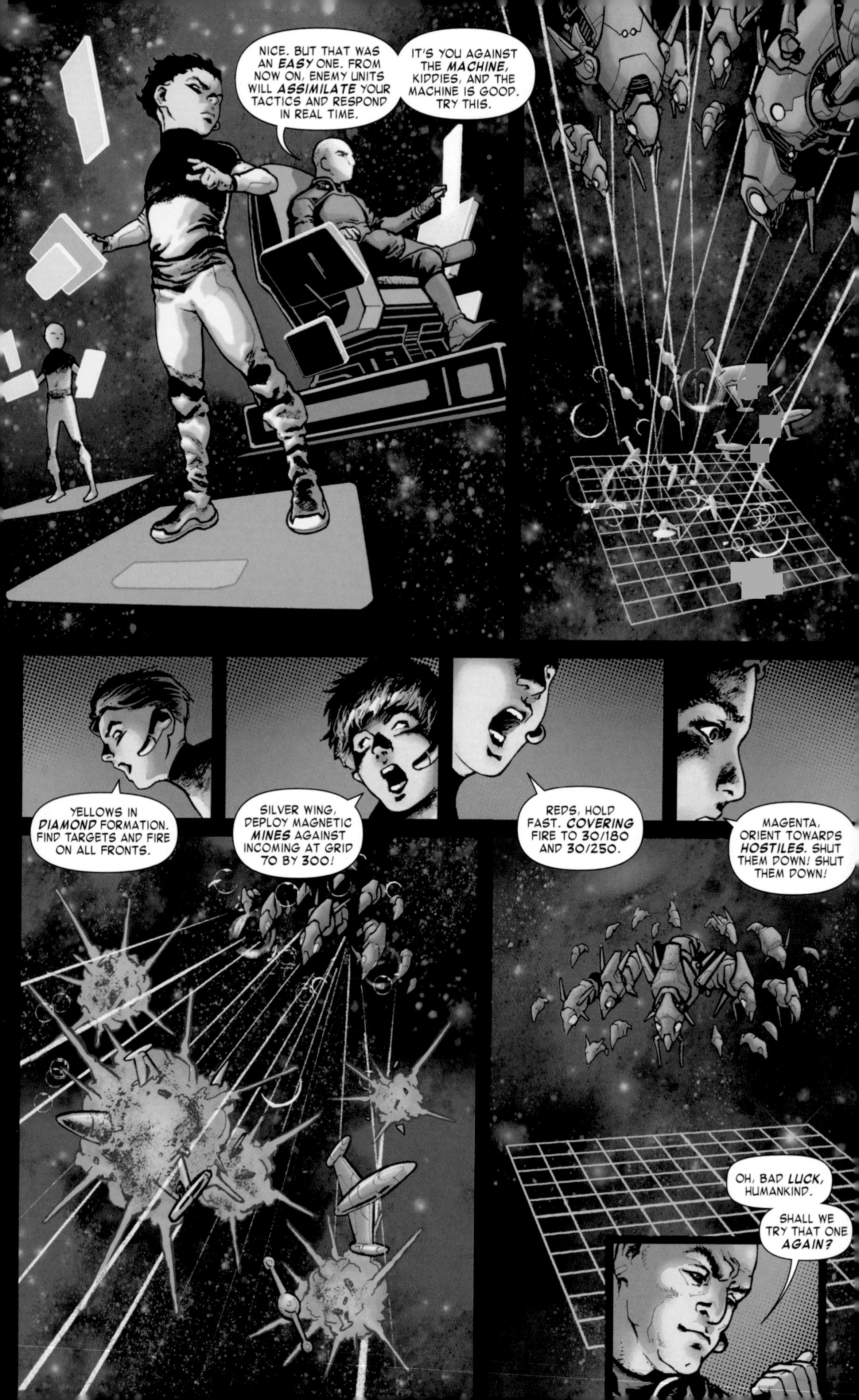
NICE. BUT THAT WAS AN EASY ONE. FROM NOW ON, ENEMY UNITS WILL ASSIMILATE YOUR TACTICS AND RESPOND IN REAL TIME.
IT'S YOU AGAINST THE MACHINE, KIDDIES, AND THE MACHINE IS GOOD. TRY THIS.
YELLOWS IN DIAMOND FORMATION. FIND TARGETS AND FIRE ON ALL FRONTS.
SILVER WING, DEPLOY MAGNETIC MINES AGAINST INCOMING AT GRID 70 BY 300!
REDS, HOLD FAST. COVERING FIRE TO 30/180 AND 30/250.
MAGENTA, ORIENT TOWARDS HOSTILES. SHUT THEM DOWN! SHUT THEM DOWN!
OH, BAD LUCK, HUMANKIND.
SHALL WE TRY THAT ONE AGAIN?

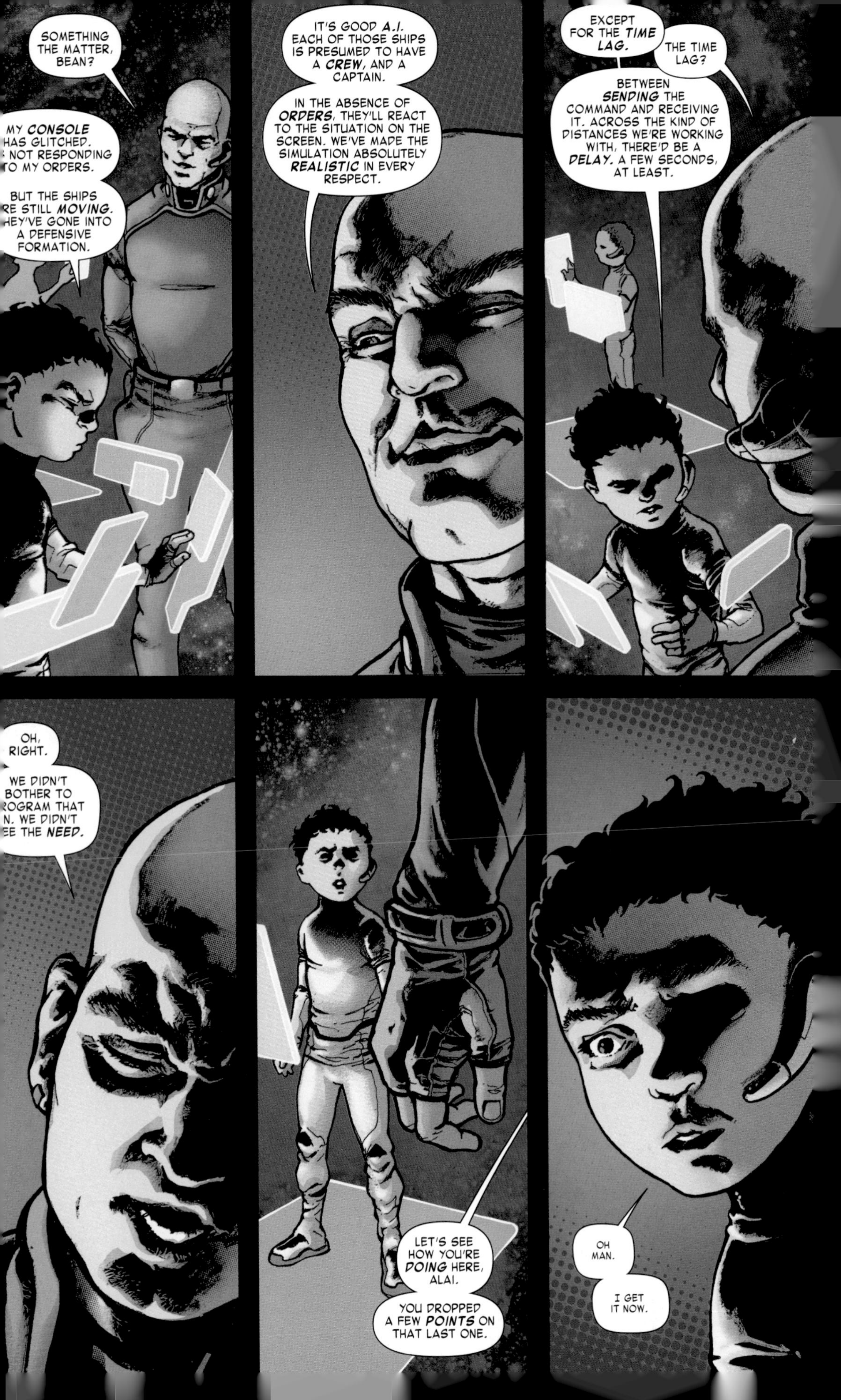

SOMETHING THE MATTER, BEAN?
MY CONSOLE HAS GLITCHED. NOT RESPONDING TO MY ORDERS.
BUT THE SHIPS STILL MOVING. HEY'VE GONE INTO A DEFENSIVE FORMATION.
IT'S GOOD A.I. EACH OF THOSE SHIPS IS PRESUMED TO HAVE A CREW, AND A CAPTAIN.
IN THE ABSENCE OF ORDERS, THEY'LL REACT TO THE SITUATION ON THE SCREEN. WE'VE MADE THE SIMULATION ABSOLUTELY REALISTIC IN EVERY RESPECT.
EXCEPT FOR THE TIME LAG.
THE TIME LAG?
BETWEEN SENDING THE COMMAND AND RECEIVING IT. ACROSS THE KIND OF DISTANCES WE'RE WORKING WITH, THERE'D BE A DELAY. A FEW SECONDS, AT LEAST.
OH, RIGHT.
WE DIDN'T BOTHER TO ROGRAM THAT N. WE DIDN'T EE THE NEED.
LET'S SEE HOW YOU'RE DOING HERE, ALAI.
YOU DROPPED A FEW POINTS ON THAT LAST ONE.
OH MAN.
I GET IT NOW.

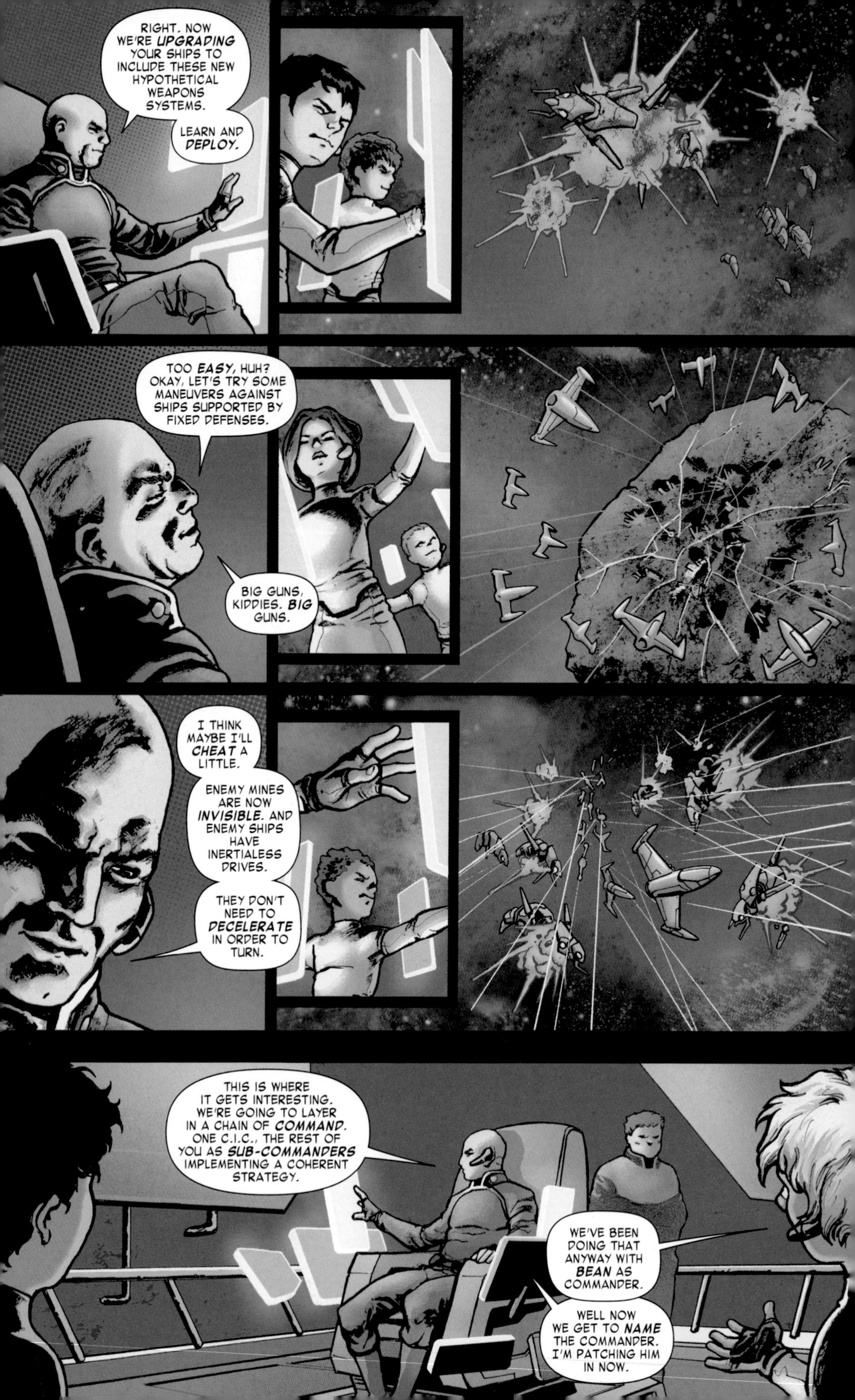
RIGHT. NOW WE'RE UPGRADING YOUR SHIPS TO INCLUDE THESE NEW HYPOTHETICAL WEAPONS SYSTEMS.
LEARN AND DEPLOY.
TOO EASY, HUH? OKAY, LET'S TRY SOME MANEUVERS AGAINST SHIPS SUPPORTED BY FIXED DEFENSES.
BIG GUNS, KIDDIES. BIG GUNS.
I THINK MAYBE I'LL CHEAT A LITTLE.
ENEMY MINES ARE NOW INVISIBLE. AND ENEMY SHIPS HAVE INERTIALESS DRIVES.
THEY DON'T NEED TO DECELERATE IN ORDER TO TURN.
THIS IS WHERE IT GETS INTERESTING. WE'RE GOING TO LAYER IN A CHAIN OF COMMAND. ONE C.I.C., THE REST OF YOU AS SUB-COMMANDERS IMPLEMENTING A COHERENT STRATEGY.
WE'VE BEEN DOING THAT ANYWAY WITH BEAN AS COMMANDER.
WELL NOW WE GET TO NAME THE COMMANDER. I'M PATCHING HIM IN NOW.

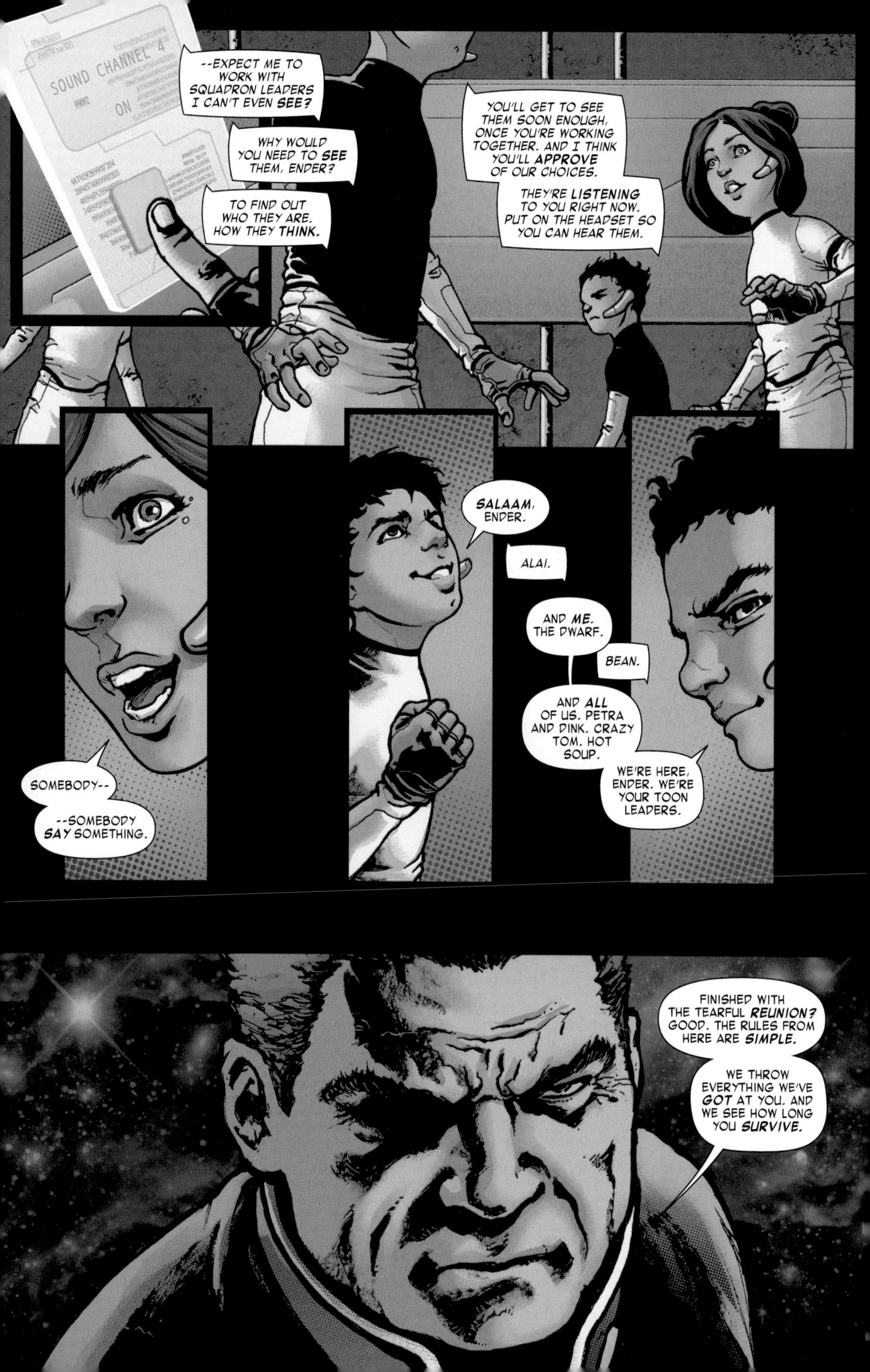
SOUND CHANNEL 4
ON
--EXPECT ME TO WORK WITH SQUADRON LEADERS I CAN'T EVEN SEE?
WHY WOULD YOU NEED TO SEE THEM, ENDER?
TO FIND OUT WHO THEY ARE. HOW THEY THINK.
YOU'LL GET TO SEE THEM SOON ENOUGH, ONCE YOU'RE WORKING TOGETHER. AND I THINK YOU'LL APPROVE OF OUR CHOICES.
THEY'RE LISTENING TO YOU RIGHT NOW. PUT ON THE HEADSET SO YOU CAN HEAR THEM.
SOMEBODY--
--SOMEBODY SAY SOMETHING.
SALAAM, ENDER.
ALAI.
AND ME. THE DWARF.
BEAN.
AND ALL OF US. PETRA AND DINK. CRAZY TOM. HOT SOUP.
WE'RE HERE, ENDER. WE'RE YOUR TOON LEADERS.
FINISHED WITH THE TEARFUL REUNION? GOOD. THE RULES FROM HERE ARE SIMPLE.
WE THROW EVERYTHING WE'VE GOT AT YOU. AND WE SEE HOW LONG YOU SURVIVE.

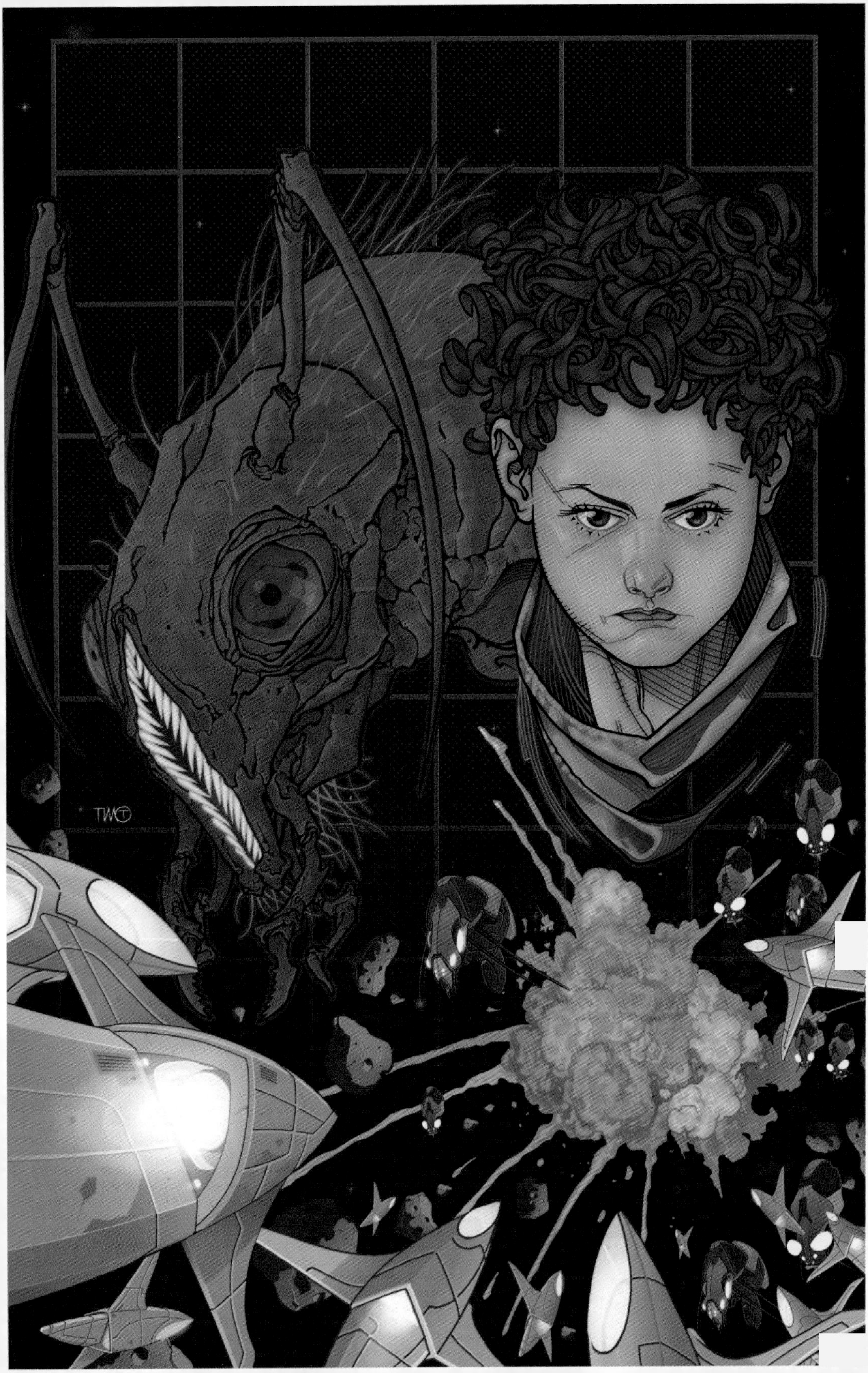

Login: BEAN
Password: *************
Station 18326
Session incept 23:12:14

Ho, Colonel. How've you been?

I know, you said these desks are private. I also know you're reading over my shoulder. Please, feel free. This report is for you, and for whoever you report to.

I've been thinking about what I'm here for. Again, this isn't something you've specifically said: I'm reading between the lines.

You need me in case Ender fails. In case you push him just that little bit too far, instead of exactly far enough, and he breaks in some small but crucial way. If that happens, I'm Plan B.

Fair enough. But I hope you've thought about what that means. Replacing Ender isn't just a case of studying his tactics, his strategies, and trying to reproduce them. It isn't even a case of empathizing with the Formics and anticipating their next move, although that's a part of it.

To replace Ender, I'd have to become Ender.

Thanks for the vote of confidence. But I don't know if a jump like that is even possible...

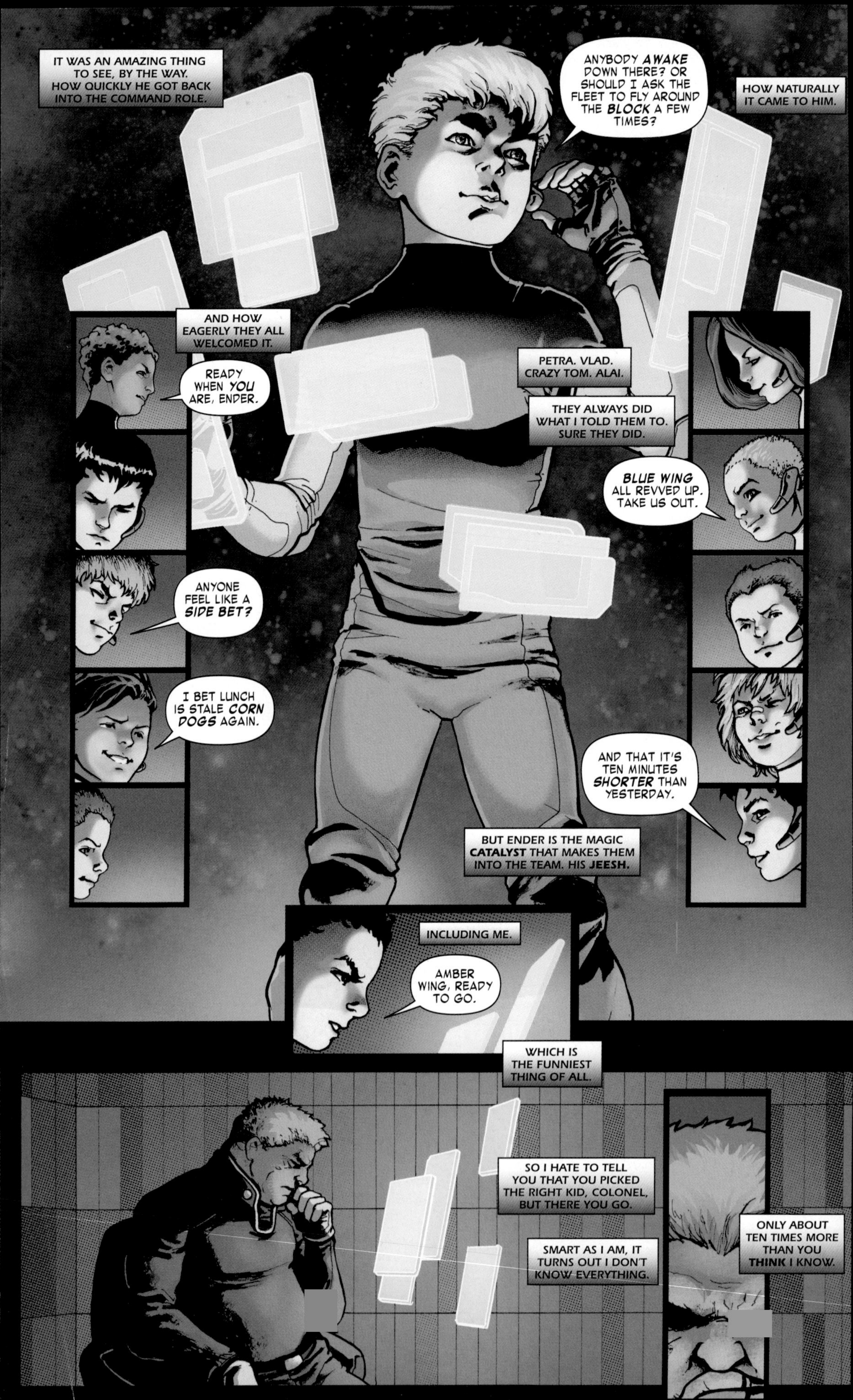

IT WAS AN AMAZING THING TO SEE, BY THE WAY. HOW QUICKLY HE GOT BACK INTO THE COMMAND ROLE.
ANYBODY AWAKE DOWN THERE? OR SHOULD I ASK THE FLEET TO FLY AROUND THE BLOCK A FEW TIMES?
HOW NATURALLY IT CAME TO HIM.
AND HOW EAGERLY THEY ALL WELCOMED IT.
READY WHEN YOU ARE, ENDER.
PETRA. VLAD. CRAZY TOM. ALAI.
THEY ALWAYS DID WHAT I TOLD THEM TO. SURE THEY DID.
BLUE WING ALL REVVED UP. TAKE US OUT.
ANYONE FEEL LIKE A SIDE BET?
I BET LUNCH IS STALE CORN DOGS AGAIN.
AND THAT IT'S TEN MINUTES SHORTER THAN YESTERDAY.
BUT ENDER IS THE MAGIC CATALYST THAT MAKES THEM INTO THE TEAM. HIS JEESH.
INCLUDING ME.
AMBER WING, READY TO GO.
WHICH IS THE FUNNIEST THING OF ALL.
SO I HATE TO TELL YOU THAT YOU PICKED THE RIGHT KID, COLONEL, BUT THERE YOU GO.
SMART AS I AM, IT TURNS OUT I DON'T KNOW EVERYTHING.
ONLY ABOUT TEN TIMES MORE THAN YOU THINK I KNOW.

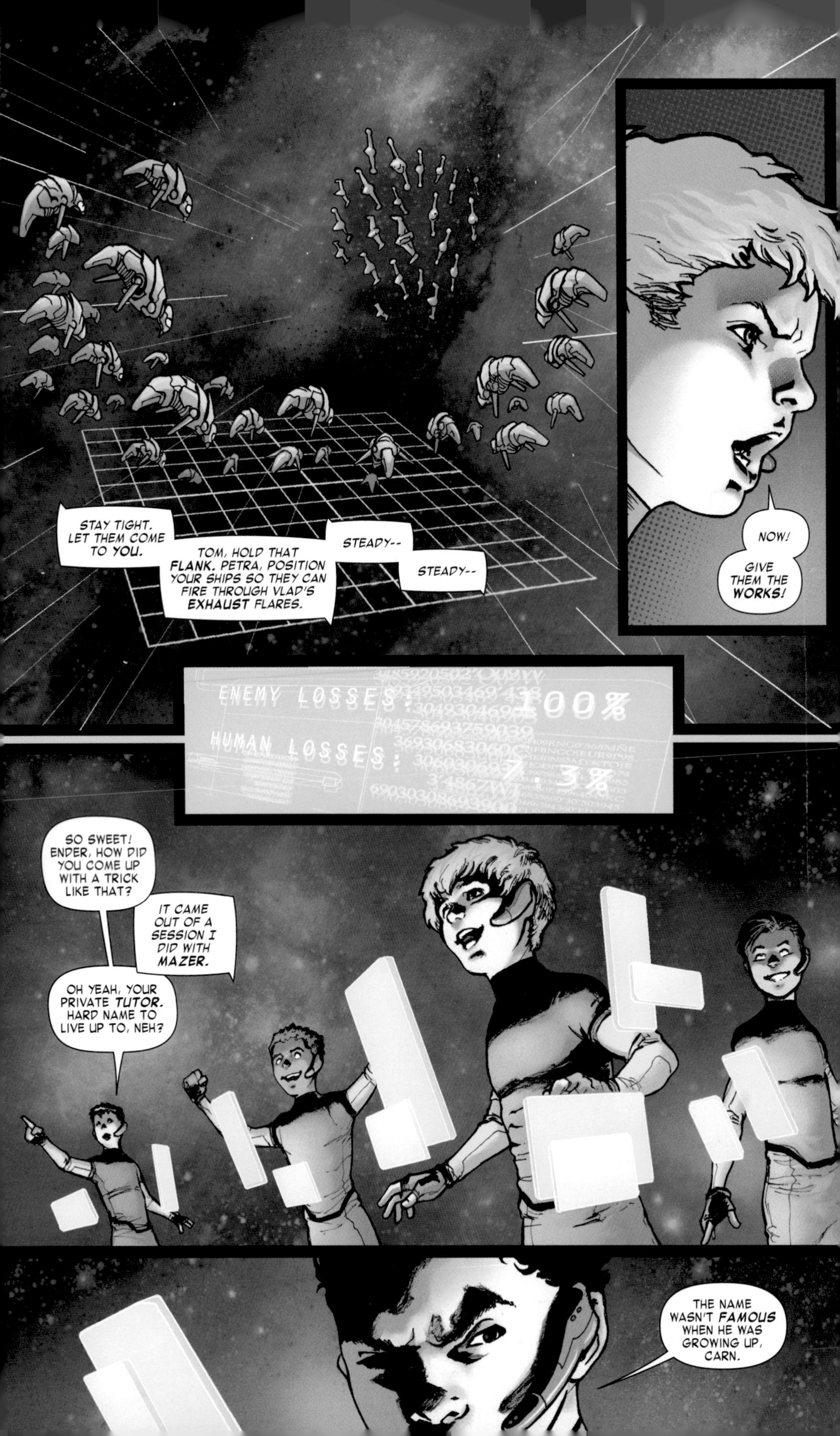
STAY TIGHT. LET THEM COME TO YOU.
TOM, HOLD THAT FLANK. PETRA, POSITION YOUR SHIPS SO THEY CAN FIRE THROUGH VLAD'S EXHAUST FLARES.
STEADY--
STEADY--
NOW!
GIVE THEM THE WORKS!
ENEMY LOSSES: 100%
HUMAN LOSSES: 7.3%
SO SWEET! ENDER, HOW DID YOU COME UP WITH A TRICK LIKE THAT?
IT CAME OUT OF A SESSION I DID WITH MAZER.
OH YEAH, YOUR PRIVATE TUTOR. HARD NAME TO LIVE UP TO, NEH?
THE NAME WASN'T FAMOUS WHEN HE WAS GROWING UP, CARN.

EARTH ABIDES!
RACKHAM DECIMATES FORMIC FLEET.

Mazer Rackham's tactical genius tipped the balance today in the ~~gement~~ of the war. The message from I.F.: "The enemy is ours. Earth abides."

Reports from fleet-based newsfeeds and from observers on orbital base Avalon confirm the total rout of the Formic armada. No figures are yet available for dead and ~~wounded~~ but it is believed that Rackham lost no more than five ships of the line ~~...~~ was the news that no I.F. officer higher

A *BLACK BOX* VICTORY. HE GOES IN AGAINST IMPOSSIBLE ODDS, AND COMES OUT A *HERO*.

BUT WE NEVER GET TO SEE *HOW* THE TRICK WAS DONE.

FIRST SIGN OF *MADNESS*, BEAN.

I WASN'T TALKING TO MYSELF, COLONEL GRAFF. I *KNEW* YOU WERE THERE.

DID YOU COME TO LET ME IN ON THE JOKE?

IT WAS PURE DUMB LUCK. RACKHAM HIT THE *QUEEN'S* SHIP, AND THE REST OF THE FORMIC FLEET STOPPED FIGHTING. THEIR PILOTS AND GUNNERS *DIED* AT THEIR POSTS.

THEY'RE *TELEPATHIC* AND THE QUEEN THINKS FOR EVERYONE. I THOUGHT THAT MIGHT HAVE BEEN ONE OF THE THINGS YOU'D ALREADY FIGURED OUT.

IS THIS BEING *RECORDED?*

OF COURSE IT IS.

YOU WANT TO KNOW HOW MANY TOP, TOP SECRETS I'VE *UNCOVERED* WITH MY COLD, INHUMAN INTELLECT.

SOMETHING LIKE THAT.

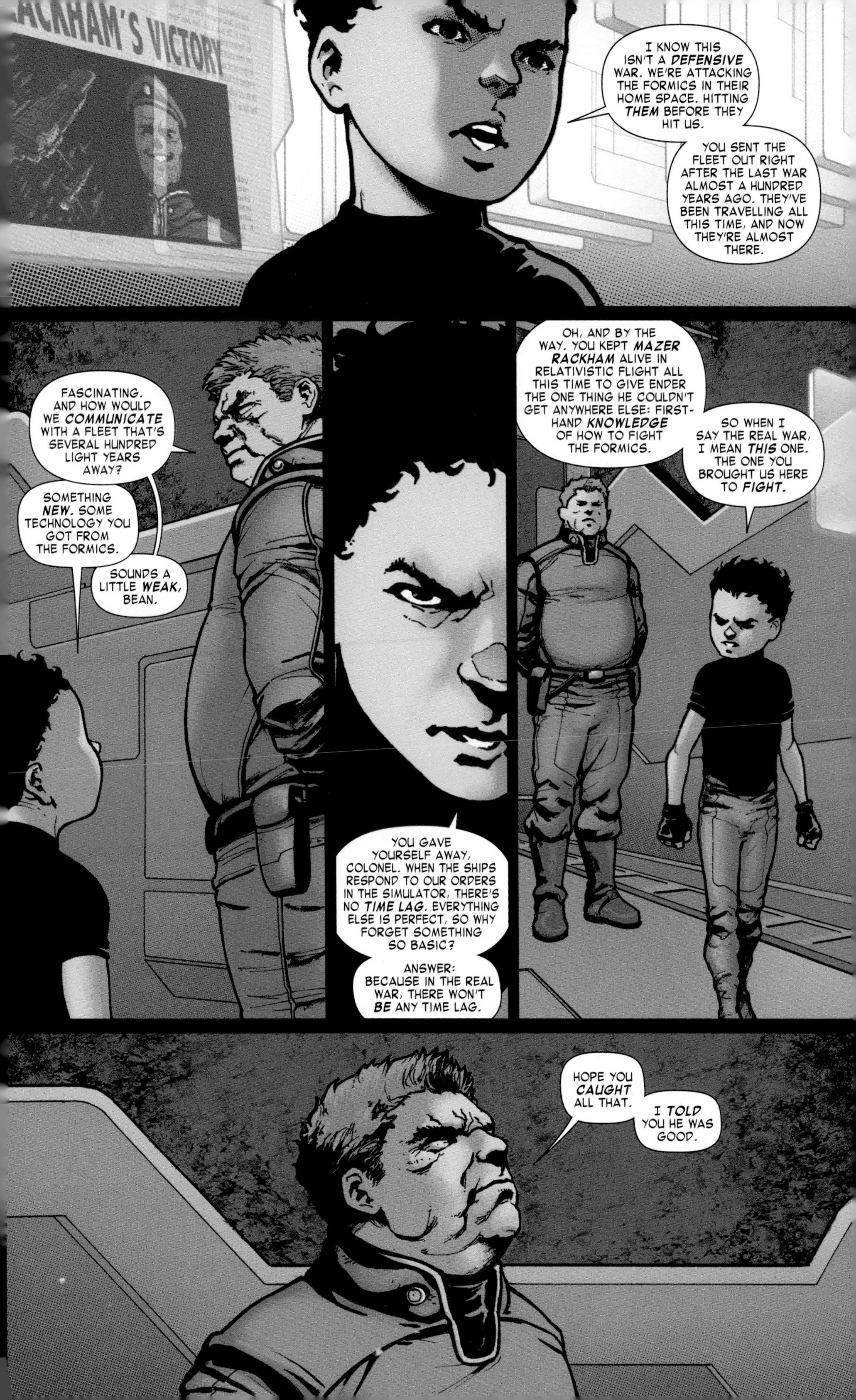

ACKHAM'S VICTORY
I KNOW THIS ISN'T A DEFENSIVE WAR. WE'RE ATTACKING THE FORMICS IN THEIR HOME SPACE. HITTING THEM BEFORE THEY HIT US.
YOU SENT THE FLEET OUT RIGHT AFTER THE LAST WAR ALMOST A HUNDRED YEARS AGO. THEY'VE BEEN TRAVELLING ALL THIS TIME, AND NOW THEY'RE ALMOST THERE.
FASCINATING. AND HOW WOULD WE COMMUNICATE WITH A FLEET THAT'S SEVERAL HUNDRED LIGHT YEARS AWAY?
SOMETHING NEW. SOME TECHNOLOGY YOU GOT FROM THE FORMICS.
SOUNDS A LITTLE WEAK, BEAN.
YOU GAVE YOURSELF AWAY, COLONEL. WHEN THE SHIPS RESPOND TO OUR ORDERS IN THE SIMULATOR, THERE'S NO TIME LAG. EVERYTHING ELSE IS PERFECT, SO WHY FORGET SOMETHING SO BASIC?
ANSWER: BECAUSE IN THE REAL WAR, THERE WON'T BE ANY TIME LAG.
OH, AND BY THE WAY. YOU KEPT MAZER RACKHAM ALIVE IN RELATIVISTIC FLIGHT ALL THIS TIME TO GIVE ENDER THE ONE THING HE COULDN'T GET ANYWHERE ELSE: FIRST-HAND KNOWLEDGE OF HOW TO FIGHT THE FORMICS.
SO WHEN I SAY THE REAL WAR, I MEAN THIS ONE. THE ONE YOU BROUGHT US HERE TO FIGHT.
HOPE YOU CAUGHT ALL THAT.
I TOLD YOU HE WAS GOOD.

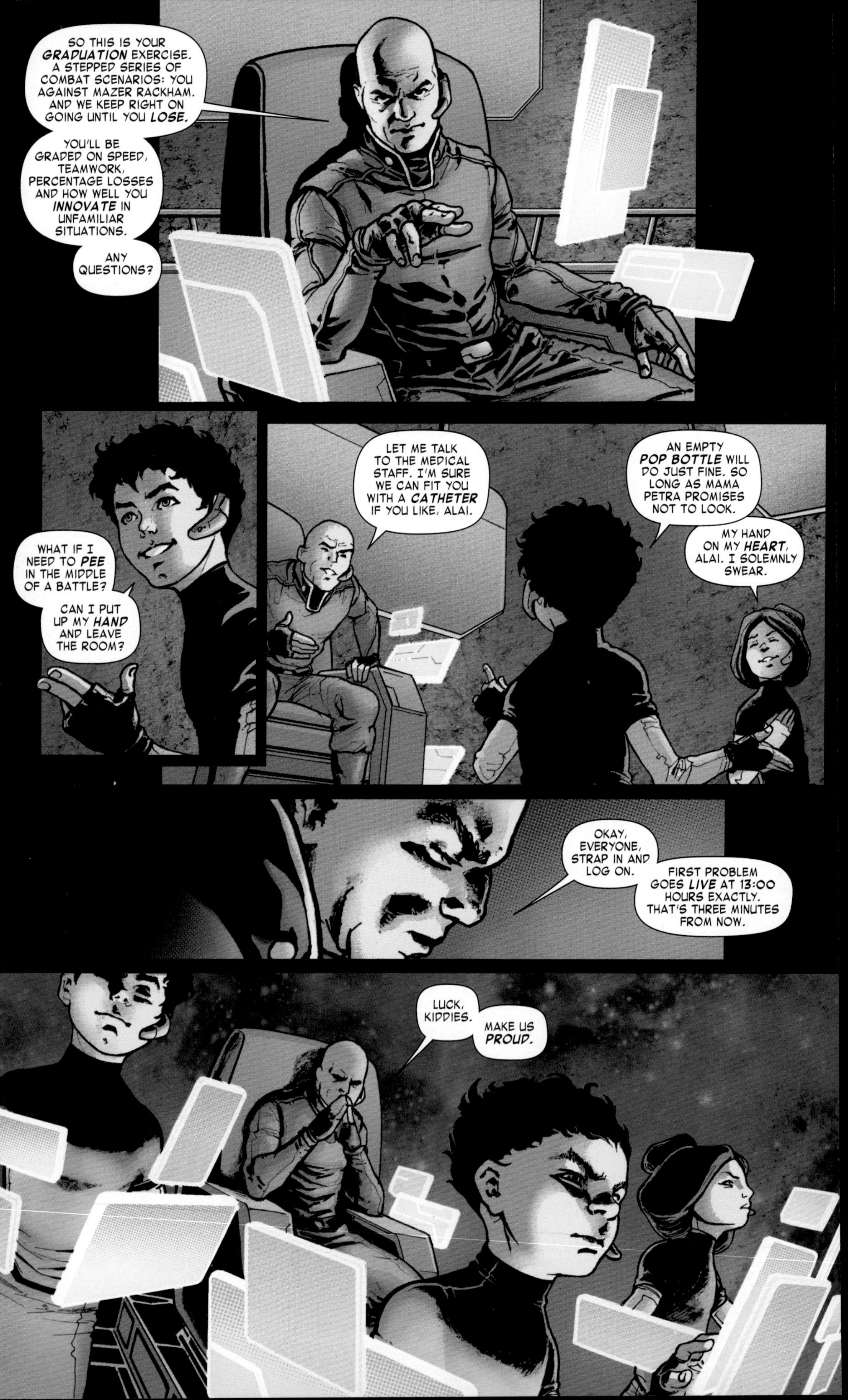
SO THIS IS YOUR GRADUATION EXERCISE. A STEPPED SERIES OF COMBAT SCENARIOS: YOU AGAINST MAZER RACKHAM. AND WE KEEP RIGHT ON GOING UNTIL YOU LOSE.
YOU'LL BE GRADED ON SPEED, TEAMWORK, PERCENTAGE LOSSES AND HOW WELL YOU INNOVATE IN UNFAMILIAR SITUATIONS.
ANY QUESTIONS?
WHAT IF I NEED TO PEE IN THE MIDDLE OF A BATTLE?
CAN I PUT UP MY HAND AND LEAVE THE ROOM?
LET ME TALK TO THE MEDICAL STAFF. I'M SURE WE CAN FIT YOU WITH A CATHETER IF YOU LIKE, ALAI.
AN EMPTY POP BOTTLE WILL DO JUST FINE. SO LONG AS MAMA PETRA PROMISES NOT TO LOOK.
MY HAND ON MY HEART, ALAI. I SOLEMNLY SWEAR.
OKAY, EVERYONE, STRAP IN AND LOG ON.
FIRST PROBLEM GOES LIVE AT 13:00 HOURS EXACTLY. THAT'S THREE MINUTES FROM NOW.
LUCK, KIDDIES.
MAKE US PROUD.

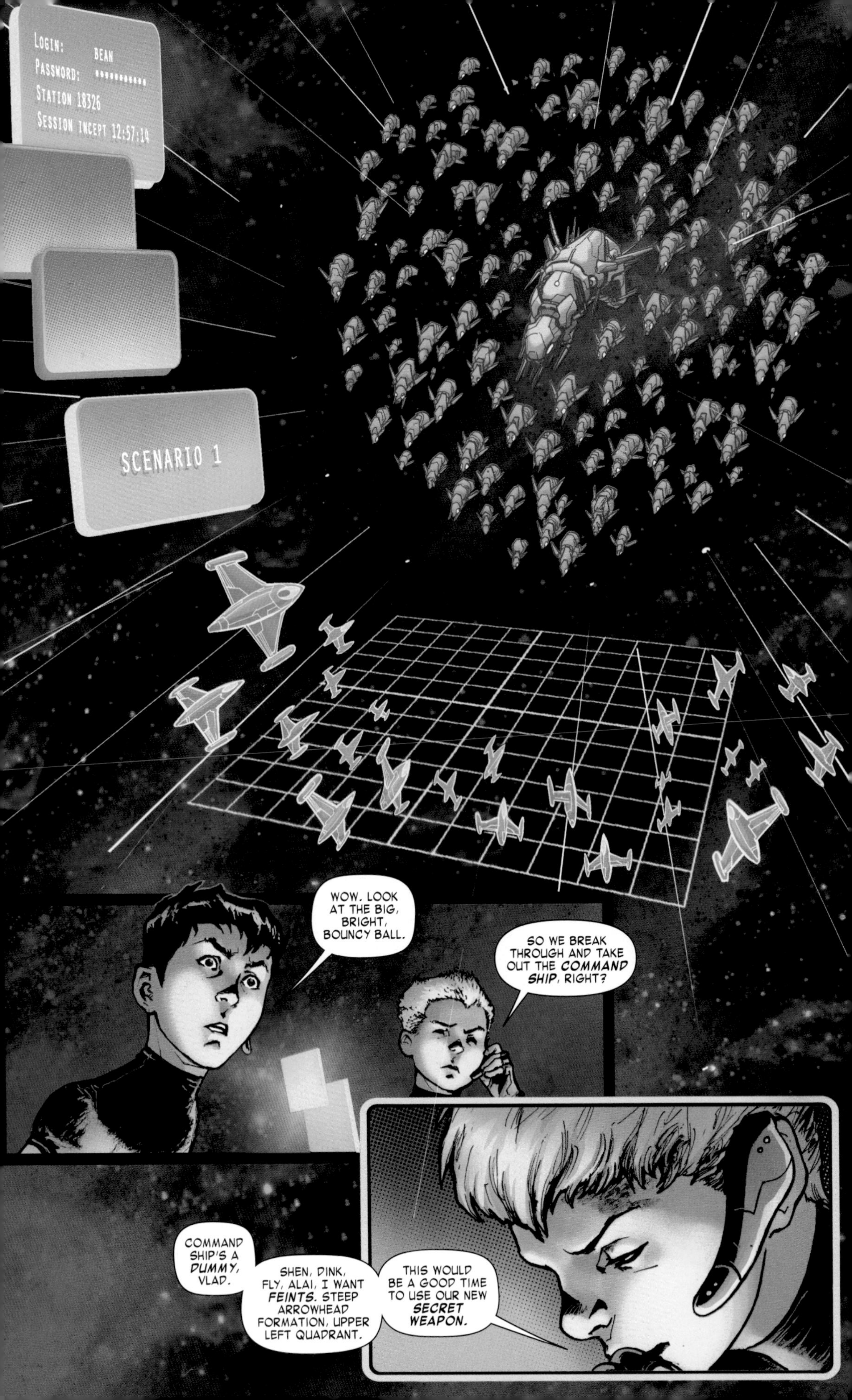

LOGIN: BEAN
PASSWORD: **********
STATION 18326
SESSION INCEPT 12:57:14
SCENARIO 1
WOW. LOOK AT THE BIG, BRIGHT, BOUNCY BALL.
SO WE BREAK THROUGH AND TAKE OUT THE COMMAND SHIP, RIGHT?
COMMAND SHIP'S A DUMMY, VLAD.
SHEN, DINK, FLY, ALAI, I WANT FEINTS. STEEP ARROWHEAD FORMATION, UPPER LEFT QUADRANT.
THIS WOULD BE A GOOD TIME TO USE OUR NEW SECRET WEAPON.

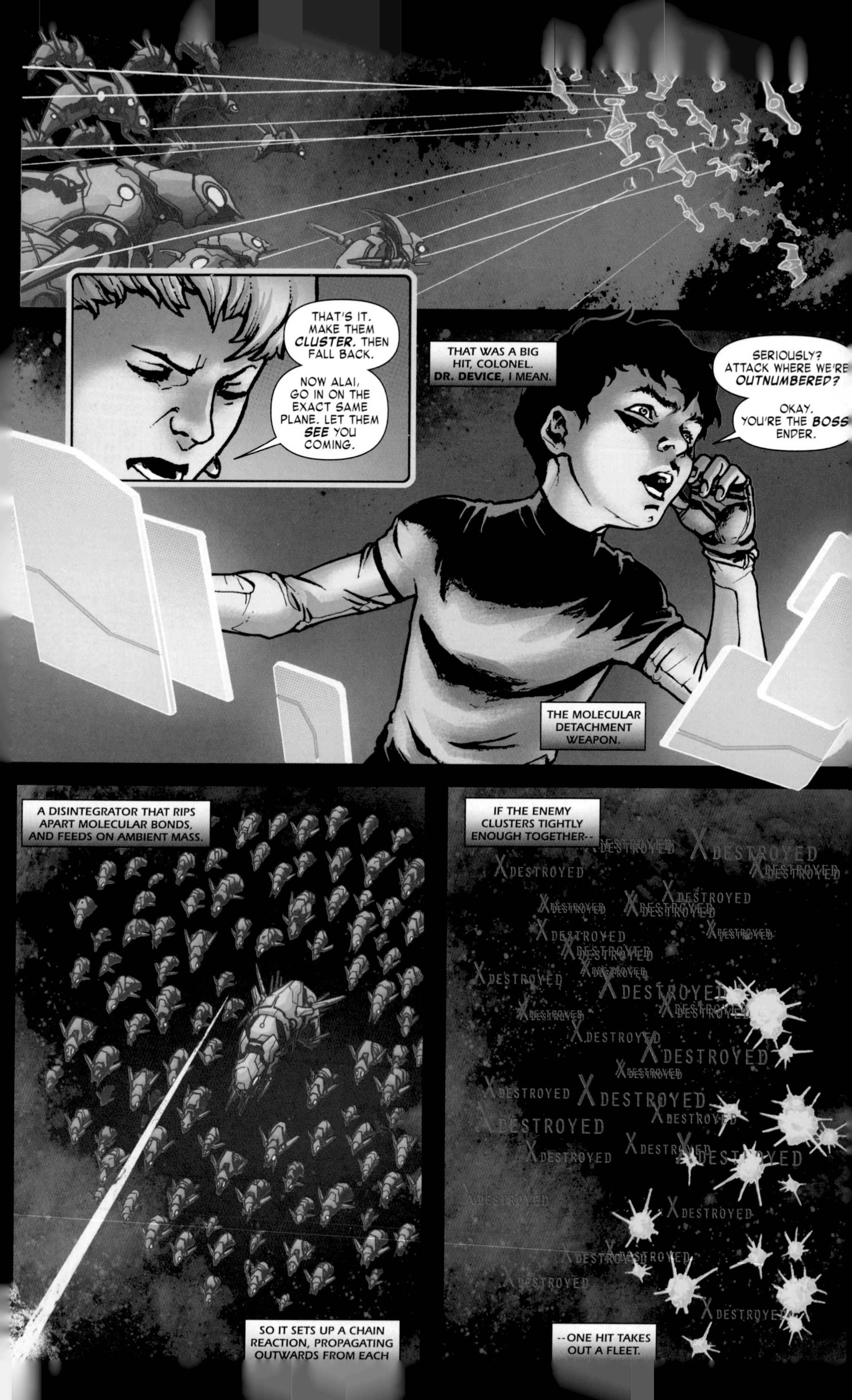
THAT'S IT. MAKE THEM CLUSTER. THEN FALL BACK.
NOW ALAI, GO IN ON THE EXACT SAME PLANE. LET THEM SEE YOU COMING.
THAT WAS A BIG HIT, COLONEL. DR. DEVICE, I MEAN.
SERIOUSLY? ATTACK WHERE WE'RE OUTNUMBERED?
OKAY. YOU'RE THE BOSS ENDER.
THE MOLECULAR DETACHMENT WEAPON.
A DISINTEGRATOR THAT RIPS APART MOLECULAR BONDS, AND FEEDS ON AMBIENT MASS.
SO IT SETS UP A CHAIN REACTION, PROPAGATING OUTWARDS FROM EACH
IF THE ENEMY CLUSTERS TIGHTLY ENOUGH TOGETHER--
X DESTROYED
X DESTROYED
X DESTROYED
--ONE HIT TAKES OUT A FLEET.

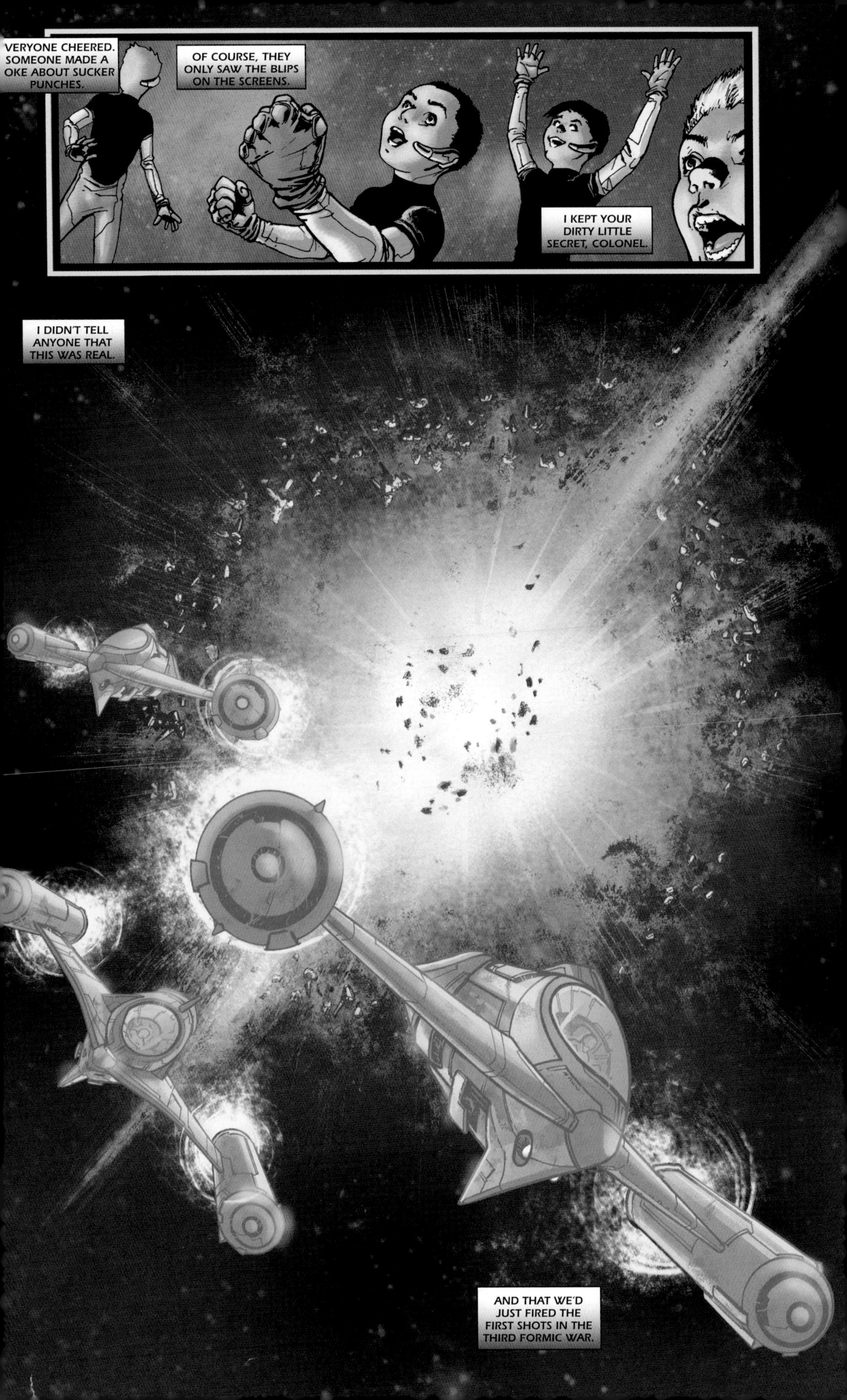
VERYONE CHEERED. SOMEONE MADE A OKE ABOUT SUCKER PUNCHES.
OF COURSE, THEY ONLY SAW THE BLIPS ON THE SCREENS.
I KEPT YOUR DIRTY LITTLE SECRET, COLONEL.
I DIDN'T TELL ANYONE THAT THIS WAS REAL.
AND THAT WE'D JUST FIRED THE FIRST SHOTS IN THE THIRD FORMIC WAR.

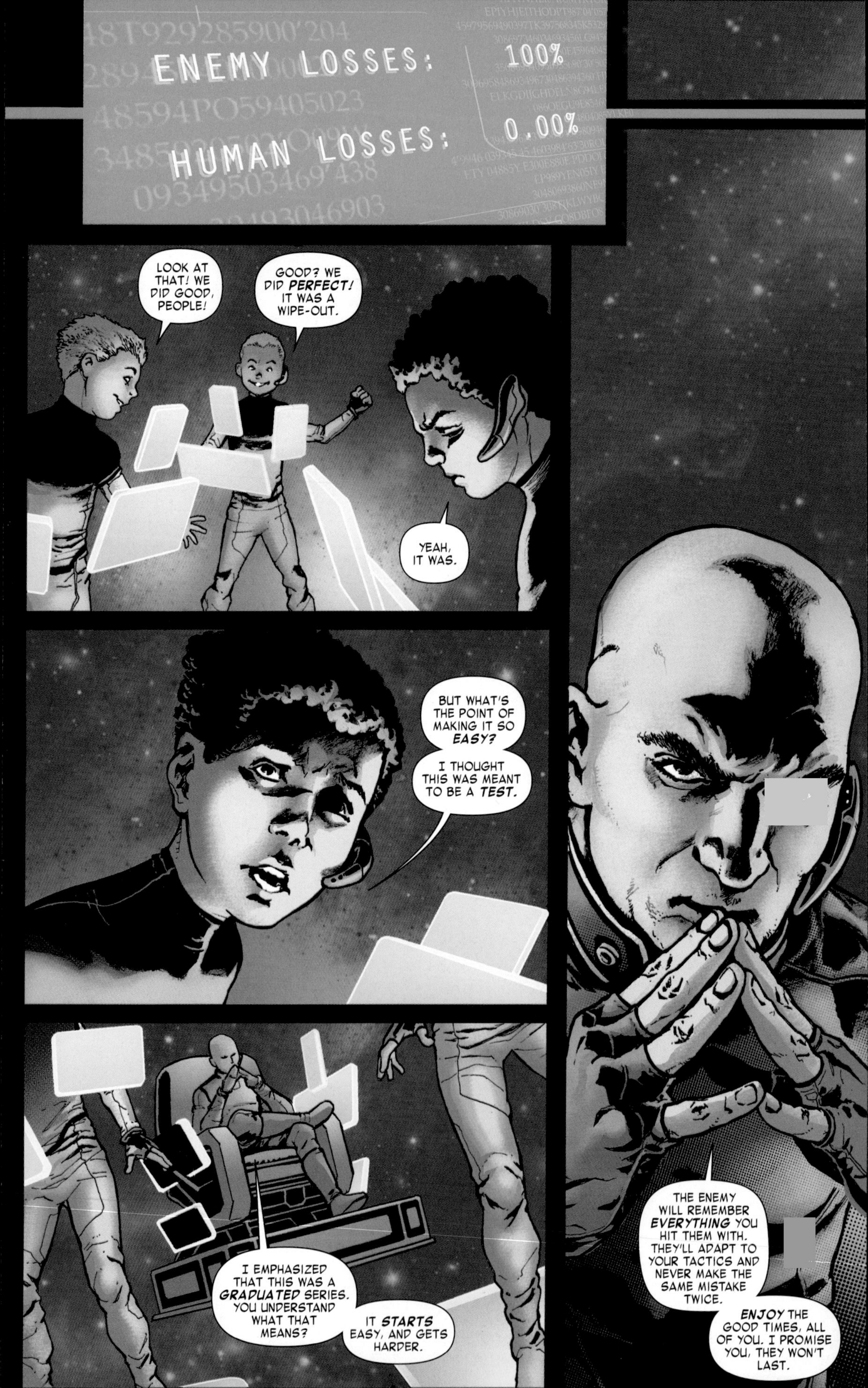
ENEMY LOSSES: 100%
HUMAN LOSSES: 0.00%
LOOK AT THAT! WE DID GOOD, PEOPLE!
GOOD? WE DID PERFECT! IT WAS A WIPE-OUT.
YEAH, IT WAS.
BUT WHAT'S THE POINT OF MAKING IT SO EASY?
I THOUGHT THIS WAS MEANT TO BE A TEST.
I EMPHASIZED THAT THIS WAS A GRADUATED SERIES. YOU UNDERSTAND WHAT THAT MEANS?
IT STARTS EASY, AND GETS HARDER.
THE ENEMY WILL REMEMBER EVERYTHING YOU HIT THEM WITH. THEY'LL ADAPT TO YOUR TACTICS AND NEVER MAKE THE SAME MISTAKE TWICE.
ENJOY THE GOOD TIMES, ALL OF YOU. I PROMISE YOU, THEY WON'T LAST.

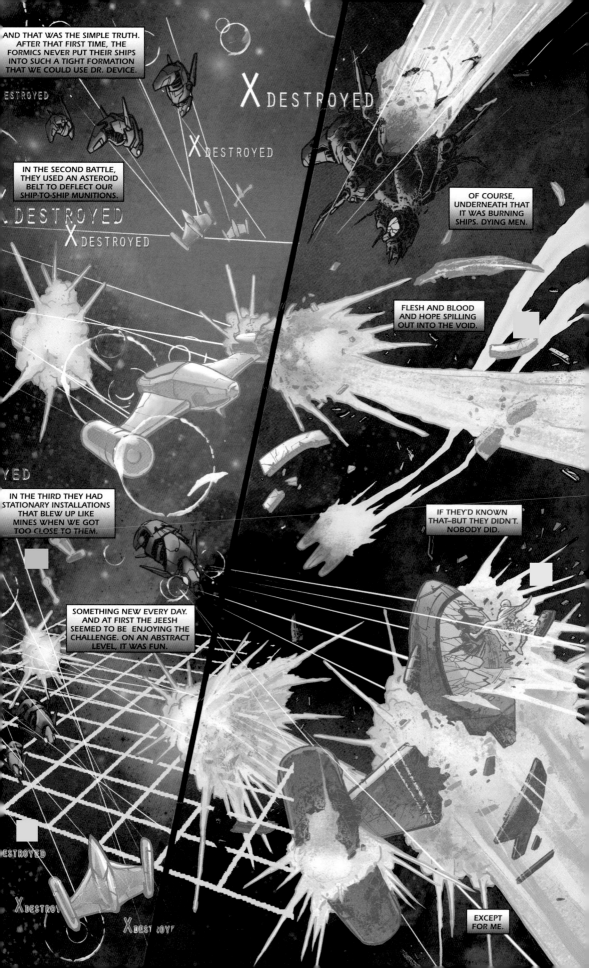

AND THAT WAS THE SIMPLE TRUTH. AFTER THAT FIRST TIME, THE FORMICS NEVER PUT THEIR SHIPS INTO SUCH A TIGHT FORMATION THAT WE COULD USE DR. DEVICE.

ESTROYED

X DESTROYED

X DESTROYED

IN THE SECOND BATTLE, THEY USED AN ASTEROID BELT TO DEFLECT OUR SHIP-TO-SHIP MUNITIONS.

DESTROYED

X DESTROYED

OF COURSE, UNDERNEATH THAT IT WAS BURNING SHIPS. DYING MEN.

FLESH AND BLOOD AND HOPE SPILLING OUT INTO THE VOID.

YED

IN THE THIRD THEY HAD STATIONARY INSTALLATIONS THAT BLEW UP LIKE MINES WHEN WE GOT TOO CLOSE TO THEM.

IF THEY'D KNOWN THAT—BUT THEY DIDN'T. NOBODY DID.

SOMETHING NEW EVERY DAY. AND AT FIRST THE JEESH SEEMED TO BE ENJOYING THE CHALLENGE. ON AN ABSTRACT LEVEL, IT WAS FUN.

ESTROYED

X DESTROY

X DEST ROYE

EXCEPT FOR ME.

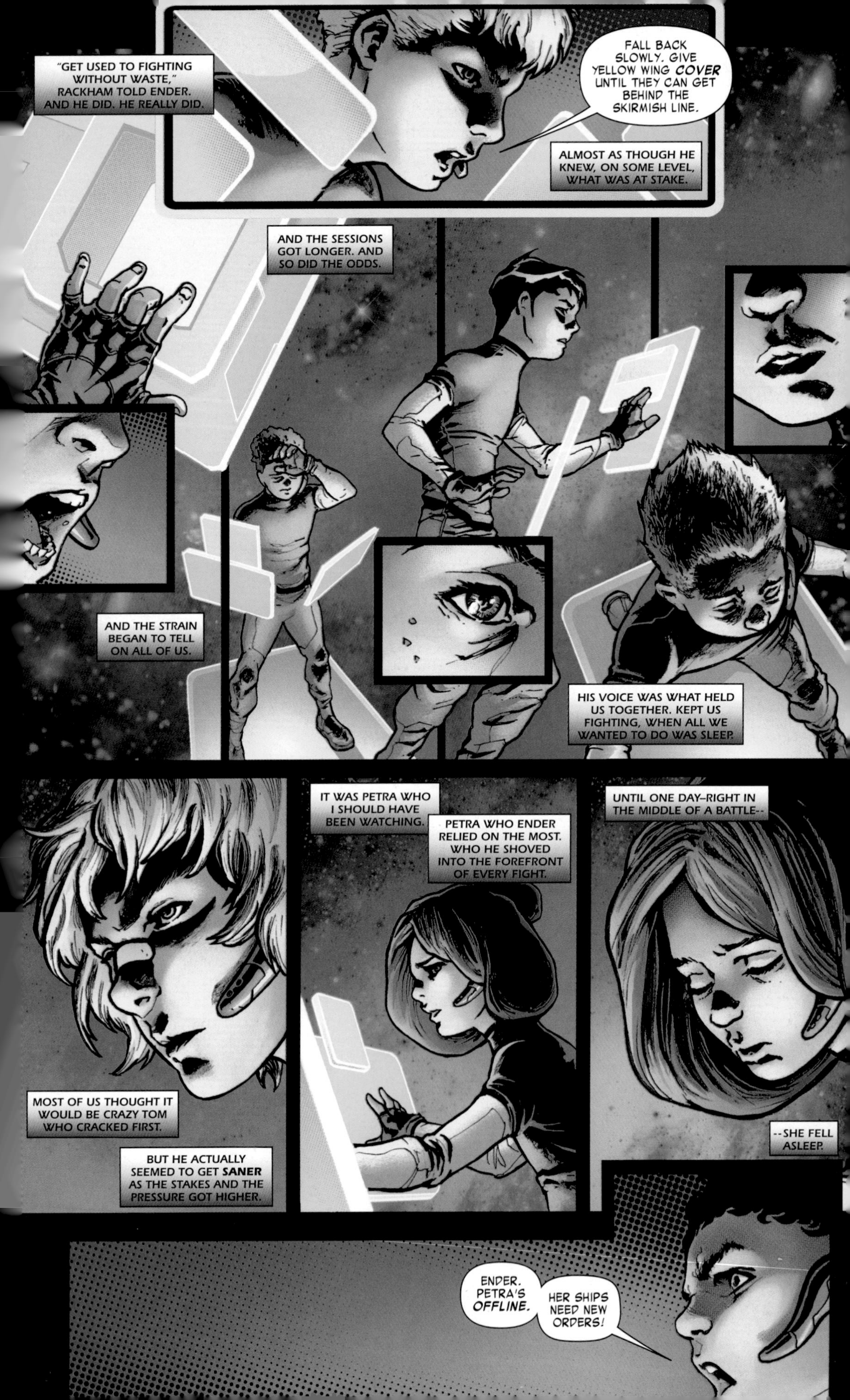
"GET USED TO FIGHTING WITHOUT WASTE," RACKHAM TOLD ENDER. AND HE DID. HE REALLY DID.
FALL BACK SLOWLY. GIVE YELLOW WING **COVER** UNTIL THEY CAN GET BEHIND THE SKIRMISH LINE.
ALMOST AS THOUGH HE KNEW, ON SOME LEVEL, WHAT WAS AT STAKE.
AND THE SESSIONS GOT LONGER. AND SO DID THE ODDS.
AND THE STRAIN BEGAN TO TELL ON ALL OF US.
HIS VOICE WAS WHAT HELD US TOGETHER. KEPT US FIGHTING, WHEN ALL WE WANTED TO DO WAS SLEEP.
MOST OF US THOUGHT IT WOULD BE CRAZY TOM WHO CRACKED FIRST.
BUT HE ACTUALLY SEEMED TO GET **SANER** AS THE STAKES AND THE PRESSURE GOT HIGHER.
IT WAS PETRA WHO I SHOULD HAVE BEEN WATCHING.
PETRA WHO ENDER RELIED ON THE MOST. WHO HE SHOVED INTO THE FOREFRONT OF EVERY FIGHT.
UNTIL ONE DAY–RIGHT IN THE MIDDLE OF A BATTLE--
--SHE FELL ASLEEP.
ENDER. PETRA'S ***OFFLINE.***
HER SHIPS NEED NEW ORDERS!

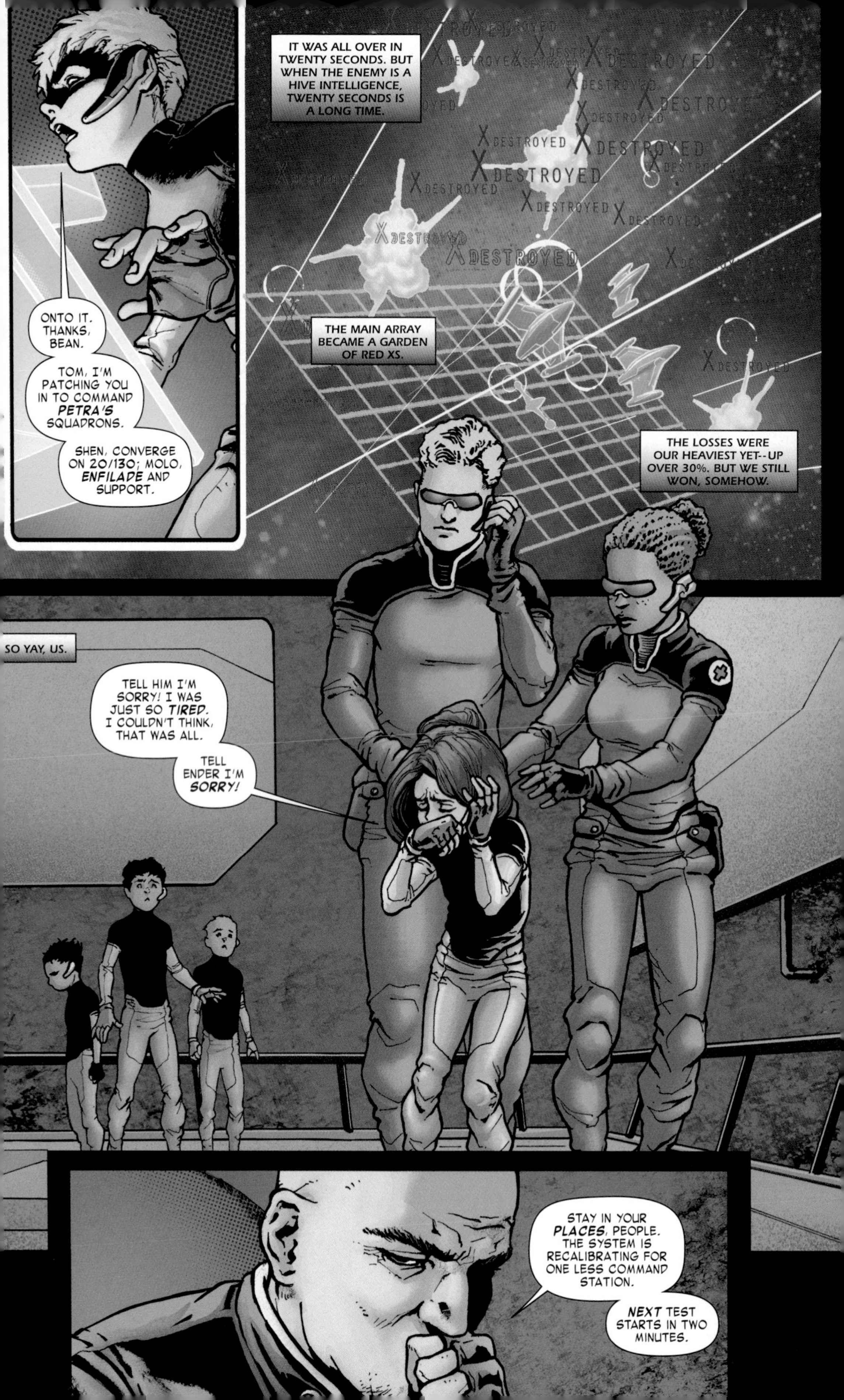

ONTO IT. THANKS, BEAN.
TOM, I'M PATCHING YOU IN TO COMMAND PETRA'S SQUADRONS.
SHEN, CONVERGE ON 20/130; MOLO, ENFILADE AND SUPPORT.
IT WAS ALL OVER IN TWENTY SECONDS. BUT WHEN THE ENEMY IS A HIVE INTELLIGENCE, TWENTY SECONDS IS A LONG TIME.
THE MAIN ARRAY BECAME A GARDEN OF RED XS.
THE LOSSES WERE OUR HEAVIEST YET--UP OVER 30%. BUT WE STILL WON, SOMEHOW.
SO YAY, US.
TELL HIM I'M SORRY! I WAS JUST SO TIRED. I COULDN'T THINK, THAT WAS ALL.
TELL ENDER I'M SORRY!
STAY IN YOUR PLACES, PEOPLE. THE SYSTEM IS RECALIBRATING FOR ONE LESS COMMAND STATION.
NEXT TEST STARTS IN TWO MINUTES.

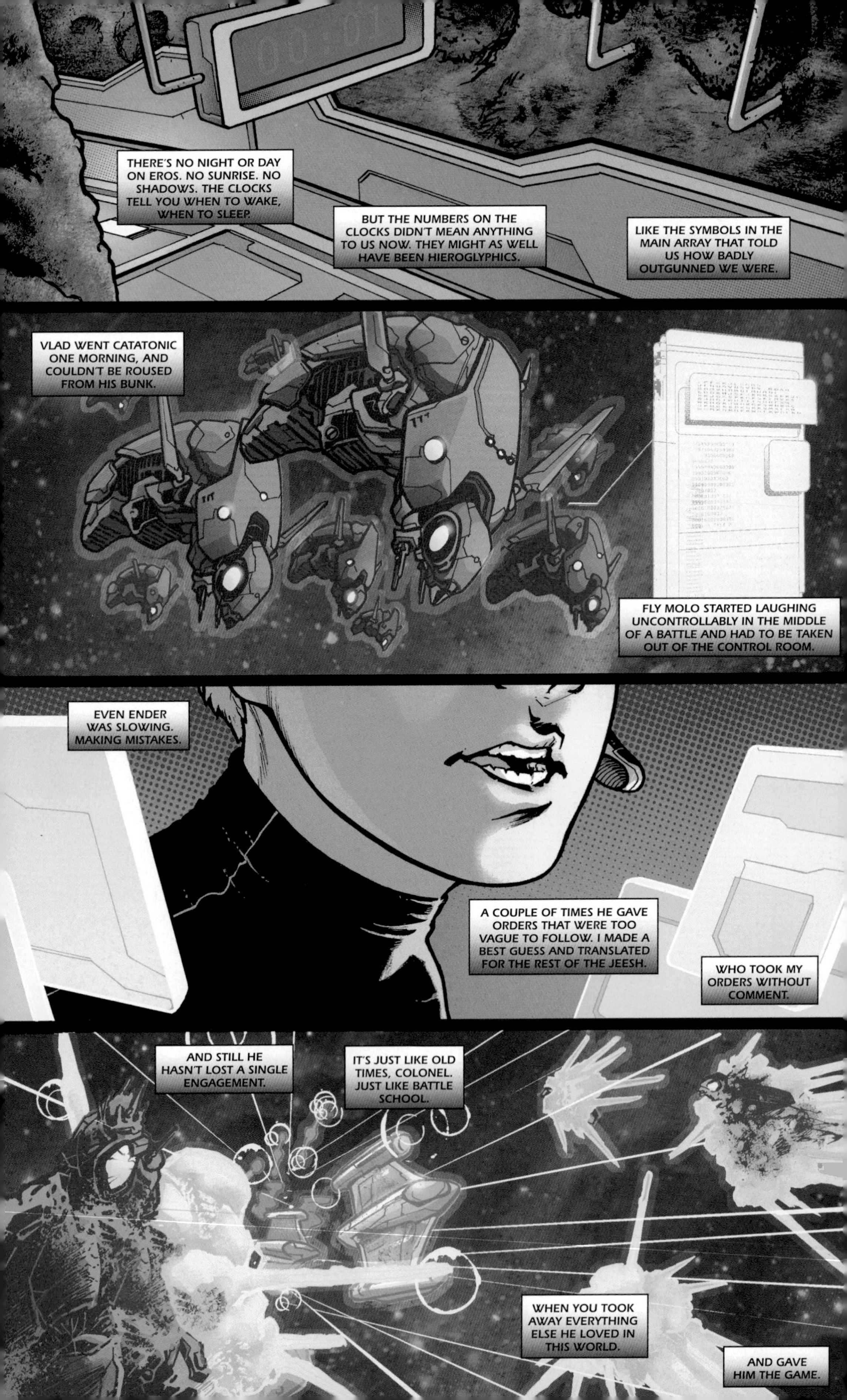
THERE'S NO NIGHT OR DAY ON EROS. NO SUNRISE. NO SHADOWS. THE CLOCKS TELL YOU WHEN TO WAKE, WHEN TO SLEEP.
BUT THE NUMBERS ON THE CLOCKS DIDN'T MEAN ANYTHING TO US NOW. THEY MIGHT AS WELL HAVE BEEN HIEROGLYPHICS.
LIKE THE SYMBOLS IN THE MAIN ARRAY THAT TOLD US HOW BADLY OUTGUNNED WE WERE.
VLAD WENT CATATONIC ONE MORNING, AND COULDN'T BE ROUSED FROM HIS BUNK.
FLY MOLO STARTED LAUGHING UNCONTROLLABLY IN THE MIDDLE OF A BATTLE AND HAD TO BE TAKEN OUT OF THE CONTROL ROOM.
EVEN ENDER WAS SLOWING. MAKING MISTAKES.
A COUPLE OF TIMES HE GAVE ORDERS THAT WERE TOO VAGUE TO FOLLOW. I MADE A BEST GUESS AND TRANSLATED FOR THE REST OF THE JEESH.
WHO TOOK MY ORDERS WITHOUT COMMENT.
AND STILL HE HASN'T LOST A SINGLE ENGAGEMENT.
IT'S JUST LIKE OLD TIMES, COLONEL. JUST LIKE BATTLE SCHOOL.
WHEN YOU TOOK AWAY EVERYTHING ELSE HE LOVED IN THIS WORLD.
AND GAVE HIM THE GAME.

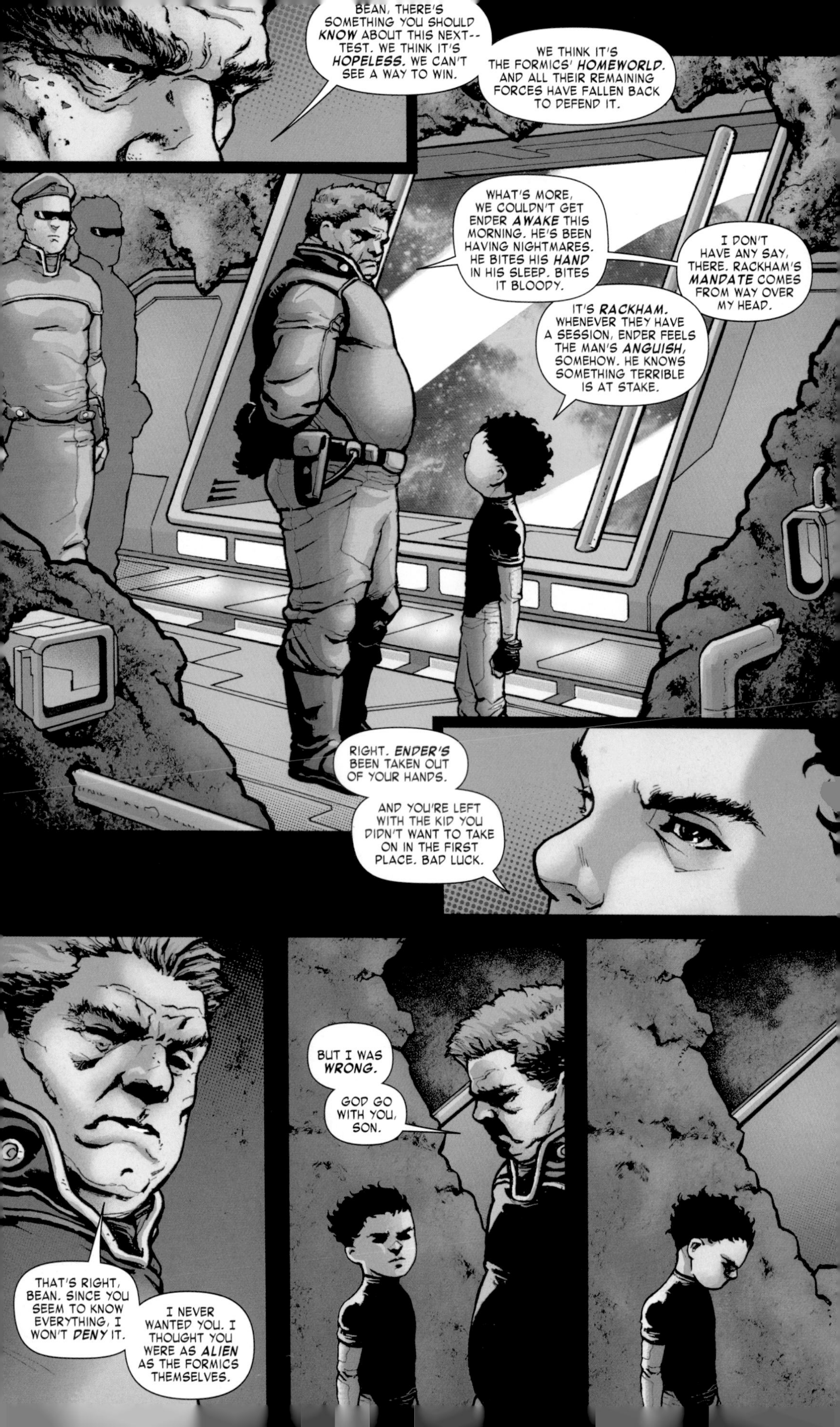
BEAN, THERE'S SOMETHING YOU SHOULD KNOW ABOUT THIS NEXT--TEST. WE THINK IT'S HOPELESS. WE CAN'T SEE A WAY TO WIN.
WE THINK IT'S THE FORMICS' HOMEWORLD. AND ALL THEIR REMAINING FORCES HAVE FALLEN BACK TO DEFEND IT.
WHAT'S MORE, WE COULDN'T GET ENDER AWAKE THIS MORNING. HE'S BEEN HAVING NIGHTMARES. HE BITES HIS HAND IN HIS SLEEP. BITES IT BLOODY.
I DON'T HAVE ANY SAY, THERE. RACKHAM'S MANDATE COMES FROM WAY OVER MY HEAD.
IT'S RACKHAM. WHENEVER THEY HAVE A SESSION, ENDER FEELS THE MAN'S ANGUISH, SOMEHOW. HE KNOWS SOMETHING TERRIBLE IS AT STAKE.
RIGHT. ENDER'S BEEN TAKEN OUT OF YOUR HANDS.
AND YOU'RE LEFT WITH THE KID YOU DIDN'T WANT TO TAKE ON IN THE FIRST PLACE. BAD LUCK.
THAT'S RIGHT, BEAN. SINCE YOU SEEM TO KNOW EVERYTHING, I WON'T DENY IT.
I NEVER WANTED YOU. I THOUGHT YOU WERE AS ALIEN AS THE FORMICS THEMSELVES.
BUT I WAS WRONG.
GOD GO WITH YOU, SON.

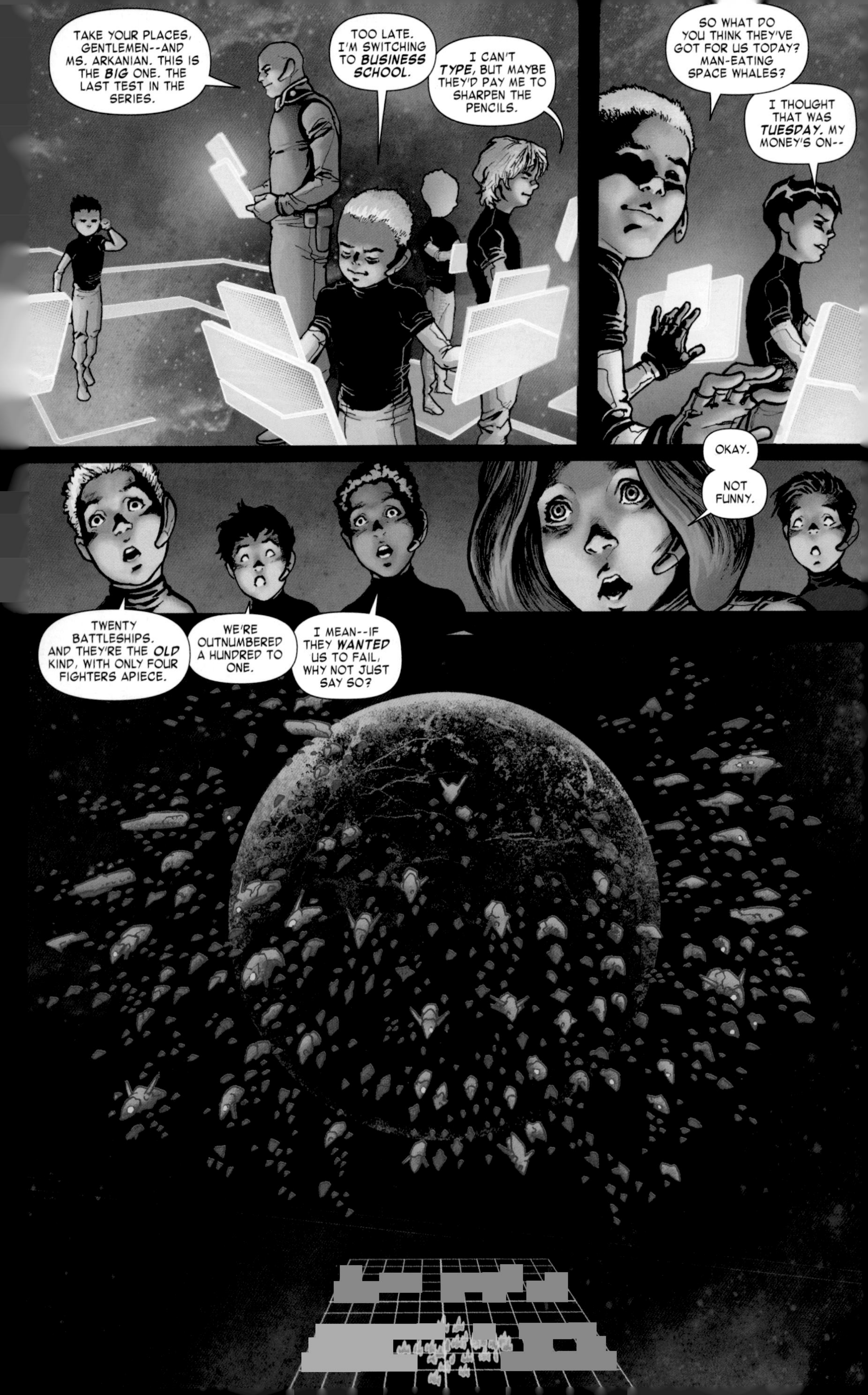
TAKE YOUR PLACES, GENTLEMEN--AND MS. ARKANIAN. THIS IS THE BIG ONE. THE LAST TEST IN THE SERIES.
TOO LATE. I'M SWITCHING TO BUSINESS SCHOOL.
I CAN'T TYPE, BUT MAYBE THEY'D PAY ME TO SHARPEN THE PENCILS.
SO WHAT DO YOU THINK THEY'VE GOT FOR US TODAY? MAN-EATING SPACE WHALES?
I THOUGHT THAT WAS TUESDAY. MY MONEY'S ON--
OKAY.
NOT FUNNY.
TWENTY BATTLESHIPS. AND THEY'RE THE OLD KIND, WITH ONLY FOUR FIGHTERS APIECE.
WE'RE OUTNUMBERED A HUNDRED TO ONE.
I MEAN--IF THEY WANTED US TO FAIL, WHY NOT JUST SAY SO?

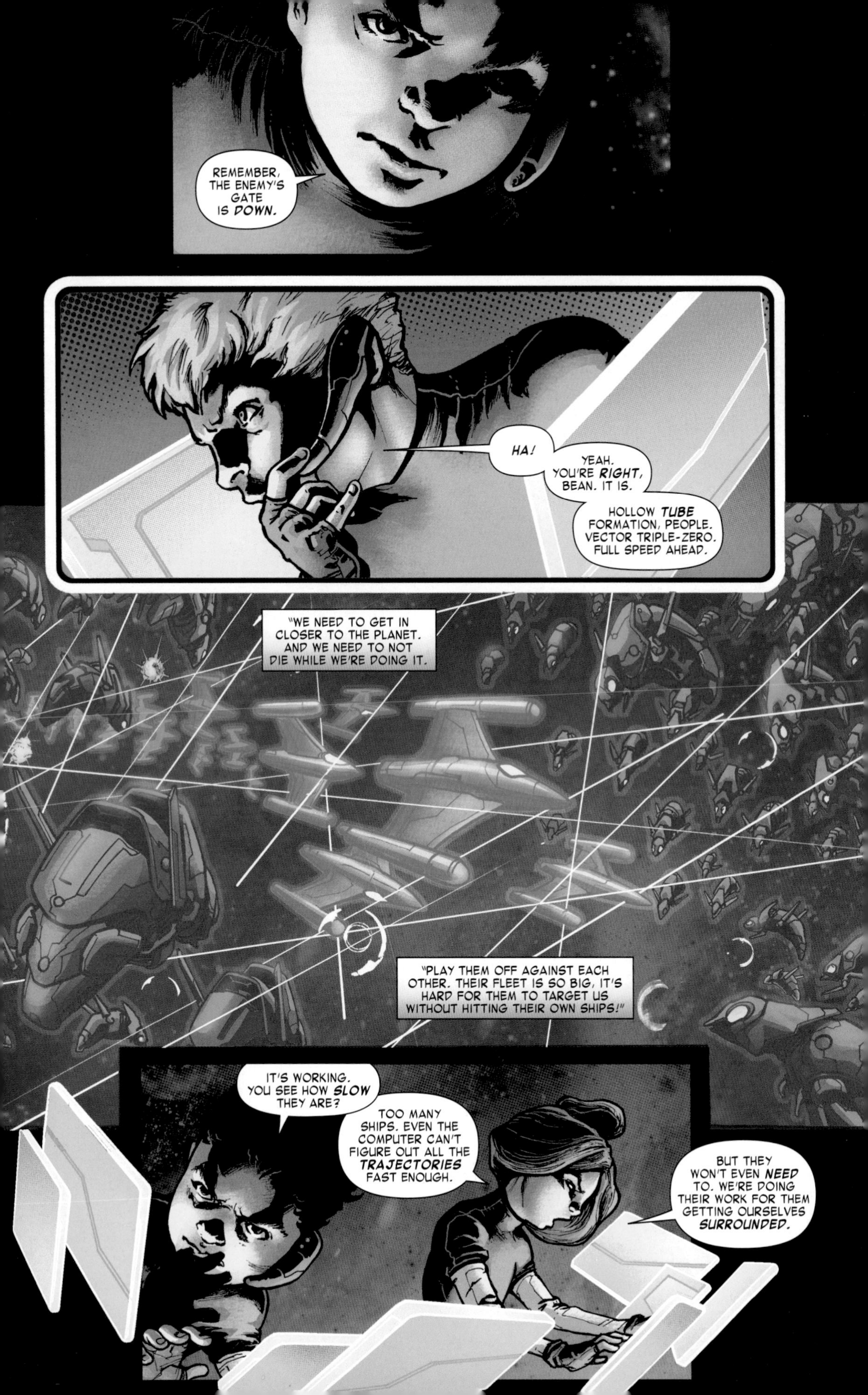
REMEMBER, THE ENEMY'S GATE IS DOWN.
HA!
YEAH. YOU'RE RIGHT, BEAN. IT IS.
HOLLOW TUBE FORMATION, PEOPLE. VECTOR TRIPLE-ZERO. FULL SPEED AHEAD.
"WE NEED TO GET IN CLOSER TO THE PLANET. AND WE NEED TO NOT DIE WHILE WE'RE DOING IT.
"PLAY THEM OFF AGAINST EACH OTHER. THEIR FLEET IS SO BIG, IT'S HARD FOR THEM TO TARGET US WITHOUT HITTING THEIR OWN SHIPS!"
IT'S WORKING. YOU SEE HOW SLOW THEY ARE?
TOO MANY SHIPS. EVEN THE COMPUTER CAN'T FIGURE OUT ALL THE TRAJECTORIES FAST ENOUGH.
BUT THEY WON'T EVEN NEED TO. WE'RE DOING THEIR WORK FOR THEM GETTING OURSELVES SURROUNDED.

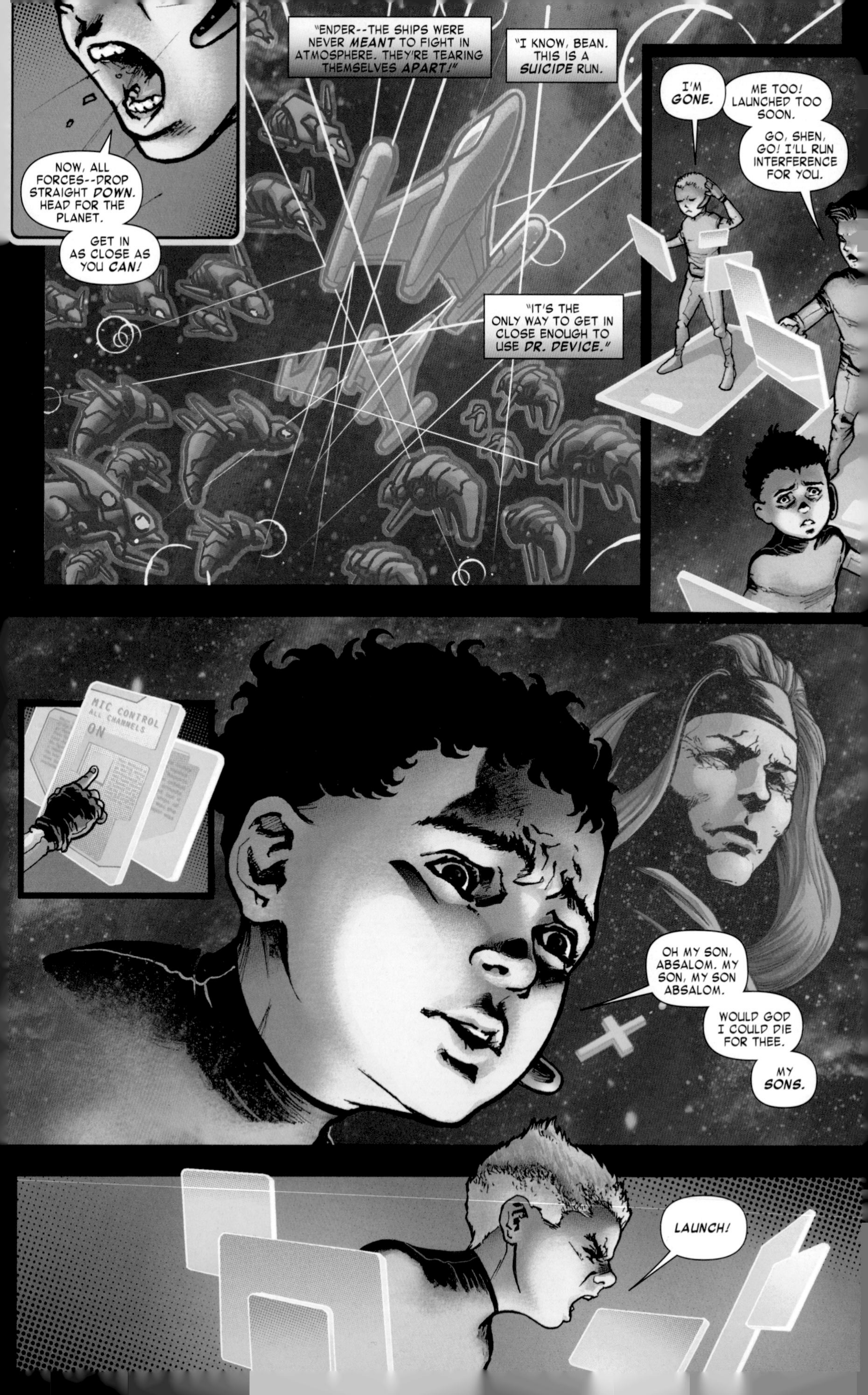
NOW, ALL FORCES--DROP STRAIGHT DOWN. HEAD FOR THE PLANET.
GET IN AS CLOSE AS YOU CAN!
"ENDER--THE SHIPS WERE NEVER MEANT TO FIGHT IN ATMOSPHERE. THEY'RE TEARING THEMSELVES APART!"
"I KNOW, BEAN. THIS IS A SUICIDE RUN.
"IT'S THE ONLY WAY TO GET IN CLOSE ENOUGH TO USE DR. DEVICE."
I'M GONE.
ME TOO! LAUNCHED TOO SOON.
GO, SHEN, GO! I'LL RUN INTERFERENCE FOR YOU.
MIC CONTROL
ALL CHANNELS
ON
OH MY SON, ABSALOM. MY SON, MY SON ABSALOM.
WOULD GOD I COULD DIE FOR THEE.
MY SONS.
LAUNCH!

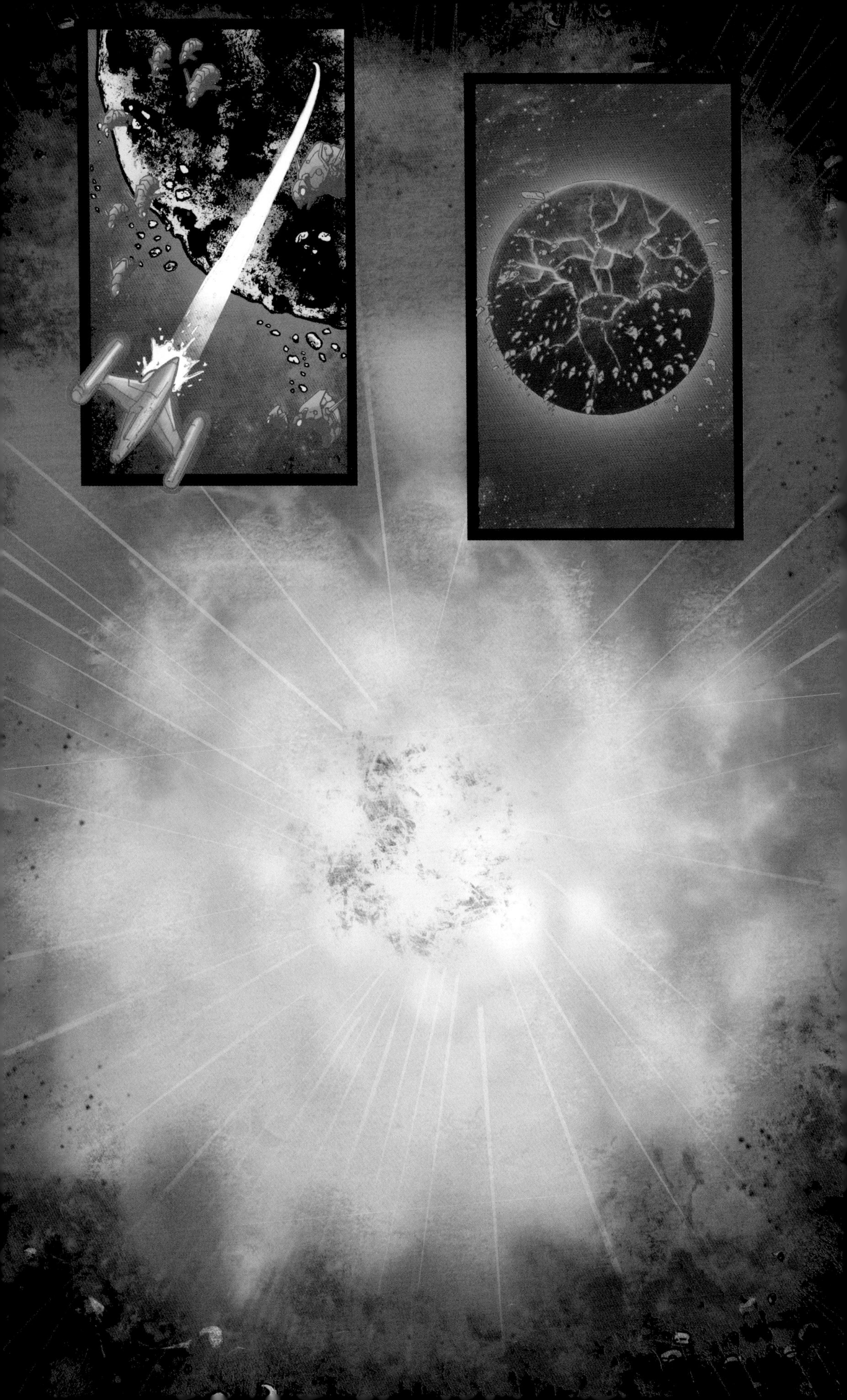

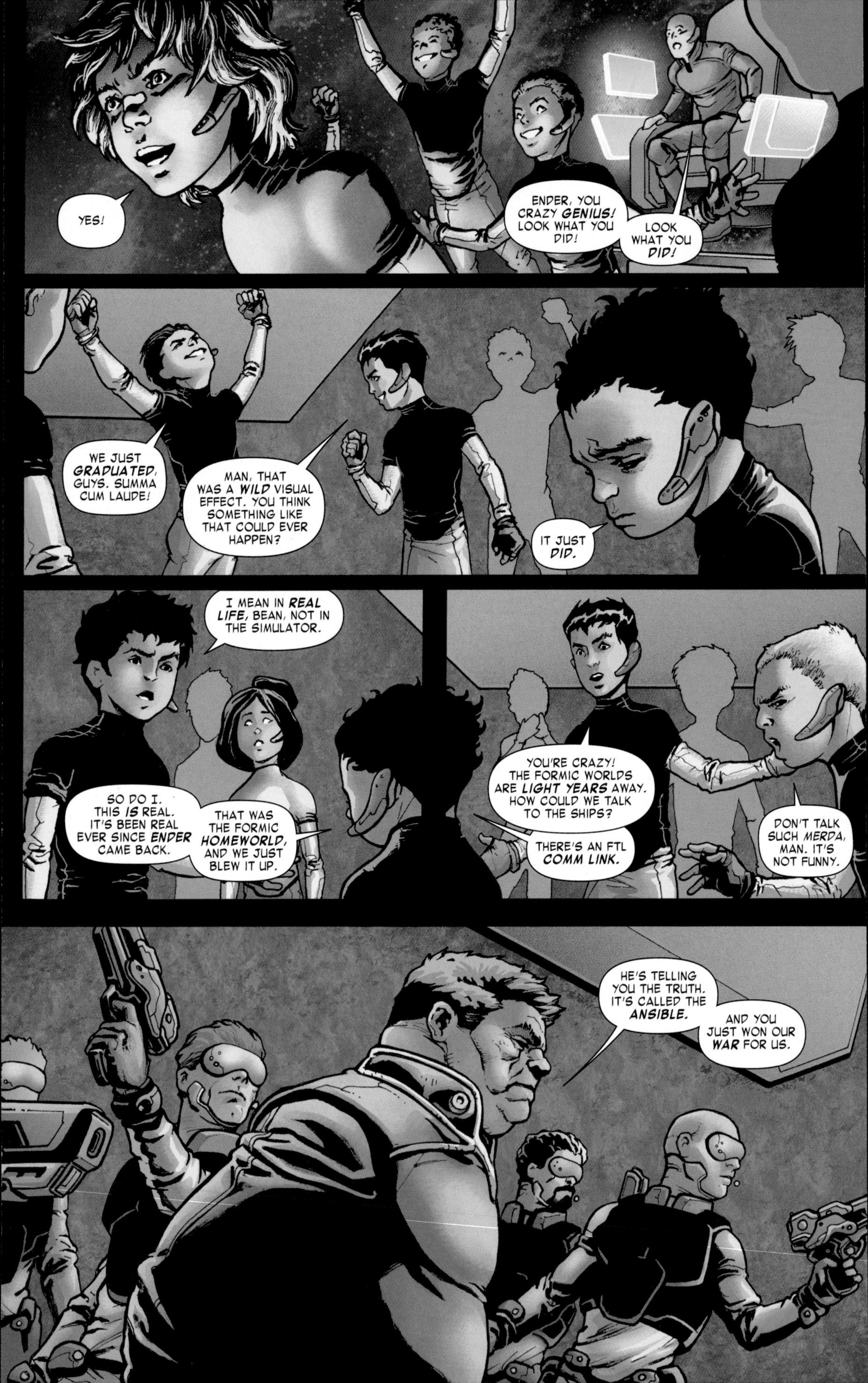
YES!
ENDER, YOU CRAZY GENIUS! LOOK WHAT YOU DID!
LOOK WHAT YOU DID!
WE JUST GRADUATED, GUYS. SUMMA CUM LAUDE!
MAN, THAT WAS A WILD VISUAL EFFECT. YOU THINK SOMETHING LIKE THAT COULD EVER HAPPEN?
IT JUST DID.
I MEAN IN REAL LIFE, BEAN, NOT IN THE SIMULATOR.
SO DO I. THIS IS REAL. IT'S BEEN REAL EVER SINCE ENDER CAME BACK.
THAT WAS THE FORMIC HOMEWORLD, AND WE JUST BLEW IT UP.
YOU'RE CRAZY! THE FORMIC WORLDS ARE LIGHT YEARS AWAY. HOW COULD WE TALK TO THE SHIPS?
THERE'S AN FTL COMM LINK.
DON'T TALK SUCH MERDA, MAN. IT'S NOT FUNNY.
HE'S TELLING YOU THE TRUTH. IT'S CALLED THE ANSIBLE.
AND YOU JUST WON OUR WAR FOR US.

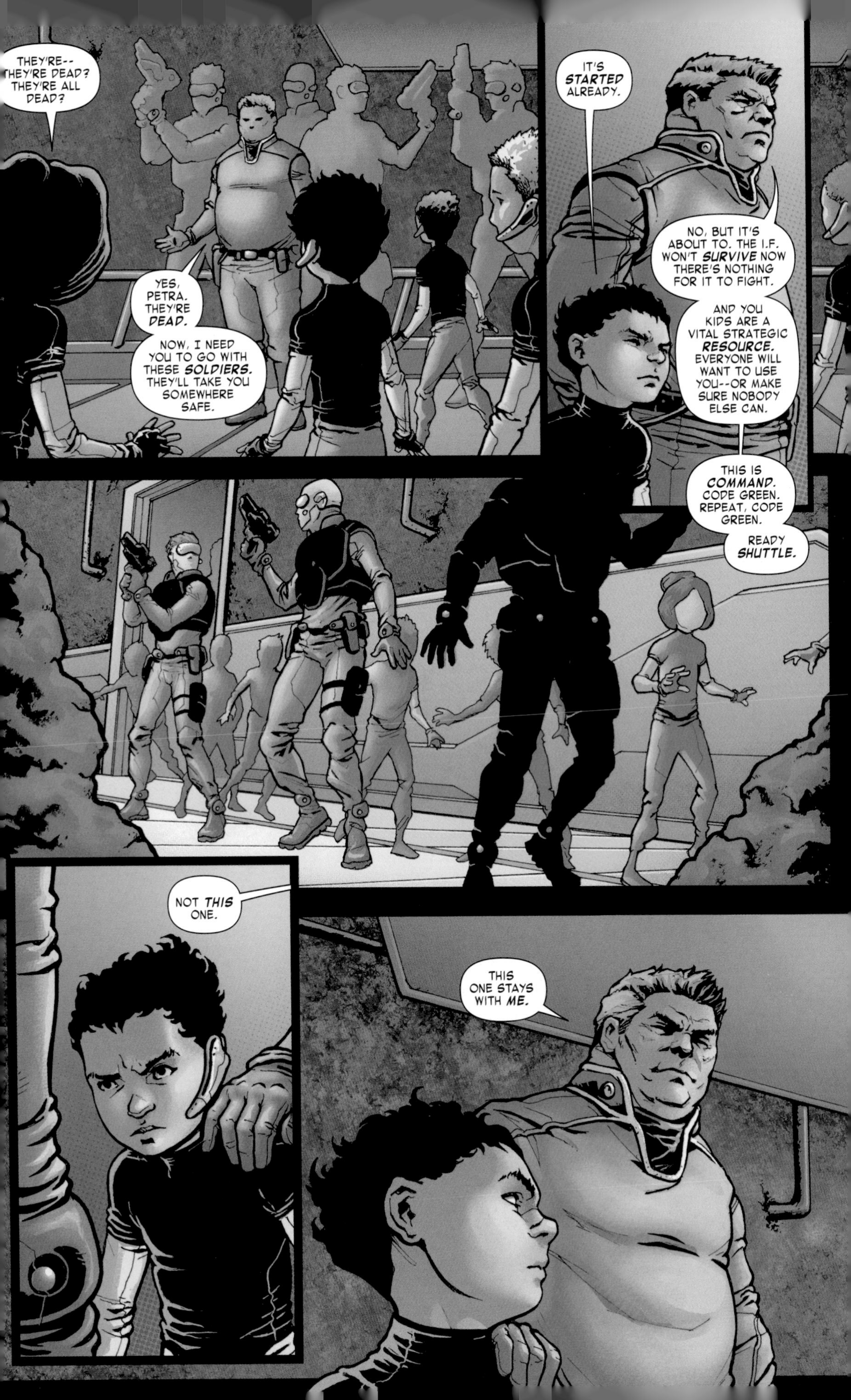
THEY'RE--
THEY'RE DEAD? THEY'RE ALL DEAD?
YES, PETRA. THEY'RE DEAD.
NOW, I NEED YOU TO GO WITH THESE SOLDIERS. THEY'LL TAKE YOU SOMEWHERE SAFE.
IT'S STARTED ALREADY.
NO, BUT IT'S ABOUT TO. THE I.F. WON'T SURVIVE NOW THERE'S NOTHING FOR IT TO FIGHT.
AND YOU KIDS ARE A VITAL STRATEGIC RESOURCE. EVERYONE WILL WANT TO USE YOU--OR MAKE SURE NOBODY ELSE CAN.
THIS IS COMMAND. CODE GREEN. REPEAT, CODE GREEN.
READY SHUTTLE.
NOT THIS ONE.
THIS ONE STAYS WITH ME.

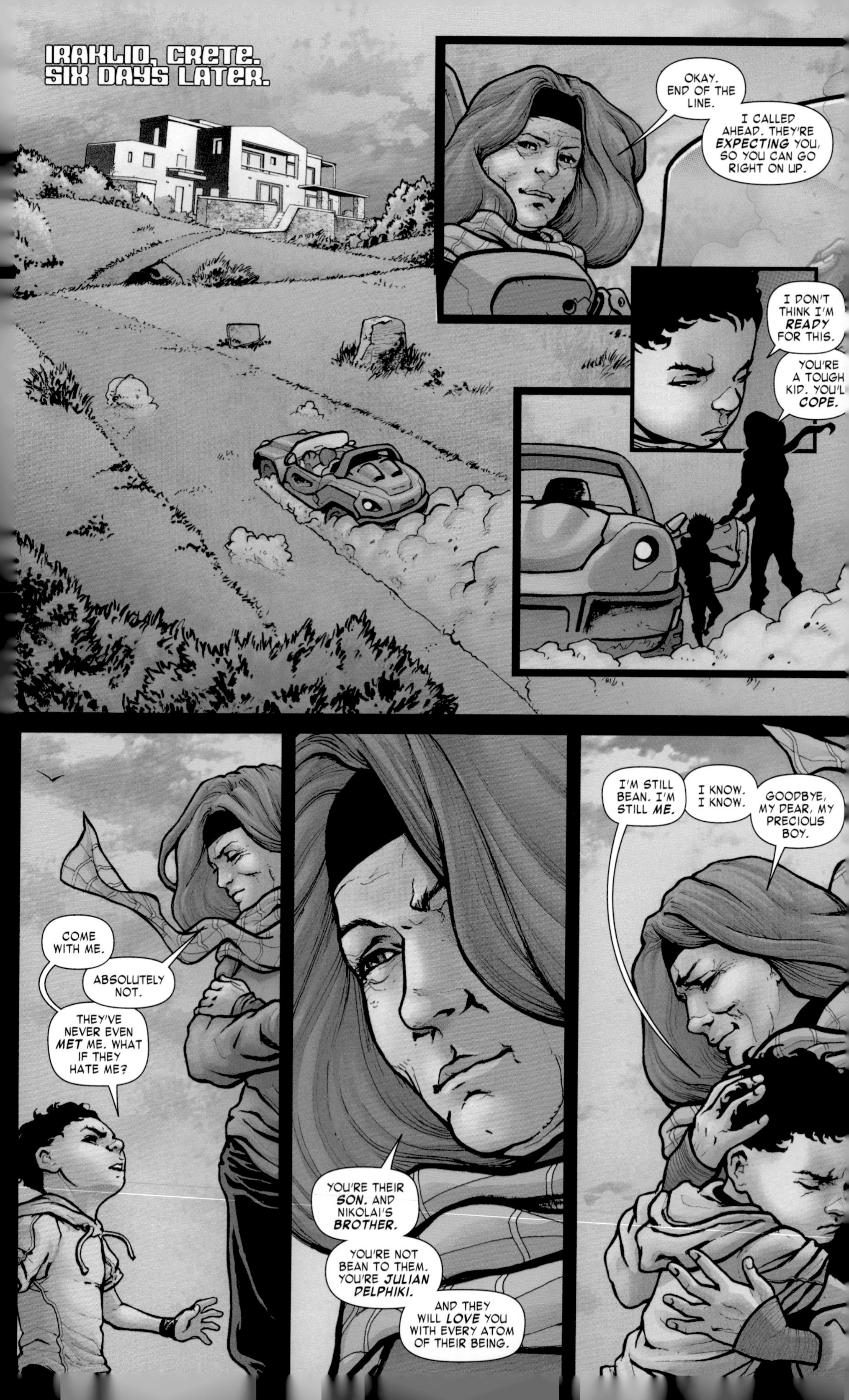
IRAKLIO, CRETE. SIX DAYS LATER.
OKAY. END OF THE LINE.
I CALLED AHEAD. THEY'RE EXPECTING YOU, SO YOU CAN GO RIGHT ON UP.
I DON'T THINK I'M READY FOR THIS.
YOU'RE A TOUGH KID. YOU'LL COPE.
COME WITH ME.
ABSOLUTELY NOT.
THEY'VE NEVER EVEN MET ME. WHAT IF THEY HATE ME?
YOU'RE THEIR SON. AND NIKOLAI'S BROTHER.
YOU'RE NOT BEAN TO THEM. YOU'RE JULIAN DELPHIKI.
AND THEY WILL LOVE YOU WITH EVERY ATOM OF THEIR BEING.
I'M STILL BEAN. I'M STILL ME.
I KNOW. I KNOW.
GOODBYE, MY DEAR, MY PRECIOUS BOY.

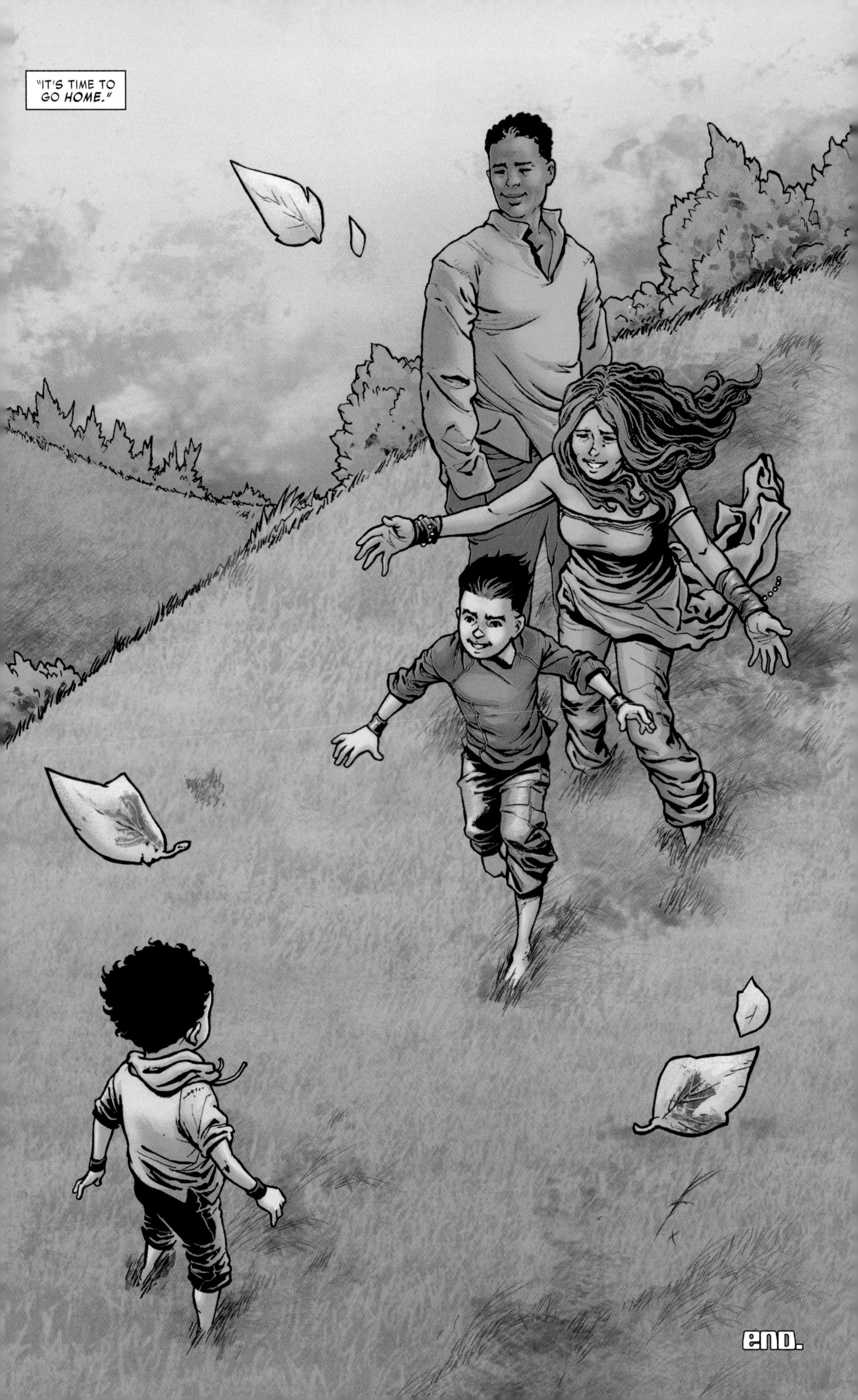
"IT'S TIME TO GO HOME."
END.

#1 COVER PROCESS
BY SEBASTIAN FIUMARA

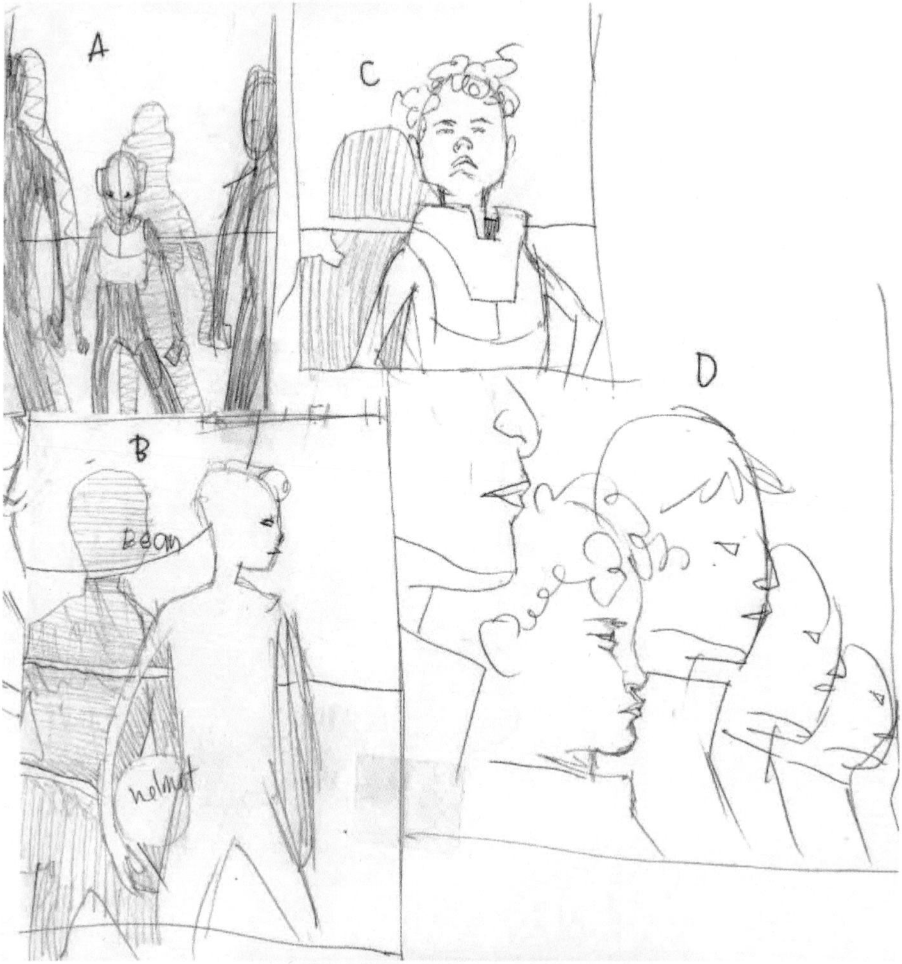
A
C
D
B
Beam
helmet

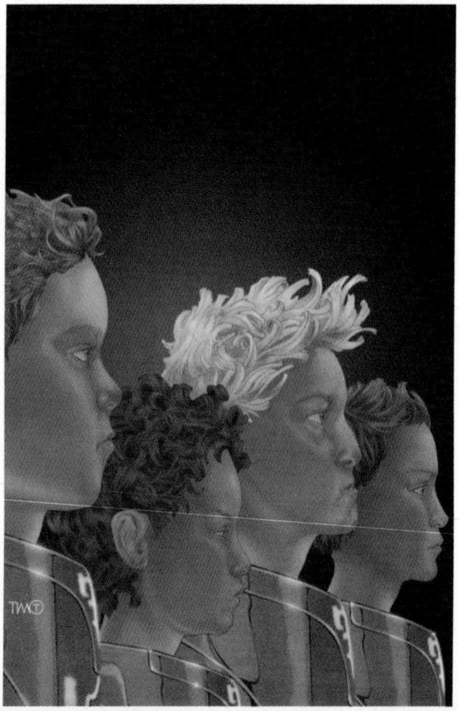

#2 COVER PROCESS
BY SEBASTIAN FIUMARA

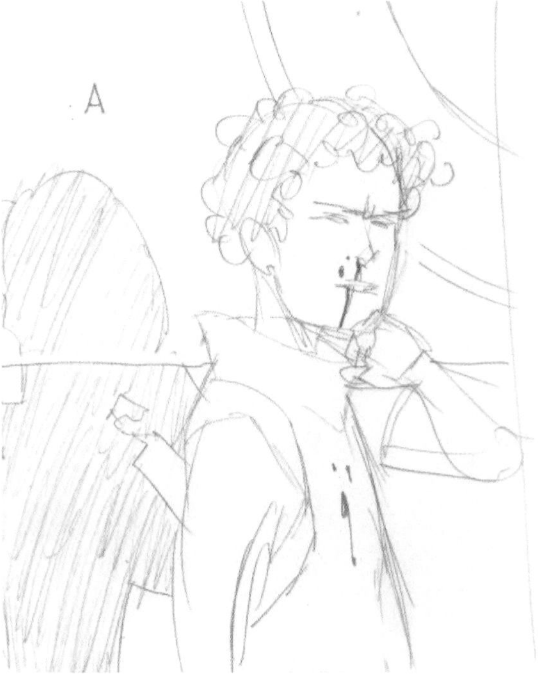
A

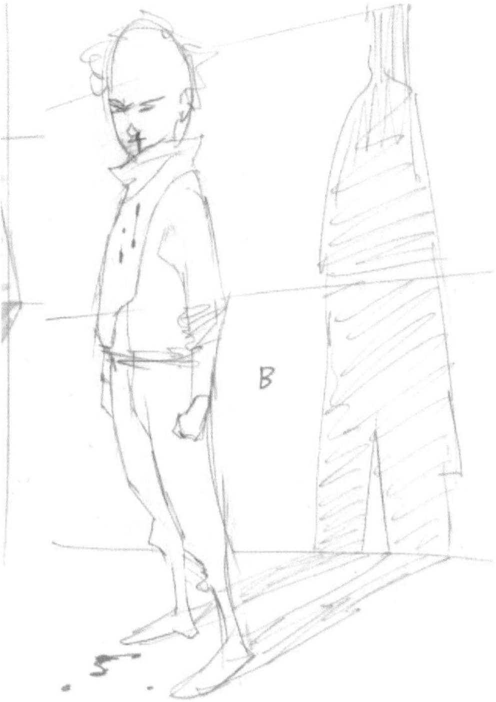
B

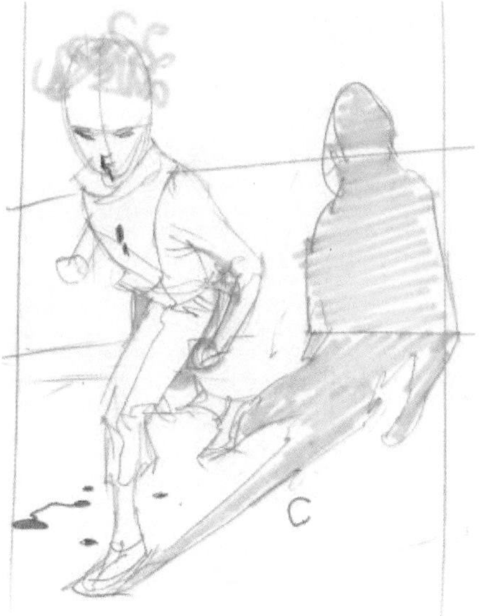
C

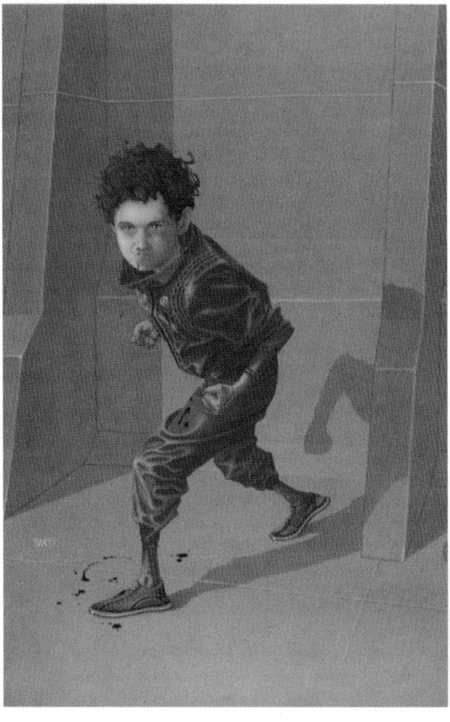

#3&5 COVER PROCESS
BY SEBASTIAN FIUMARA

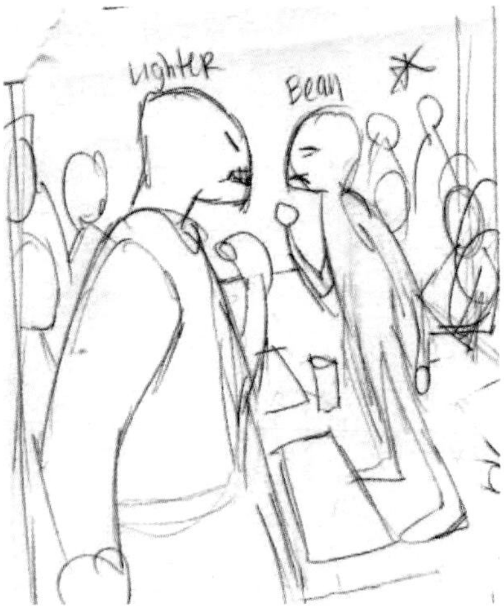
Lighter
Bean

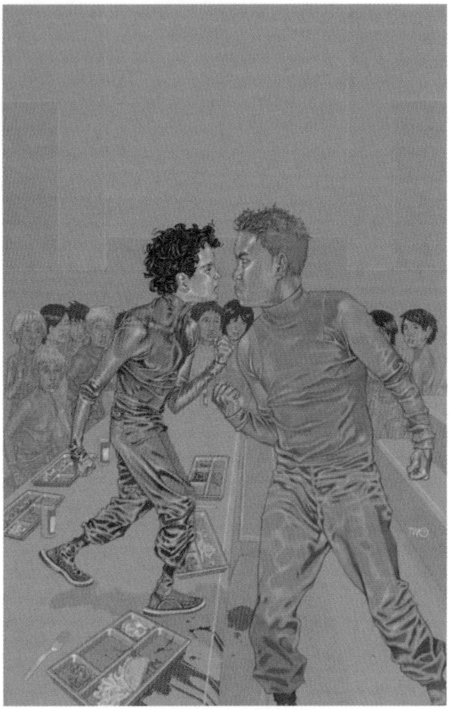

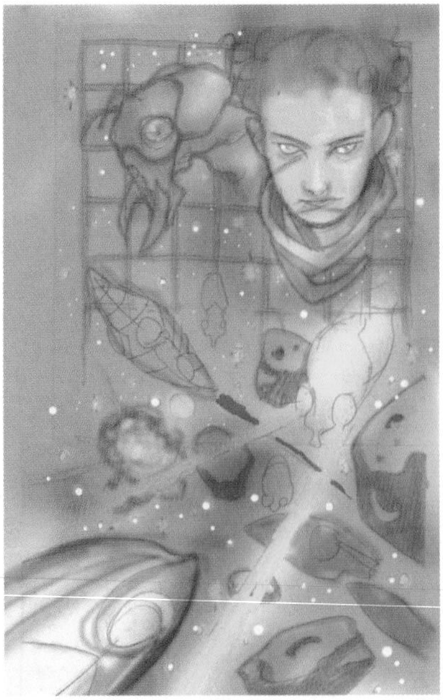

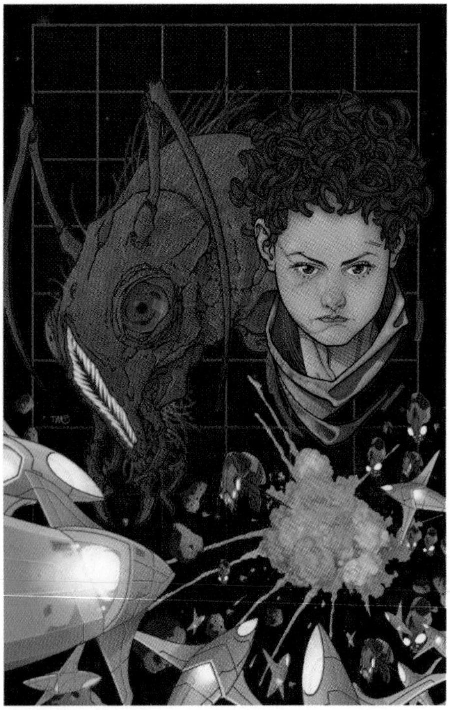

#4 COVER PROCESS
BY SEBASTIAN FIUMARA

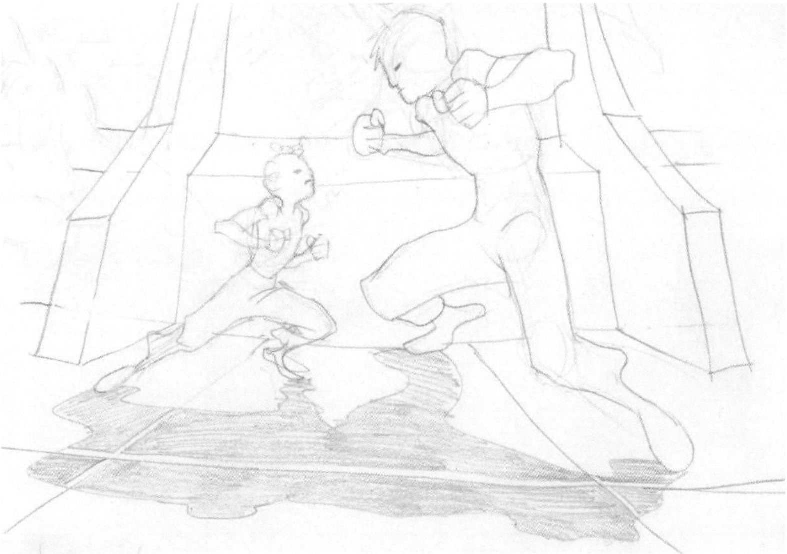

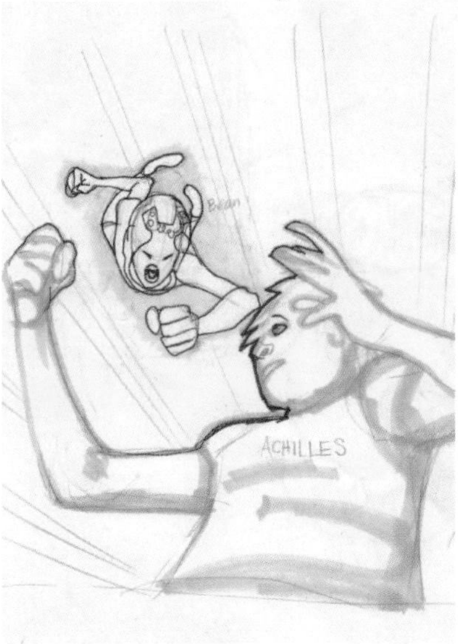
ACHILLES

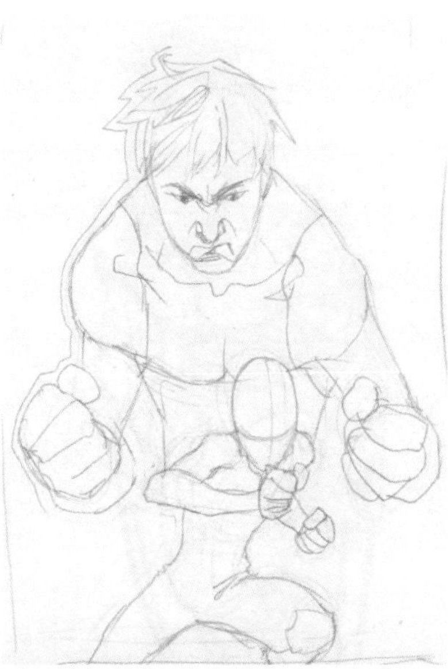

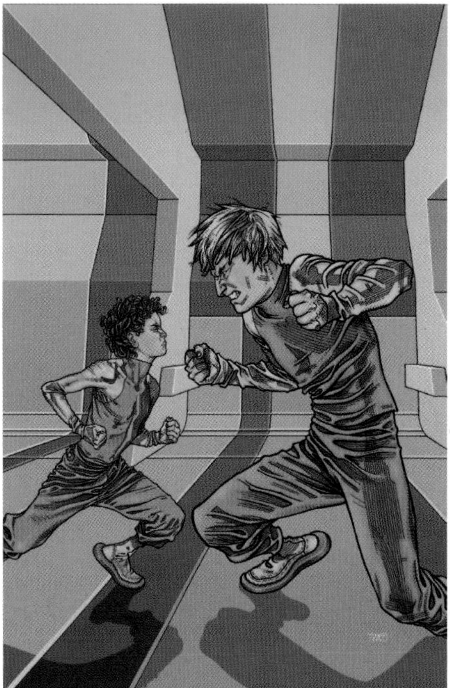

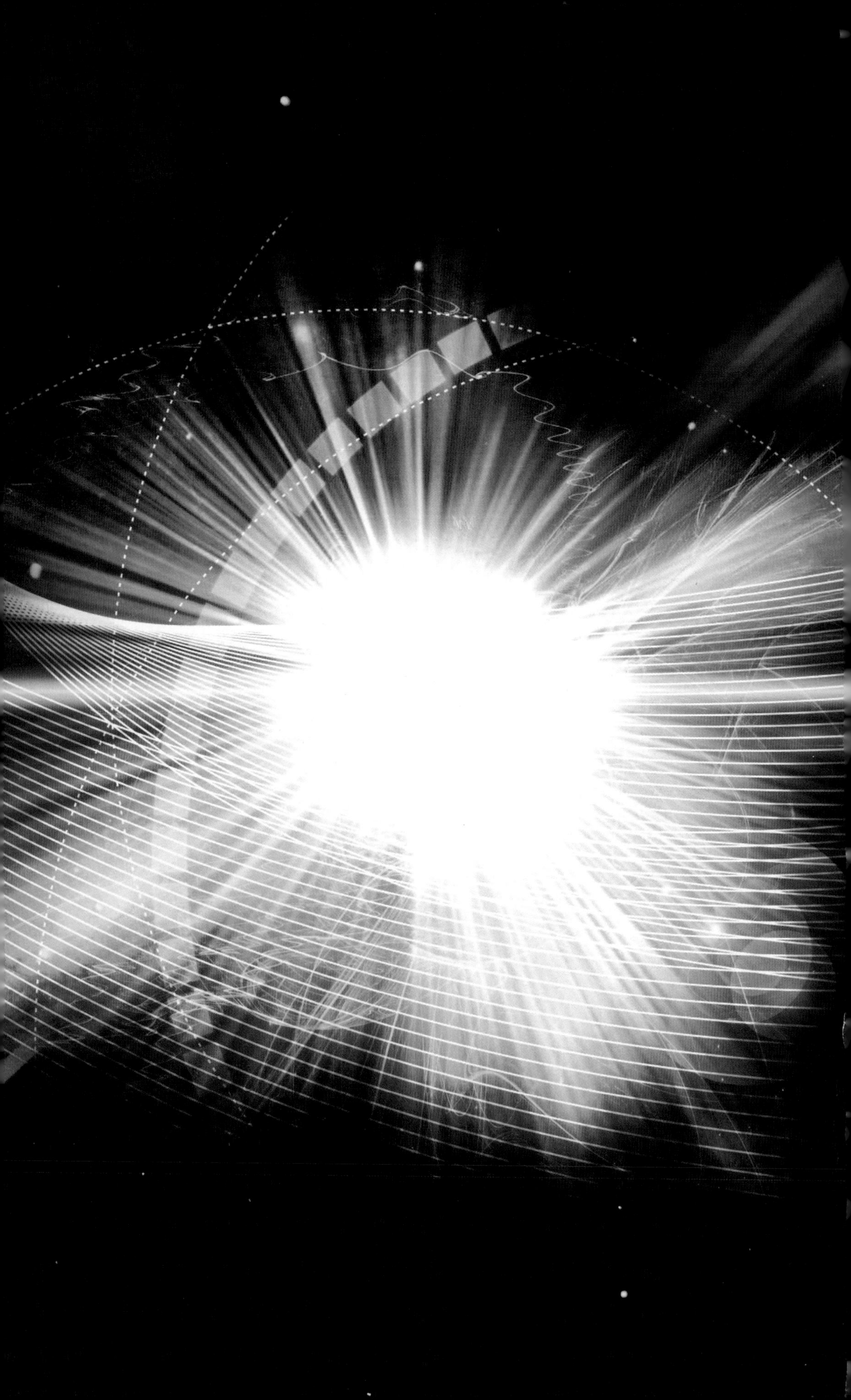